A poignant portrait of vanished places and times, as well as a heart-wrenching testimony to some of the cruelest parts of western history, *Lost Letters from Vienna* is a book to savour and treasure, also for its author's clear-eyed candour in telling her family's tale of persecution and survival. Course recreates the past with immediacy and vividness, and tenderness, yet with not even a hint of sentimentality. This is a work of integrity and compassion.

— Lee Kofman, author

An epic family history. A profound portrait of marriage. A book of magical detail.

— Tim Bonyhady, cultural historian

History is us, wrote the Italian singer-songwriter Francesco de Gregori.

History doesn't stop at the front door.
History breaks into our rooms, burns them,
History does wrong, and it does right.
History is us.
It is we who write the letters.
It is we who have everything to win, and everything to lose.

Sue Course's gripping, evocative family memoir reveals how history and ordinary life are woven together. History broke into her Jewish family's opulent rooms in Vienna, burnt them, it did her family wrong, it did them right, and it sent them to the other side of the world to begin very different lives. Her story is often grim, at times exciting, refreshingly frank, and told with a positive and imaginative spirit, without any self-pity.

— Tim Colebatch, journalist

Sue Course's memoir takes us inside the lives of a large wealthy Jewish Austrian family fractured by war and scattered across the globe. Her intimate, moving stories of persecution, poverty, death and survival trace the legacies of war across generations and continents. We are reminded again of the horrors so many millions endured in WWII, as well as the richness of culture and history they brought as refugees to their host countries.

— Professor Katie Holmes, La Trobe University

About the Author

Sue Course was born in Vienna in 1933 and came to Melbourne as a four-year-old refugee with her parents. Growing up in suburban Melbourne, Sue became a nurse and activist. In 1973 while raising a family of four, she helped save 33 hectares on the banks of the Darebin Creek, now called the Darebin Parklands, one of the nation's earliest and most remarkable urban land conservation victories. As one of the last remaining members of the migrant Jewish families born in pre-war Vienna, she tells her family's story.

LOST LETTERS *from* VIENNA

Sue Course

Published by Wild Dingo Press
Melbourne, Australia
books@wilddingopress.com.au
www.wilddingopress.com.au

First published by Wild Dingo Press 2019

Designer: Debra Billson
Editor: Catherine Lewis
Printed in Australia.

Cover credits:
Stack of letters: Agnes Kantaruk/Shutterstock
Map of Vienna 1858: Source: John Murray, Albemarle Steet, London
Author: J & C Walker Sailp; Wikimedia Commons
https://commons.wikimedia.org/wiki/File:Wien1858.jpg
Chair: Adolf Loos, Chair from the Langer apartment, c. 1903,
National Gallery of Victoria.

Course, Sue 1933- author.
Lost Letters from Vienna / Sue Course.

 A catalogue record for this
book is available from the
National Library of Australia

ISBN: 9781925893052 (paperback)
ISBN: 9781925893120 (epdf)
ISBN: 9781925893137 (ePub)

Acknowledgements

This book has been a huge project spanning many years. I had no concept of what I was letting myself in for. It had its beginnings when I found the letters of my grandparents and continued with the collection of hundreds of other family letters and additional material.

I am indebted to a wide number of family and friends from all over the world who in their various capacities supported, advised and actively assisted. So many people have contributed that unfortunately I cannot mention everyone by name. You know who you are and I thank each and every one of you.

Some of these wonderful people are no longer with me to celebrate the great achievement—the result of their dedicated work. For a start I would like to mention particularly my childhood friend, Barbara Niven, and my American cousin, Henry Bohm, both of whom, in spite of failing health, made themselves available with their expertise and assistance. They taught me a lot on the way and persuaded me to donate the primary material to the State Library of Victoria.

Before we could do anything else, we had to translate around two hundred letters written in German, which took a lot of teamwork. After beginning with Henry Bohm's translation of some of my grandparents' letters, the task was carried on by Arthur Klimes, while my sister-in-law, Elizabeth Langer, undertook the translation of all Aunt Pauline's letters. Erica Price worked on the translations of my father's letters and many official German documents. I thank her for her enormous support and advice over many years.

The students of the Banyule German U3A class of the early 2000s enthusiastically embraced this project, especially Judith Hannah, Loretta Forsey and Janette Creed who often deciphered difficult handwritten letters and continued on even after the class folded.

My appreciation also goes to my relatives in England, the US, Canada, Switzerland, South Africa and Australia, including Heidi Rohel, my brother Martin Langer, Dennis Stone and Alfred Muller who added to the actual written material; and others such as John Kary, Nick Kary, Claudia Kary, Andrew Jakins, Tim Bonyhady and Diana Dumouchel, who provided extra information which was able to be included. Lastly to Joele Bohm, Henry Bohm and Pauline Stone (Kary), all long deceased, for their forethought in recording their family stories that guided my approach to this book. A special thanks goes to Gordon Boath who, with his interest in genealogy, drew up the family trees to make the family connections easier for the reader.

I am indebted to Terence Lane for his expertise and contribution on the Adolf Loos material. I am grateful for the many who, with their expertise, supported me at various steps along the way and in a variety of ways did their best to keep me motivated, including: Eve Recht, Robert Upe, Susan Marshall, Michael Smith, Catherine McCardle, Janet Butler, Susan Sheldrick and Pao Franco.

This book could not have been written without Jeanette Leigh who assisted me in weaving together the past and the present.

A special mention goes to my cousin Jonathan Jacobson who took on the task of reading several drafts of the book as they became available and made comments on information and errors that had been overlooked.

Warmest thanks go to Catherine Lewis who took the project out of a dream into reality and to all her diligent team at Wild Dingo Press.

Finally, much gratitude to my children, Tony, Di, Gill and Phil for their loving support and help. I particularly thank Phil who pursued the project with me the whole way.

*This book is dedicated to my children and grandchildren
and to all my extended family across the globe.*

The author's maternal family tree

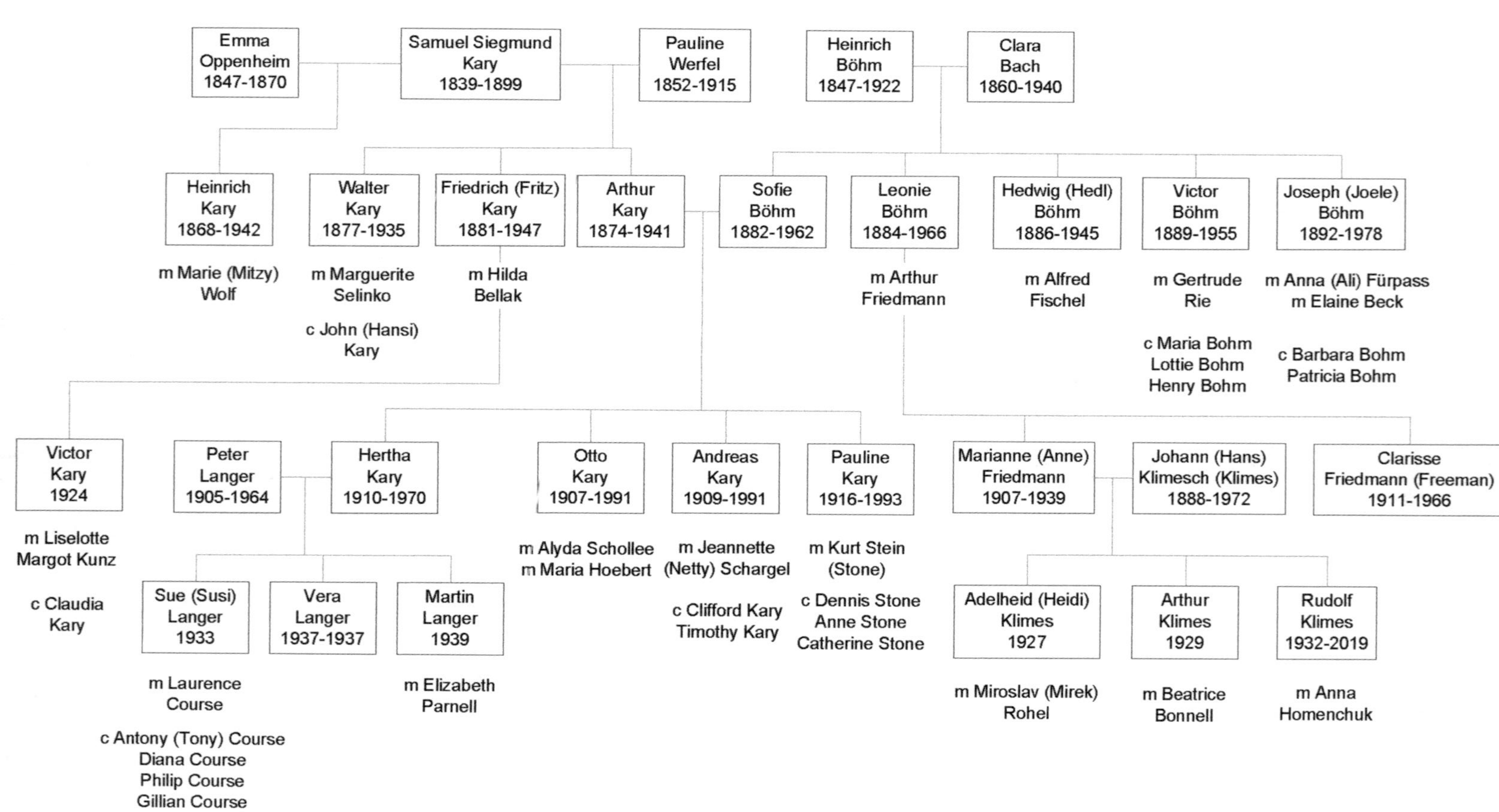

The author's paternal family tree

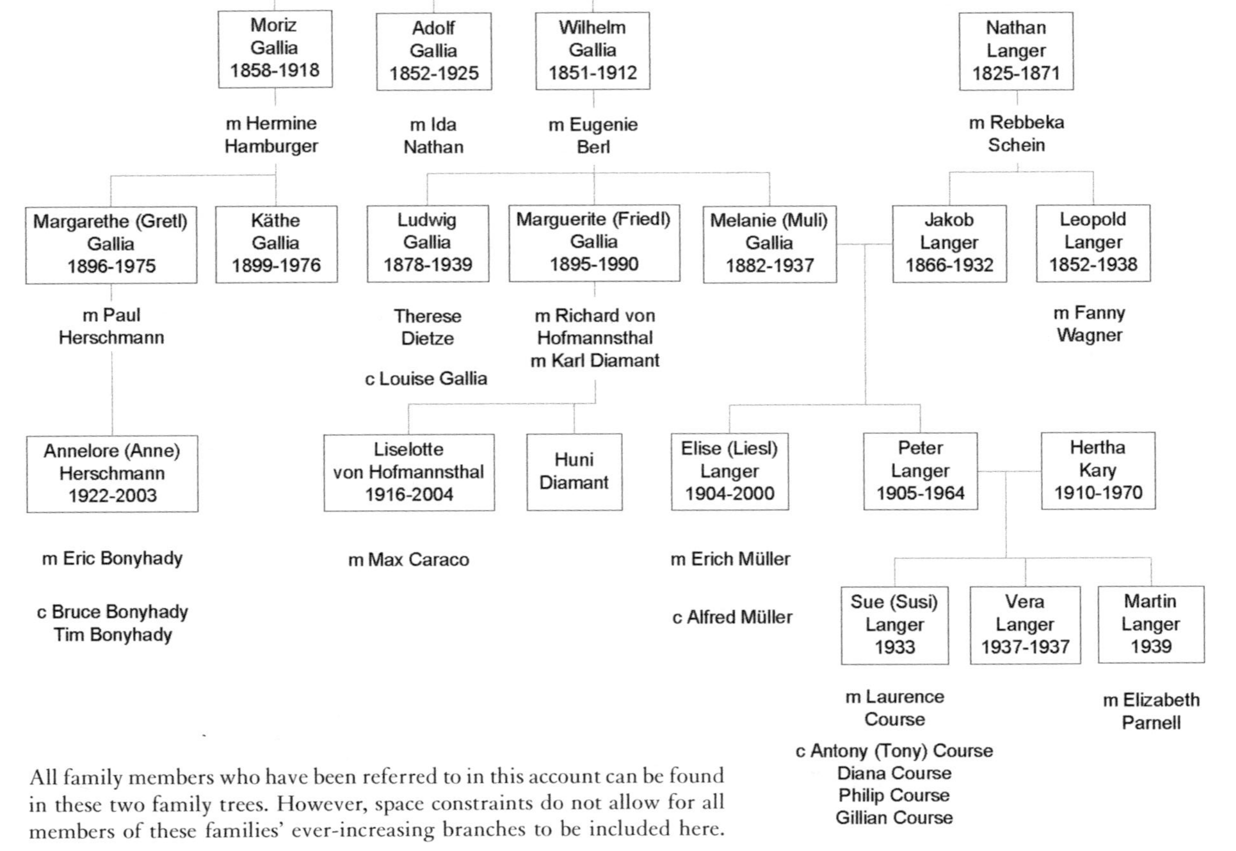

All family members who have been referred to in this account can be found in these two family trees. However, space constraints do not allow for all members of these families' ever-increasing branches to be included here.

Contents

1

INTRODUCTION

I was four years old when the Germans marched into Austria. Being a toddler, I was probably only aware of my parents' distress on a subconscious level. Our home was Vienna, and it was the age of the Anschluss, that forced, feckless union with Hitler's Germany. You will know what followed: a holocaust of epic proportions. Survivors talk about the shock of it all. People simply could not believe what was happening; that their lives could break down so profoundly.

The story of escape and restoration that follows is one I can tell now from the comfortable distance of time because of a special discovery. There I was in my modest suburban Melbourne home in 1969 with two young children. I was seven months' pregnant, had a high-maintenance husband, and I had just brought my mother across from New Zealand because she was gravely ill with cancer. In her luggage were boxes of letters and papers, all written in German. Well, I certainly had no time for dealing with them at the time, so they were relegated to the top of a cupboard, where it was nice and dark, and easily forgotten.

Life passes quickly. The calendar page turned over to the year 2000, the year I retired from nursing and when my favourite aunt, Aunt Liesl, died. To assuage my grief, I cleaned and cleared. So, there I was, getting into the cupboards, pulling out old bags, books, hats and clothes, my husband Laurie's briefcase, missing since 1962, and there was that cookbook I was looking for in 1965. Squashed in behind all of this were hundreds of letters and war accounts, some handwritten and some typewritten, and all written in German.

The cardboard box collapsed as I removed it from the cupboard, the letters dropping like shot birds falling from the sky. I began leafing wildly through the skin-thin airmail pages. My German was rusty; I could read it but not scan it. However, what I could determine was that the letter I was holding was written by my mother, Hertha Langer, in 1938, and that others were from her parents, Arthur and Sofie Kary, from that year forward. I was completely overwhelmed.

I emailed my Viennese cousin, Henry Bohm, who lived in the United States, and asked him to help with the translation. Because of the enormous volume, I conscripted other Viennese relatives and friends to assist with the mammoth task. As the decoding progressed, German giving way to English, it was like reading an historical novel. The letters revealed a family history that I had no idea about. No one had ever told me about any of these events.

The mail service of 1930s' Europe was probably way better than Australia's today. Can you believe that letters sent from Vienna took only ten days to get to Melbourne in 1938? And remarkably, the postman delivered regularly within Europe even after the various Nazi invasions, which meant my family was able to stay in touch while in flight.

At that time, writing was a vital point of contact for everyone, and throughout this period of an extensive family's dislocation and dispersion, the letters poured to and from across oceans almost as regularly as the waves. Letter by letter, I relived the stories of escape, resettlement and the fate of those left behind. Frank and detailed accounts portrayed communities lost to time, immersing me in the deteriorating conditions and increasing restrictions experienced by Viennese Jews as Nazification continued on its deadly path.

My parents and I were the first of our family to leave. In 1938 the trip to Australia from Vienna was relatively easy, and I was still very young. Before me now were the stories of all the people I had lived amongst who had such a terrible time of it. What did this all mean? Why was it coming out now? I was dumbfounded.

My family was so close before the war and then suddenly we were wrenched apart. Those letters had kept everyone connected, and I felt that their reappearance would only strengthen those ties. I began engaging my extended family, urging them to add titbits of information and stories to fill the gaps. In more recent years, when relatives visited from Canada and the United States, they sat for hours reading the letters. They never said much but I could tell they were deeply affected.

In 1968 I returned to Vienna for the first time since I was four, with my nine-year-old daughter Diana. We left our modest *pension* near the imposing Hofburg Palace in the city centre to walk to my great-aunt, Marguerite Kary's house. She lived in my family's original home on the Ringstrasse and was my only surviving relative in Vienna. Nearby, I saw a group of Austrian soldiers standing on a street corner with rifles slung over their backs, and had an instinctive urge to flee. Something must have happened in those pre-war months for me to have that pure, chest-tightening fear, but no details remain in my conscious mind. I can recall that feeling still.

Years later, I visited the Hundertwasser Museum in Vienna. It is an extraordinary art museum created by artist Friedensreich Hundertwasser, a Viennese-born Jew who avoided persecution by being baptised into Catholicism in 1935. His mother was Jewish, but his father was Catholic. I bought a postcard in the museum shop with a quote of his that struck deeply:

> Wer die Vergangenheit nicht ehrt, verliert die Zukunft.
> Wer seine Wurzeln vernichtet, kann nicht wachsen.[1]

I had it framed for my living-room wall to remind me of how lucky my family was. We were forced from Vienna and dispersed,

---

1   Those who don't honour the past lose the future.
    Those who destroy their roots cannot grow.

but thanks to an efficient postal service we were able to weave an invisible connective web around the globe.

History consists of a series of stories; our daily events, moment by moment, are relegated to history. The deeply personal sagas, our subterranean stories, are most important because our past guides us at an unconscious level. I think history allows us to make sense of our lives. I am sharing this one because everything that happens shapes our world.

For generations my family lived on the 'Ring', the famous Ringstrasse in the very heart of Vienna. Our family home was one of the many palatial buildings constructed along the grand boulevard which replaced the mediaeval ramparts that had been paid for from the ransom of Richard the Lionheart.

Our lives were rich with privilege because from the early 1800s through to 1938, the family businesses were multinational corporations. On my mother's side were the Böhms, who owned one of the biggest hat manufacturing companies in the Austro-Hungarian Empire. And then there were the Karys who were big in silk textiles, the biggest in Europe. My father's clan, the Gallia family, were also successful, in the gas lighting business, and were keenly involved in the Secession art movement in Vienna.

My ancestry was full of high achievers. You need go no further back than my great-uncle, Franz Werfel, who wrote a book you may have heard of, *The Song of Bernadette*, which was made into a major Hollywood film starring Jennifer Jones. One of my aunt's cousins, Annemarie Selinko, wrote *Désirée*, the bestselling story of Napoleon's first love, and my great-aunt, Hermine Gallia, is preserved in one of Gustav Klimt's most famous portraits.

This was the setting where generations of Jewish people were intrinsically enmeshed in the cultural and economic life of Vienna, the European hub for cultural pursuits. The scene collapsed when the Nazis invaded on the 12th March 1938, uniting Germany and Austria in a marriage made in hell, known as the Anschluss.

But let's go back to Vienna at the turn of the 20th century when it was the European hub of great artists, thinkers and composers. The capital of the Austro-Hungarian Empire abounded with these modernist geniuses who were taking convention and turning it on its head. My grandparents could walk down the street and enter a café for strudel and coffee and overhear discussions between the luminaries of the day. When my grandparents went to the opera, great composers such as Gustav Mahler and Richard Strauss were actually conducting.

In the 1920s and 30s, on the boulevard on which I lived, on any day, you would have been likely to see several of the world's greatest talents. Sigmund Freud often strolled down the Ringstrasse on his way to his favourite haunt, Café Landtmann, a place of historic elegance. Other masters frequenting that café were writers such as Thomas Mann and Bohemian modernist poet, Peter Altenburg. More recently, it has hosted Marlene Dietrich, Hillary Clinton and Paul McCartney. The café has been there since 1873 and today continues to attract tourists.

Families of our social standing were schooled in the arts, so some of my relatives were fine musicians, including my father, Peter Langer, a complicated man who would become a cellist in the Melbourne Symphony Orchestra in 1946. Our education focused on music, literature, languages and philosophy. This began at an early age, especially for young women.

Disproportionate numbers of Jews within Vienna made up the creative intellectuals engaged in the adventure of discovery and knowledge, including film director, Fritz Lang, palaeontologist and evolutionary biologist Othenio Abel, philosopher Martin Buber, neurologist and psychiatrist Viktor Frankl, creator of psychoanalysis Sigmund Freud, and the pioneer shopping-mall designer Victor Gruen. Then there was Hugo von Hofmannsthal, the famed novelist and librettist, who was related to my great-aunt Friedl by marriage.

Many of these Jewish luminaries converted to Catholicism or Protestantism. Some even to Lutheranism, the most anti-Semitic Christian sect of them all. Why did they do this? The answer is expedience: to fit in. Anti-Semitism pervaded most professions. A composer or conductor, no matter how prodigious their talent, could never reach their career pinnacle while being a Jew.

Immediately after Gustav Mahler converted to Catholicism in 1897, he was appointed director of the esteemed Hofoper, the Vienna Court Opera, a role that was denied to Jews. Ironically, or perhaps as one might expect, Mahler was never really accepted as a Christian, nor did he fully embrace it in his heart. After his conversion he famously commented:

I am rootless ... as a Jew everywhere in the world. I am thrice homeless: as a native of Bohemia in Austria, as an Austrian among Germans, and as a Jew throughout the world. Everywhere an intruder, never welcomed.

It was commonplace for religious conversions to occur to secure that top job, but total acceptance was mostly elusive; at the end of the day, once a Jew, always a Jew, according to those who find Jews odious.

At the beginning of World War I, Vienna had the largest Jewish community in western and central Europe with record numbers of Jewish people attending *Gymnasium* (academic senior secondary school that led to university entrance). Although my parents and grandparents were Jewish, they were secular in their leanings. My parents were married in a synagogue but they never attended for worship, nor did they observe the holy days. In fact, they were so secularised that they had me baptised in the Anglican church in Vienna on the 8th August 1938 before coming to Australia because they believed it would be easier to get along in life as a Christian. My father also converted, although had his father, Jakob, lived to see this he would have been horrified. Jakob was deeply committed to his roots and supported many Viennese Jews, including the provision of financial support for penurious members of the community.

For centuries, secular Jews chose total assimilation; in Vienna they were well accustomed to acting flexibly when it came to their identity in order to make the cogs of life mesh more smoothly. Despite their legislated rights and the fact that Austria was a modern liberal state, the devoutly Catholic Habsburg Empire made sure that Jews remained on the periphery. Around 9,000 converted to Christianity between 1868 and 1903.

Back in 1848 under Emperor Franz Joseph I, it seemed that a new world for Jews was surfacing in Austria. He granted them some civil rights including the right to establish an independent religious community. This was more of a property deal than an altruistic act, but more about that later. Full citizenship rights were granted in 1867. This volte-face, where Viennese Jews finally had freedom and could function normally in society, saw a burgeoning in their numbers from 6,000 in 1860 to around 185,000 in 1938.

So, at the end of the 19th century, one could accurately say that Jewish people were not only major players in the arts in Vienna, they carried it: in other words, they paid for it. On my paternal side, my great-great-aunt Hermine and great-great-uncle Moriz Gallia were two of the most significant Secession artist patrons. The Gallias had more bohemian leanings than my mother's family. When Hermine Gallia modelled for revolutionary painter Gustav Klimt, it thrust her into a fame that outlasted her lifetime; the portrait now resides in the National Gallery in London.

Then, March 1938 saw everything change—we went from being doyens of the arts to objects to be disparaged, dislocated and discarded. Suddenly, the air needed purifying of the stench of greatness that we had become. Aryanisation and Nazification sent my family fleeing across the globe.

Over the coming years, more than six million European Jews were dislocated from their lives, stripped of their dignity and murdered along with some millions of other 'undesirables' such as

Roma, homosexuals, people with disabilities, political opponents, etc. No less tragic, although perhaps less frequently acknowledged, are the other casualties of that insane war: the estimated 70 to 85 million people who were wiped out as military and civilian casualties right across the world.

Most of my family did not suffer these shocking acts but they had their wealth and businesses taken from them and were forced by the German army to house strangers in their homes; and when they were completely humiliated and disempowered, most of them managed to flee Europe. Just a few of my relatives were carted off to concentration camps alongside other mothers, fathers and children, to be subjected to the most sadistic cruelty and brutality during the 'Final Solution'.

Yes, we were lucky. The loss of belongings and our homes was a small price to pay for our lives, but I am filled with sadness at the injustice. A consonant and a vowel, a language and hundreds of years of history, plus the oceans I crossed, separate Austria from Australia. At various junctures, Vienna, city of music, city of dreams, has called to me across the chasms of time, distance and history. What an interesting time it has been, this life of solving family puzzles. Now I am one of the last remaining members of the Jewish families born in Vienna; and at this ripe age of 86, husband long gone, with four kids and eight adorable grandchildren, I am grateful that they have not had to tell a story of escape.

So, time-leap with me back to the Vienna of September 1938— me in father's arms, my mother's unworldly dark eyes glancing back, not daring to shed tears, as we boarded the Deutsche Luft Hansa Junker plane.

2

AN ANTIPODEAN LANDING

The two-hour crossing from Vienna over the Alps to Switzerland was horribly turbulent. Even though I was just four, it is a trip that I clearly recall. Both my parents had a relentless grip on their sick bags; it was a nightmarish, nauseating flight in an unpressurised plane.

A train hurried us to Marseille. The port of the ancient city was swarming with people desperate to emigrate. After pausing in Algiers and Port Said, the ship took us through the Suez Canal and on to Colombo. In Singapore there was a vessel change and we travelled the remaining stretch on board the *Nieuw Zeeland* via Indonesia. My mother wrote vivid descriptions of the journey to her parents, Arthur and Sofie Kary, who were still stuck in occupied Vienna. Nothing gets left out, including my father's struggle with sea sickness. Especially glowing are the accounts of their time visiting Borobudur and Bali in Indonesia; the mix of eastern cultures and spicy exotic foods was so alien to their European palates. You would have thought they were on holiday.

I guess my parents had the ability to shut off for a time from the awful drama they had left behind. The letters gave my anxious grandparents a strong sense of our journey with its highs and lows. But they were especially keen to hear about Australia, which was also to be their ultimate destination. Early November 1938, Grandfather Arthur wrote:

We have followed your journey as though we had actually been with you.

Then just four days later another letter arrived:

I can scarcely wait to get your first report from Melbourne. Our breakfast, when we read your letters aloud, is now the best part of the day for us.

The letters, written during that fearful pre-world war period held us together for dear life. The trip across to the faraway land of Australia may have been long and reasonably uneventful, but the move was a terrible wrench. Our extended family had lived together in the same apartment buildings for generations and we were unused to being apart.

Our first Australian port of call was Brisbane where we arrived on the 7th November. My parents eyed the new terrain, so different from Vienna, with trepidation, wondering how they would manage in such a strange, austere land. As we waited in that port, news of the *Kristallnacht* pogrom, the Night of Broken Glass, reached us. My grandparents never wrote anything about that, for good reason.

Kristallnacht hailed what was to come from one of history's most despicable regimes. It happened in response to the action of a 17-year-old Polish-Jewish student in Paris, who shot a high-ranking Nazi official. In retaliation, German propaganda minister, Joseph Goebbels, organised pogroms across the Reich on the night of the 9th November. It was known as Kristallnacht because of all the shattered glass from Jewish-owned shop windows littering the streets across Nazi Germany, as well as occupied Austria and Sudetenland.

Right across these territories, civilians joined in the free-for-all with the Nazis. Mobs formed, unhindered by police, and burnt down synagogues. Jewish-owned buildings, cemeteries, hospitals, schools and homes were ransacked, and thousands of

Jews were shipped off to concentration camps. Fortunately, most of my family managed to escape harm during this ill-fated event.

The next round of family news caught us up on our arrival in Sydney Harbour. My parents sighed with relief on finding that none of our relatives had been too badly affected by the rioting, plus they felt more heartened on seeing Sydney's more inviting landscape—things were looking up. Days later, we sailed into Station Pier in Port Melbourne from where, in two years' time, Australian troops would leave to help the allies defeat Germany.

My parents scanned the wharf for our sponsors, Dr and Mrs Wishart, who were old acquaintances of my grandparents. Without their help, we may not have been able to get out of Austria so quickly because Australia and other western nations were maintaining strict immigration quotas, despite the terrifying events that were unravelling Europe. The other key aspect of our early escape was that the Nazis still had some semblance of concern about how they appeared to the outside world. So they were allowing some of us Jews out—with conditions: you had to obtain the right visas, relinquish your estate and pay substantial exit fees.

From the ship's deck, my father glanced beyond the Wisharts' sign—'Welcome Langer family'—and across to the Dandenong Ranges in the distance. He wondered where the real mountain ranges might be. Flat Melbourne was a disappointment after picturesque Sydney and compared with the rich character of Vienna, it seemed particularly stark. Nothing in this Antipodean scene alleviated the heartbreak of being unceremoniously ejected from home and country.

Letters from my grandparents urged my father to have courage. Grandfather Arthur judiciously reminded him that they may actually be in paradise, and that they should be grateful not to be back in Vienna in the face of the Nazis. In Vienna, my father had practised as a lawyer, but since his departure Jewish lawyers had been stripped of their right to work. Conditions were deteriorating fast. Grandfather wrote:

There are new regulations now that allow for very few lawyers [to practise]. In Berlin for example, only forty, and especially not Jews. There are many announcements that further worsen our situation such as the special 'J' label in passports.

Grandfather told him to keep his head down and practise tact in dealing with this enormous adjustment. My father had the propensity to be difficult. He spoke his mind, often leaving circumspection and tactfulness to their own devices. This trait began in childhood and was left largely unchecked by his parents. I remember his sister Liesl telling me that he would say dreadfully inappropriate things to visitors. One time, at around age six, he went around the room asking the guests how old they were. Then he would act as if he were surprised, asking, 'And how is it that you are still alive?' His mother would make ineffectual attempts to stop him. This could be dismissed as merely childish silliness, however, but he did not learn to modify this kind of behaviour and as an adult he never restrained his opinions. His stridency could only serve to compound our challenges in Australia, considering we were from a nationality and religion that were not flavour of the month in most places in the world. Arthur's prudent advice was:

[Don't be] critical about your new country. Praise everything you see and make no comparisons with Vienna. People in foreign countries don't like that ... and don't grumble, and above all, don't make unnecessary demands on the Wisharts.

Most of my grandfather's advice was helpful and insightful, but some of his ideas were somewhat naive. Later in that 'don't grumble' letter, he advised that first impressions are not reliable and that we would soon discover new interests in water sports, lawn games and much else. In fact, there were a whole lot of things to consider before water sports. My family's initial experience in Australia was no holiday.

The Wisharts looked after us well. They drove us to the short-term accommodation they had organised for us in a boarding house at Parliament Place in East Melbourne. From there we moved to a guest house at 159 Cotham Road, Kew, where we lived for four months. The accommodation was once a grand, prestigious Federation-style house situated near the shopping centre. It was well beyond its heyday and had been subdivided to house boarders. Our rooms had large windows opening directly onto the red-tiled verandah and the front garden. The weather was stifling hot and to open a window meant battling push after push of invading flies—small black ones and large blowflies. There was not a breath of fresh air, and the sky was perpetually overcast with a grey haze from bushfires.

That first summer of 1938–39 was hot, *so* hot. January 1939 saw Melbourne reach the stunning temperature of 114.1° Fahrenheit (45.6° Celsius). The impending war in our homeland was now so far from us, but the Black Friday bushfires were raging in the nearby hills and across large areas of Victoria, burning an estimated area of 5 million acres (2 million hectares) and destroying several towns. The death toll was 71. The smoke obliterated the sun and everywhere was consumed by haze and ash. My parents had never experienced such conditions. Understandably, they were despondent and could barely raise the energy to look for work. Is this what Melbourne is always like, they wondered?

As for me, a fair, curly haired four-year-old, tall for my age and quite forthright, I would have played happily under the garden hose. But I, too, could feel the general air of despondency, although I did not understand why my parents were feeling so low. My attempts to get their undivided attention were met with irritation as they sat in the shared living room, dispirited, listless and reluctant to move from their place by the solitary electric fan. Even my father who was so childlike and generally loved playing games, became grumpy with me. '*Nein Susi! Geh weg. Wir können jetzt nicht spielen'* (No Susi! Go away. We cannot play now), my father would bark.

I felt very lonely. It was inexplicable to me that they had not brought my black Scottish terrier, Putzi, with us. He had been my constant companion and I talked about him all the time. My parents were very fond of me but they were unused to a little girl constantly pressuring them for attention. In Vienna, my nanny was always at hand to take me to the *Stadtpark* (city park) to play.

The elderly boarding-house owner took pity on me on those stinking hot days, squirting me with the garden hose as we communicated through play because we had no common language. And how strange the English language sounded, the words so loose, like an endless run-on of twangs compared with the clipped precision of German. Everything was different, including the food. The boarding-house breakfast consisted of slabs of white bread and butter, occasionally a boiled egg, and small, pallid sausages that emitted an unappetising smell; incomparable to our smoky, spicy Viennese sausage. We could not bear to look at them, and the hot weather made them even less palatable.

As respite from the stifling heat, we strolled in the coolness of the early evenings. No one greeted us with *Grüss Gott* as we passed in the street, and no one shook our hands. Whenever my parents tried to greet people or ask for directions, they would look at us as if we were somehow not right in the head.

Now and again friends and acquaintances from Vienna arrived. They came with terrible stories and sad faces. I overheard words like 'arrests', 'imprisonment', and 'concentration camps'. I watched their troubled faces as they talked, not understanding the enormity of what they were saying.

As my young self gradually adapted to the new world, the memories of Vienna, my grandparents and other relatives retreated into a dim space in my consciousness. Only my Putzi's face remained.

3

DOWNSIZING

By early March 1939, after a six-month search, my father had found a job in a metal factory as a cost accountant. Being a lawyer and having to do such menial work was quite depressing for him I am sure, but the family needed to be taken care of.

His salary enabled us to move into a rented red clinker-brick house at 15 Knutsford Street in Balwyn. Balwyn was (and still is) a lovely suburb with wide roads lined with oak trees. Our house was probably the most modest in the street. Big properties with tennis courts surrounded us but our garden was of average size with plenty of huge overhanging trees from the neighbouring property. It was perfect for me as I loved climbing trees. From the top of the fence, I accessed the branches and from there, I clambered into another world. I was a climber from way back—way back in the cot.

Confined spaces presented me with a challenge as a child in Vienna; they just dared me to escape. As a two-year-old I preferred to start the day early, well before any of the adults were awake. The high sides of my cot, however, presented an apparently insurmountable obstacle, so I observed carefully as one of my parents or our maid unlocked the clasps. Naturally, at some point, I tried to unlock the clasp myself, but when I did, only one of the two hinges yielded to my efforts, leaving the cot side lopsided. The hard, metallic rails dug painfully into my adventure-seeking body as I climbed out, which always hurt, but it was better than lying around.

As difficult as it was to adjust to many aspects of Australian life, my parents absolutely loved our garden. Our Viennese apartment had no garden, nor a balcony other than the *Klopfbalkon*, a special balcony where the dust was beaten out of the carpets. Fortunately, the Stadtpark had been just five minutes' away, so when I was a baby, my mother took me there for walks in the pram. Always immaculately outfitted in a smart hat, gloves, a simple necklace and a fashionable dress—fashion was a passion of my mother's—she would escape the confines of domestic life and stroll among the English-style gardens, gilded by the many monuments to great Austrian composers.

Then one day, a pronouncement came from on high; our ruling matriarch, my Great-Grandmother Clara Böhm put a stop to this activity. My mother's younger sister, Pauline, wrote about it in her memoir:

My own sister felt the sting when a friend of Clara's met her in the park, walking her newborn baby. Such behaviour was not acceptable. What would people think? From then on, Hertha, not able to afford a nurse, had to stay home to cook and clean and send the maid to the park.

According to the mores of the day, it was unbecoming conduct for the daughter of an affluent businessman to walk her own child. This was the nanny's role. Just a note here about Clara. She was the archetypal matriarch, demanding obedience and adherence to her wishes from everyone within her purview. Under her scrutinising eye—and I mean eye, as she only had one having lost the other in a botched cataract operation—she passed judgement on everything, from behaviour to marriage proposals. Children had to be presented to her for inspection. If they were less than good-looking, artistic or intelligent, they were reproved.

Come snow or rain, the nanny took me to the park to run around in the designated play areas. Park rules were strict. I had to remember to remain only on the paths because it was forbidden to venture onto the grass; like the flowers, trees, statues, ducks and swans, grass was to be viewed from a distance—Vienna had many protocols.

In Melbourne, we were released from the grip of such suffocating mores and my parents delighted in the freedom of their backyard, luxuriating on the lawn and reading books in their deckchairs.

As luck would have it, the week we moved in coincided with the arrival of our container of household furniture and goods from Vienna. You can just imagine the excitement as the truck pulled up, and anxiety regarding the condition of the contents. My father filmed the unloading on his 8mm movie camera, not something Australians would have done at that time. In fact, few Australians would even have owned a movie camera.

The removalists decanted all the familiar furnishings from the enormous crate marked, 'Joseph Popper, Vienna, Intern Transport 330'. Out came beds, bed linen, Persian rugs, a Bechstein grand piano, armchairs, tables, *objets d'art*, trinkets, blankets, tablecloths, kerosene heaters, pictures, books, photograph albums, letters, hand-me-downs and hand-me-ons—the objects of the life my parents had chosen in Vienna. All these settled comfortably into our modest home like dust settling on a shelf, except for the bidet which, of course, we never installed. Bidets were certainly not common in Australia. I doubt people would have known what it was or what to do with it, or even how to plumb it in.

It was with great optimism that we affluent Viennese Jews had packed our crates, and as history would have it, many of the goods would never actually reach their destination, being pillaged by the Nazis before they were loaded onto the ships. In his history of the Gallia family, *Good Living Street*, my cousin Tim Bonyhady wrote:

Nineteen thirty-eight was a good year to be a removalist in Vienna. As tens of thousands fled the city following the German annexation of Austria, the Nazis seized their businesses, required them to pay punitive departure taxes, prevented them from converting their remaining money into foreign currency and stole much of their art. The refugees usually were able to leave with their household goods, however, because the Nazis were eager to maintain the pretence that Austria's Jews were leaving voluntarily and wanted other countries to take them. The result was a surge in demand for removalists in a city where it was common to rent the same apartment for life.

Grandmother Sofie wrote to my mother from Vienna:

I am so happy that you got your things, also in such good condition. I had big worries that everything would disappear and reclaiming here does not help. Netty [the wife of my mother's brother, Andreas] sent two post packets with her best table and bed linen and nothing arrived.

These household goods were the remainders of a wholly different life. According to custom, well-to-do Jewish Viennese families stayed close. Generations of our extended families lived, procreated and died in the same apartment blocks. My parents and I had lived in the same block as my maternal grandparents and most of our extended family. The seven-storey building was located on a section of Vienna's famed Ringstrasse called Stubenring. On the floor above us lived my grandfather's brother Walter, his wife Marguerite and their son Hans. The building at Stubenring 14 was designed by well known Austrian architect Jakob Gartner and erected in 1905. Gartner's apartment and commercial buildings were renowned throughout the empire, as were the many synagogues he designed. Grandfather Arthur inherited our building from his mother, not because he was the eldest, but because he was the favoured son of six siblings.

When my parents married, my mother did not leave the family home. She and my father were given the apartment next door to live in. Our place was half the size of my grandparents' apartment but to give you an idea of the scale, my grandparents' place had a

27-metre-long living room. These apartments were palatial, with ornate ceilings as high as 3.8 metres, marble staircases, quarters for servants and guests—all of a bygone grandeur and scale not seen in most modern buildings.

In a way, my family's DNA forms part of the fabric of the historic Ringstrasse. Our street was at the eastern-most end of the 'Ring', which was constructed on the site of 13th-century mediaeval fortifications. The building of the original ancient city walls, gates, and fortifications that encircled the city centre occurred sometime around 1200. These were funded by the ransom payment for the release of Richard the Lionheart (Richard I of England). Then, in 1857, 27-year-old Emperor Franz Joseph ordered that the old ramparts be demolished to make way for his new vision—the grand horseshoe-shaped, five-kilometre boulevard that would surround the inner city. The ancient city walls were certainly obsolete after the invention of explosives, which would have brought them down in the blink of a detonator.

The Ringstrasse was to be a regal monument to the grandeur of the Habsburg dynasty. The emperor's plan was to line the wide boulevard with imposing civic and domestic buildings in a variety of neoclassical architectural styles including renaissance, Gothic and baroque. The redevelopment also marked a new era for Viennese Jews. Prior to the 1848 revolution, Jewish people residing in Vienna had no rights whatsoever and they were even required to pay a tolerance tax. When the emperor decided to undertake the project, he needed money to finance it and so three months before the cleared lots went on sale, he expediently issued a decree giving Jews the right to own land and dwellings for the first time in Viennese history.

Determined to take their rightful place in society, wealthy Jews were quick on the uptake. They built their own palaces just like the aristocracy. The future seemed optimistic. The homes of various branches of my family sat among government, educational, and cultural structures. Halfway between the two residences of my mother's and father's families was the gothic form of St Stephen's Cathedral, perhaps the most famous Viennese landmark even today. It can be seen from many parts of the city and you can hear the 21,283-kilogram Pummerin bell ring across the city on special religious days.

Directly across the Ringstrasse from Stubenring 14 are two major cultural institutions that occupy the entire block: the University for Applied Arts (*Universität für Angewandte Kunst*), formerly the Austrian School for Applied Arts, and the renowned Museum for Applied Art (*Museum für Angewandte Kunst*, or MAK), formerly the Austrian Museum for Art and Industry. One block north sits the imposing Government Building (*Regierungsgebäude*), originally the Imperial Ministry of War (*Kriegsministerium*), constructed between 1909–1913. Today, the Government Building continues to house the offices of several federal ministries.

The Stubenring segment of the Ringstrasse now also houses shops, offices for small businesses such as interior designers and lawyers, and boutique hotels. Any property along the Ringstrasse is certainly prime real estate. It was then and it is now. And so my family lived in the culturally rich heart of Vienna. I still refer to the Stubenring building as 'ours' because no one actually bought it from us—it was stolen by the Nazis.

Less than ten minutes' walk from there was Lobkowitzplatz 1, another prestigious address where my paternal grandparents, Melanie and Jakob Langer lived with my father and his sister Liesl. Melanie's brother and sister, Ludwig Gallia and the widowed Friedl von Hofmannsthal, lived nearby the Stubenring in the Landstrasse district at Ditscheinergasse 3 in the family home that they had occupied since the time of my great-grandparents, Wilhelm and Eugenie Gallia.

Just 15 minutes from there, Grandmother Sofie's family of origin resided at Mariahilferstrasse 97, a bustling shopping street. Her grandfather, Bernhard Böhm, and his brother Naftali, the founders of the Brüder Böhm hat empire, engaged prominent Viennese architect Emil von Förster to design their apartment house on land just a short walk from their factory in 1883.

The whole Böhm clan lived there even after the children grew up and married. Pauline remembered it fondly in her memoir:

The house had two staircases to accommodate at least ten families and its rear gave onto a lovely, if a bit sooty garden. My mama and all her sisters and brothers were raised in that house.

Nestled within its four storeys were four large apartments occupied by Naftali and Bernhard, and the families of Bernhard's two sons. My great-grandparents, Heinrich and Clara, brought up their children Sofie (my grandmother), Leonie, Hedl, Victor and Joele in their 15-room apartment, which also housed a cook, three maids, a governess and a butler. Each storey had two spacious apartments on either side of the building running front to back. The house also contained four smaller apartments that initially were intended to be income-producing rental units, but ultimately housed members of the extended family. On the ground floor facing the street were two small retail arcades. It featured a courtyard in the middle and an expansive rear garden, which only the very wealthy could afford in downtown Vienna. These days, the Böhm family apartment building houses a large retail store and several offices. Mariahilferstrasse continues to be a premier retail and shopping thoroughfare in Vienna.

When Grandmother Sofie married Arthur in 1901, they lived with her family for 15 years until Arthur's mother Pauline died. Arthur inherited the Stubenring apartment and persuaded Sofie to move there. Pauline wrote:

When Papa dared to move his family a 20-minute trolley ride away, I doubt if he was ever forgiven. Mama cried for years, she told me, because she was that homesick.

The Ring's monumental buildings were completed by the time the emperor died in 1916. Emperor Franz Joseph was 86 years old when he passed away; my mother was just six. Along with family and friends, she watched the spectacle of the funeral procession from the comfort of their long balcony above the street crowds. For kilometres along the tree-lined avenue, the views were superlative from their box seats.

Grandmother Sofie was unable to play hostess that day because she was in hospital having just given birth to her youngest child, Pauline. All her other children had been born at home but this was the beginning of the era of hospital births. So, she missed the regal procession transporting the Emperor's body in the ornate black imperial horse-drawn hearse along the snow-lined streets in late November.

The spectacular albeit solemn funeral pageant was a thousand strong, with European royalty, flanked by plumed and gilded military and horses. More than half a million Viennese lined the streets to watch as the cortege headed to St Stephen's Cathedral, just five minutes stroll from our home. St Stephen's was crammed with diplomats, kings, crown princes, prelates, statesmen and archdukes blazing with colour in their bright blue, beaver-collared Hussar coats—a colourful contrast to the female mourners from the Austrian Imperial family who were draped top to bottom in black crepe veils. After the service, the entourage accompanied the emperor's coffin another four blocks to his final resting place at the Church of the Capuchins imperial vault.

Photos from those earlier years, a lifetime and half a world away, fill me with sadness as I consider the fragility of the era. I was a happy child with a sometimes troubling need for independence. I remember at the age of three standing in my grandparents' spacious bedroom and being a prisoner. Good manners were very important to them and I had neglected to say, 'Good morning'. My grandmother reminded me but I obstinately refused to comply. I decided that I would just leave the room but the enormous panelled double doors were shut. The door handle was too high and no one would open it for me until I uttered the greeting. I remained defiantly silent. Even now, I do not like routine or monotony, never have.

My bookshelves contain old photo albums, monuments that outlived my relatives. Photos captured our happy family and portray me so nicely turned out in dresses, hats and coats. There I was in my father's or mother's arms, and another snap is of me being held by my paternal grandmother, Melanie, who is wearing a dirndl. The one of me on the lap of my infant nurse, in her neat starched cap and apron transports me into a different world, as does the one of my doting maternal grandparents and me taking the spring waters in the Austrian holiday resort town of Altaussee. The thought of Altaussee makes me sentimental, even though I do not recall those holidays too well. I disappear into the old scenes where aunts and uncles ski in the nearby Alps, and my father, uncles and grandfathers are lawyers and industrialists. It was just our everyday life, not knowing that disaster was approaching.

The year I was born, 1933, was in the midst of the Great Depression. This did not affect my family too much, however, because although my father found it difficult to find work after qualifying as a lawyer, fortunately his uncle, Dr Ludwig Gallia had a law practice and took him into the firm.

Being the first grandchild for both sides was a major cause for celebration, and in fact, I was the only grandchild to experience some family life in Vienna. My parents hired an infant nurse whose sole responsibility was to look after me during my first two months of life. After that it was just our *Fräulein* (maid) who performed the household chores as well as helping with my care. My mother had to learn some domestic skills because Fräulein could not do everything. These skills turned out to be a great asset in the turbulent years that followed.

When my mind returns to those early years a few memories stand out, not so much of the people, but certainly of my dog and some of our apartment. I recall the pot-bellied heater opposite the entrance door, the high ornately decorated ceilings like an old museum, and the nursery with bars on the windows to prevent me climbing out and falling to the street below.

A highlight was being allowed to catch the huge lift up to our apartment on the first floor, which was a novelty because mostly we walked up the wide stone staircase encircling the lift. The deep stair risers were difficult for a three-year-old to climb and the way up from the spacious lobby was poorly lit and gloomy. The roomy lift with its metal lattice grid transferred me into a world of changing scenes as we rose slowly and serenely to the first floor. The button was unreachable for me but the lift's slow upward passage was a source of joy. I watched people walking up the stairs at the same speed as the lift's sedate pace and marvelled as the caretaker in the lobby was reduced to a tiny figure.

Yes, the way we all lived in Vienna was a far cry from the leafy outer suburbs of Melbourne on the edge of the Australian bush with not a servant in sight. From a life plump with privilege we plummeted into a penurious existence. Things were going to be especially hard for my long-suffering mother.

I always admired her courage, the way she worked so hard to take care of us under the most difficult circumstances, especially financially. My father, as wonderful as he was in many ways, thought money grew on trees and he was never one to consider that a lack of it was a barrier to whatever he might like to pursue. My mother had been dealing with his extravagances from the early days of their marriage. When she died, I discovered a diary that, unbeknown to me, she had kept since 1919 when she was nine years old. On the 4th May 1936, she wrote:

Peter has been in Prague for 3 days with the Hockeymannschaft [hockey team]. I was to have gone there as well with my parents. Unfortunately, it was too far for them and I stayed with a heavy heart in Vienna because I didn't want to spend the money to make the trip with Peter. I spent the days very quietly and saved a lot.

When Peter returned, I couldn't suppress my bitter face in spite of myself when I heard how much money he had spent, an amount which can't be brought in normally. I didn't want to say to him what I have said so often, that it is only I who gets to feel his extravagance in the end. Unfortunately, he noticed my upset.

He has the ability to enjoy life without thinking of the result. I can't decide to go away [on holiday] if I know that I, the apartment, the child need different things urgently. I am not at all at ease.

Each time financial hardship struck, she made the necessary adjustments. In Australia she would take in lodgers or find something to sell—and always with some humour.

'One must accept what one cannot alter,' she would say. But it was definitely not the life she was expecting.

4

THE GERMANS INVADE VIENNA

Two months before the Anschluss, on the 17th January 1938, Grandfather Arthur suffered a stroke and for weeks after he fought for his life; it was months before he could talk and move again. Overnight he aged and, in fact, he would never completely recover.

Our slice of the world was very attractive to Adolf Hitler. An enduring issue from the end of the Holy Roman Empire was unification of the German-speaking realms, and Hitler was about to fix that problem. At the time, Kurt Schuschnigg was Chancellor of the Federal State of Austria and was a strong opponent of the Nazi Party.

Hitler was mightily displeased when Schuschnigg called a referendum asking the Austrian people whether they wished to remain a free and independent country. My mother's cousin, Henry Böhm, remembers the posters on every street and trolley car urging the public to support the cause. The Austrian military dropped leaflets from the sky throughout the city, encouraging a vote for Austrian independence. In the end, Hitler just sent the troops in. Henry wrote in his unpublished family memoir:

Then, two days before the scheduled vote, came several hours of no announcements, no leaflets, and suddenly the word was put out that the referendum had been cancelled! Twenty-four hours later, on the morning of the 12th, I woke up to the extraordinary sound of a great many airplanes flying at low altitude over the city. When we looked out of the windows, and then went onto the terrace, we saw the black swastika in a white circle surrounded by a red field painted on the tail of each plane, and the Maltese crosses on the wings. The radio proclaimed the Anschluss with great enthusiasm.

As the situation worsened, my mother wrote in her diary:

On 11th March 1938, Austria collapsed. I shall never forget what went on before this time, fever and excitement. I am also not capable of describing it. The universal depression in the last year was unbearable. The many men, the young lads who were out of work was an unbearable and depressing sight and I often asked myself, where was the way out. I saw none. I see no possibility of change if the old system is kept.

The thought that the only possible end was union with Germany is unthinkable. The invasion of Hitler was terrible to many Austrians, and especially us Jews. We tried to be blind and fought for a lost cause. At our head stood a man whom even today I have an inexpressible admiration for, Schuschnigg, who after the death of Dollfuss had become a bureaucratic and unpopular Bundeskanzler [Chancellor], grew in a superhuman way during Austria's last weeks.

The speech he delivered in answer to Hitler's speech and the speech in Innsbruck, in which he announced the referendum, filled many people with enthusiasm and won them over for Austria's fight. In those days I believed in the possibility of a future for Austria.

On Wednesday the elections were announced. On Thursday the excitement became unbearable. Hordes of mostly Nazi sympathisers swept through the streets and organised gatherings. The unemployed and troublemakers were on the side of the Nazis who paid better. Nevertheless, it was possible to hope for a decisive majority for Schuschnigg. The Germans were never liked in Austria.

On Friday at 6 o'clock in the evening it was announced on the radio that the elections had been called off. This news hit us terribly. We knew what it meant. I cannot describe our mood in words. We hung on the radio. Suddenly, just before 7.30, Schuschnigg spoke without being announced. He told us that Hitler had invaded. 'I bear witness before God and the world that I am only yielding to force ... God protect Austria.'

As soon as we could think about ourselves again, we knew that there was no possibility for us in our homeland anymore. We had to find a new home. My father and his relatives and friends were astonished about this decision. They did not suspect that they would soon come to this decision.

The suddenness of the Anschluss generally elicited a sense of disbelief about the malodour in the wind of the impending horrors. Chancellor Schuschnigg was forced to resign and was subsequently arrested, interned in a number of concentration camps and survived to be liberated in 1945 by the US army.

The people of Vienna listened to Hitler's 19,500-word speech on the 28th April 1938, and it seemed that my Grandmother Sofie was initially taken in by the rhetoric, although I think that the references to 'Jewish parasites' may have raised some alarm bells. However, she wrote:

Our impression was that it was a peace speech so that we don't need to worry for the time being.

Luckily, my parents decided not to wait and see. At that point no one else in the family agreed with them, but it wasn't too long before they soon changed their minds. Within two days the Viennese scene altered drastically. Mass arrests began in the evenings and violence lacerated street life during the day.

Previously, illegal Nazi Party members crawled out of the woodwork, happy to air their membership and proudly display their uniforms and badges now that it was 'lawful'. They took over political administrative posts and became commissars charged with overseeing Jewish properties and businesses. Years later

I would read in my mother's diary about how the Nazis rushed at the Jews, arrested or murdered them, stole their businesses and began the process of throwing them into concentration camps. It was unfathomable for everyone living through the nightmare, but a small child will only be aware of a mother's distress, and now of course for me, this time is a blank.

Our last few months in Vienna in 1938 were consumed with preparations to leave. Soon after, the rest of the extended family tried to obtain visas for the USA. Henry Böhm wrote:

We very quickly concluded and agreed that the best chance for all to eventually get out was to emigrate which meant going through the intricate and difficult manoeuvres required for legal departure. Some, probably the younger adults, might have attempted illegal border crossings, most likely not only without German exit permits, but mostly without valid entry visas to elsewhere. Success would have compounded the departure barriers of those who remained behind and failures would be sent to concentration camps.

The only legal way out of Vienna was to obtain an exit visa plus a visa for another country. American, British and French visas were the most sought-after. Daily, lines of Jews waited outside foreign consulates. These queues were an opportunity for Nazis to round them up and brutalise them. Many people were beaten severely, and/or arrested, then taken to prisons and shipped off to Dachau. It was reported that many fled to the Vienna Woods, and many, with a sense of hopelessness and doom, took their own lives.

Before the Holocaust began in full force, my extended family joined the long daily queues for American immigration visas only to be told there was a waiting period of two years. Knowing they would be unlikely to survive that long, they applied for any country that would take them, such as Britain and those parts of Europe not yet embroiled in the conflict. Henry was a small child when his family escaped Vienna. They went to Czechoslovakia because the main factory of the family business, the Brüder Böhm hat empire, was there. There was a catch though: no one could leave without first paying the 'exit tax'.

For my parents, being young and with few assets other than my mother's inheritance and a share in their Stubenring apartment, it was a much simpler task to obtain the exit visas compared with Grandfather Arthur, whose assets took up 30 pages of documents.

It has been estimated that confiscated Jewish wealth paid for around a third of Germany's war effort. They stole a phenomenal 120 billion marks, which is more than $ 17.4 billion in today's money. My family contributed considerably to the war effort in this manner.

5

FROM KITCHEN TABLE
TO EMPIRE

My mother's family made their fortunes in cloth. The silk textile business of the Kary family began in a tiny Hungarian village and grew into the most prosperous silk and cloth business in the Austro-Hungarian Empire. It was started by my great-great-grandfather Siegmund Kary, and continued through the generations to eventually be run by my grandfather Arthur, with the help of my mother's two brothers Otto and Andreas. In 1864 Siegmund established S. Kary & Co. The firm was later called Seiden Kary (Kary Silks).

When the Nazis took power in 1938, the Seidenhaus business headquarters were in the Regensburger Hof in the heart of Vienna behind the Gutenberg monument. Rebuilt in 1897, it is a magnificent turreted, neo-baroque edifice overlooking the historic Lugeck Square. It also housed a retail haberdashery section selling silk, satin and brocade by the metre to the public. Arthur owned that handsome building. Today the Lugeck building is another grand monument to a stolen life, and houses a classy restaurant, the place to go for good schnitzel. They also owned a manufacturing plant in Fischamend, Lower Austria, until the Russians came along and destroyed it at the end of the war.

A typical Nazi tactic at that time was to send small groups of officials to visit Jewish-owned businesses and factories. They would call the owners and workers into a meeting and 'encourage' the employees to denounce their bosses by suggesting that they were subjecting them to poor treatment, or that they were cheating on rates of pay or overtime. This gave the officials cause to arrest them.

Bespectacled Arthur was a proud and arrogant man with a stern gaze and heavy moustache. Family accounts suggest that he and his two sons, Otto and Andreas, were never all that kind to their employees so it is likely that their staff were quite willing to denounce them. My cousin, John Kary, (Walter and Marguerite Kary's son, originally named Hans) wrote and told me:

The sons, Otto and Andreas, were not good employers and treated staff with scant long-term thought, with the result that Nazi union pressure caused them even bigger problems than other Jewish people.

The Karys were thrown in jail whereas the Böhm brothers, Victor and Joele, who were Grandmother Sofie's brothers, were actually protected by their workers because they always treated them with the utmost consideration. The brothers ran a hat manufacturing company that had serviced a global market, plus a domestic market of around 55 million people prior to the breakup of the Austro-Hungarian Empire. Their business originated in 1840 at the kitchen table of my widowed great-great-grandmother Fani Böhm and her two sons, Bernhard and Naftali. They lived in Nikolsburg, Moravia, an ancient city that now forms part of the Czech Republic. On that table (and as I write I am trying not to think about the hygiene aspect), they prepared hare skin for making hats.

The Böhms moved from Nikolsburg to Vienna during the 1840s and opened another business, this time trading in hare skins for the manufacture of fur hats. The business expanded in 1850 when they established a shop on Vienna's Gumpendorfer Strasse, now part of the Mariahilf district, which is a hip wining and dining destination. There, in this once unremarkable street, they cleaned, carroted and cut the skins to create the fully prepared material from which to make the headwear *du jour*. (Carroting was a process used since the 1700s in which rabbit, hare and beaver skins were treated with a diluted solution of mercuric nitrate, a mercury compound. When the skins were dried in an oven, the thin fur at the edges turned orange, hence the term carroting. The process emitted toxic vapours and resulted in the hatters being poisoned by the mercury. This is probably where the term, 'mad as a hatter' derives from because it caused mood and behaviour changes.)

In 1848, Brüder Böhm (Böhm Brothers) hat manufacturers was officially formed, and in 1862 they erected a factory at Schottenfeldgasse 30, in the Neubau district in Vienna. From there they expanded their empire, and in 1881 they built a much larger factory in Prague. By the 1920s, they had built another two factories in Neutitschein, Moravia (now Novy Jicin, Czech Republic) and employed 2,400 employees, making Brüder Böhm one of the largest hat manufacturers in Europe.

By the time of the Anschluss, Brüder Böhm had been handed down to the third generation of brothers—my great-uncles, Joele and Victor. Intense and determined, Victor became the technical head of the company. Joele, who was a charming man, headed up sales. He was the youngest of the five children and his mother's favourite. Being a bit of a playboy, he was 38 before he settled down and married.

Their business was also commandeered by the Nazis. In this case one of their travelling salesmen, Fidel Haas, was appointed 'commissar', and although he became an influential member of the Nazi Party, he remained completely faithful to the Böhms. Joele wrote in his 1969 family memoir:

He was one of the misled ones, basically a decent simpleton who assured Victor and me that it is all a formality, that we should carry on heretofore and should just keep him informed of what we are doing. He considered that his main duty was to protect us and the factory against any encroachment or interference or molestation by 'party hoodlums'—and he kept his promise to the end.

In a very dangerous situation, it was the entire factory personnel that saved Victor and me in a dramatic way from arrest and imprisonment … When the three-man Nazi commission appeared in the factory and called a meeting of the entire crew, among the 200 assembled workers there was not a single one who took advantage of the situation and complained, not even after the commission told them they have obviously become such cowards and serfs that they don't even dare to air their just complaints and grievances. It was such complaints which their red tape needed for our arrest as we learned from other cases in other factories with less fortunate results.

Quite a few of them [the Nazi commissars] were misled themselves and utterly misinformed about the real goals of their party. Some such former business friends came to see me during these first few days and assured me that my family and I have nothing to fear, that we are not the kind of people they are up against and they only want to free society of 'usurers and parasites'. Some went so far as to offer their personal guarantee for my family's safety and their immediate intervention 'if any crackpot would dare to inconvenience us.' They really meant it. Two of them committed suicide when they saw what their cherished party really was.

Before the first week was over, Victor agreed with me that the factory and all our property is lost, that all our efforts must be concentrated on getting out of the country and this sole aim would be greatly endangered through any delay for the hopeless attempt to save the factory.

Obtaining an exit visas was becoming increasingly difficult. Victor and Joele possessed many assets that the Nazis wanted but at that time it had to be seen to be done legally. The Nazis did not want it to appear as though the assets were being seized, so they put business owners through extraordinary bureaucratic hoops.

The brothers were 'required' to sell the business, which they offered to some of their Austrian competitors. Some said they simply had no money to offer. However, the Böhms were not asking for money; they just wanted to exchange the business for exit visas for the entire family which they hoped their competitors could arrange through their Nazi connections. One person said

he would not be involved in a deal that meant 'stealing the factory from us under Nazi duress'. As it turned out none of their leads actually had worthwhile contacts to get those visas.

A month later, their faithful commissar Haas brought them a man with the necessary connections: Othmar Reich, the owner of a Bavarian hat factory. Nevertheless, the deal took another five long months of wading through reams of red tape.

Meanwhile, Haas moved into an apartment within the Böhm family block and developed an even more fervent loyalty towards them, especially Clara. He repeatedly chased roving Nazi molesters out of their home and once personally hurled two uniformed SA (storm trooper) hoodlums out of the factory.

In the end, Othmar Reich paid millions of marks for the business but the brothers did not receive a schilling of it. The same went in the case of the sale of their Mariahilferstrasse apartment block and the various factories—no money reached the family; everything went to the Nazi treasury for punitive taxes.

In August 1938, great-uncle Victor and his family were finally given a time to report to the relevant officer for the issuance of passports and exit visas. The passports of his wife Gertrude and children were available, but Victor's and his daughter Maria's had been 'mislaid'. Henry Böhm wrote that:

At that point the problem was how to find the unobtrusive, polite, non-threatening, yet effective path of bribery to the right official who would find these passports within a day or two … As a consequence of successful financial lubrication, the two passports miraculously appeared the next day and we departed by train for Czechoslovakia, I believe on September 14, 1938.

Giving up their 90-year-old family enterprise was devastating, but there was absolutely no choice. Once Victor and Joele received their visas they had to leave immediately because the visas expired within days and then they would have had to go through the whole process again. This also meant they could not wait for their mother, Clara, or widowed sisters, Leonie and Hedl, to get their visas. No one in the family dared accompany them to the train station. When Victor's and Joele's families finally left Austria, all the cash the Nazis would allow them to take with them was 10 marks each. The stitches of my very close-knit family were well and truly unravelling.

6

NEW BEGINNINGS, DEAD ENDS

The light, filmy airmail letters, stamped with the eagle and the *Hakenkreuz* (swastika), continued to sustain our tenuous connections. My grandparents kept everyone updated about everything that was going on through writing a regular bulletin they titled, 'Children's Newsletter'. These were often typewritten on the thinnest of airmail paper and continued until beyond the end of the war, providing insights into their experiences. These included the latest news from Europe, the deteriorating situation in Austria for the Jews, various individuals' escape plans, and news from other family members as they scattered across Europe, the Americas and the Antipodes to escape their otherwise inevitable deaths.

Victor and Joele Böhm, however, fully expected to remain in Europe. They flew to Czechoslovakia because having a business base there meant they had permanent visas. Joele wrote that things were not as rosy as they were expecting.

When we arrived, tremendously relieved, at the Czech border station, we found Richard and Otto [their cousins, Otto Wolf and Richard Böhm, who ran Brüder Böhm's Czechoslovakian operations] waiting for us. But when we greeted them with, 'Finally, free and safe!' they gasped and said, 'Don't you know that the Nazis have broken their promise to Chamberlain? They were not satisfied with occupying the German-speaking northern part of the country but are advancing into the rest of the country. It's a question of days rather than weeks before the whole of Czechoslovakia will be occupied!' We had no idea how bad things were.

However, Joele and his wife, Ali, and Victor, Gertrude and their three children were caught in a precarious position because they had no documents to go anywhere. A long-term business friend Fritz Feldheim, who was in the leather business, arranged for the Belgium Foreign Office to issue visitor visas for Brussels. They flew from Prague to Brussels on the 28th September 1938, aboard the last civilian plane permitted to fly over Germany.

So Victor's and my family took a non-stop flight to Brussels, crossing over German territory and dearly hoping that no unscheduled stop would be made on German soil. We had heard of such landings in Germany where the refugees were simply taken off the plane and nothing was heard thereafter.

On our safe arrival, Feldheim was waiting for us ... He helped us settle into a furnished apartment and brought us some urgently needed money, which we had previously managed to deposit as an emergency with his company. The Czechs had not allowed us to take more than some pocket money out of the country.

A few days later, Victor and Gertrude whisked their two daughters across to the relative safety of St Winifred's Girls' School in Kent, England. Their emigration was facilitated by the sponsorship of another uncle who was a British citizen. They did not send their son Henry because he had Legg-Perthes disease, a rare and debilitating childhood condition that affects the hip. At that time, he was only able to walk with a heavy brace and needed constant care. He was enrolled in a Belgian school.

Now, with some breathing space, they could attempt to secure their financial situation and plan a move to Britain where they would need to meet the obligations of Britain's preferential quota status. This meant committing to establishing some kind of industry outside London in an area of high unemployment. This ruling was intended to address some of the strain of the 1930s depression. Even so, it was not ideal because the family preferred to be in London, where they planned to bring their mother, Clara, who had by then made it out of Vienna to Paris with her two daughters, my great-aunts Leonie and Hedl.

It was a race against time to sort out what was left of the Czechoslovakian and international side of their operations. The period between May and the end of August was the time when Brüder Böhm traditionally shipped their goods to customers in the UK, USA, Europe, Australia and New Zealand, with most payments flowing in during September. To get around having their business totally pillaged by the Nazis, they executed a cunning plan.

The click-clacking of typewriters could be heard 18 hours a day. Victor and Joele, and their wives, and Otto and Richard, who had succeeded in getting out of Czechoslovakia and had joined their cousins in Brussels, churned out volumes of letters and telegrams to their customers explaining their current situation. They requested that everyone pay their invoices immediately into a Belgian bank account before the Nazis could surreptitiously send invoices on official Brüder Böhm stationery and collect the payments. Because their business was a partnership and not a corporation, they were legally entitled to collect these claims personally. Joele wrote:

Our main handicap in this work was, of course, the lack of books, files and records of any kind pertaining to these claims, but with the help of our foreign agents and our excellent memories, we could reconstruct most of the major claims on our numerous customers.

The campaign met with reasonable success, but in some cases it took months and in others, years before the considerable amounts of funds became available. For the meantime, we had to rely on the minor emergency funds we had created some time ago in London, Brussels, Amsterdam and Zurich.

However, the German army was advancing quickly and after one month in Brussels, it became a matter of urgency that they leave. There were no visas available [for Britain] in the normal way. It was only through contacts there that we could arrange visas.

In the freezing temperatures of January 1939, they endured the 16-hour nerve-wracking ferry trip from Ostend to Dover. Victor and Gertrude visited their daughters at St Winifred's before proceeding to London where they found a temporary apartment in the affluent suburb, Swiss Cottage, an area where many Jewish refugees settled and set up synagogues. Some 50 years later, it became a very desirable area for celebrities such as Daniel Craig, Jude Law, and Jamie Oliver to live but in 1939, it was teeming with refugees from Vienna and other parts of Austria and Germany, including Sigmund Freud and his daughter, Anna, a close friend of Victor's wife Gertrude, who were able to help them settle into the new environment. Even Henry's paediatrician was there, Dr Josephine Stross, who was able to recommend some good doctors for him. They were joined in London two months later by great-grandmother Clara and her granddaughter, Clarisse, (the daughter of Leonie, my grandmother Sofie's sister).

Victor and Joele immediately began the search for a suitable place for a new hat manufacturing business. They were drawn to Lancashire, which was once a centre of the industrial revolution in Britain and would soon become the location of armaments and uniform factories to service the war effort. They found an abandoned factory in Preston that provided an ideal location for the new enterprise. Preston very much needed an economic boost as it had boomed between the two world wars after suffering with the decline of the cotton industry.

The family initially hired six employees. Within months they had 80 people employed in a profitable new business called Bohm Bros. Ltd. They built good relations with their staff, their new community and, as enemy aliens, they even developed a friendly relationship with the local policeman, Constable Smith. Victor's son Henry wrote in his memoir:

The most lasting and important memories of Ingol [the Preston suburb where they lived] revolve around the family of the local constable, Mr Smith, to whom my mother, an adult enemy alien, had to report daily …

Mr. Smith's understanding of his duty as a constable demanded that he not only keep an eye on the Böhm family to protect the country's security, but, within that parameter, also assure for them normal, not unfriendly surroundings…

I have no idea from whence this man and his wife, not widely travelled or highly educated, had the humanity and kindness to make welcome a strange, foreign family from a different educational background, amidst this small unsophisticated neighbourhood. They permitted their son Ian to play with me (not a forgone conclusion as several boys in the area were not permitted by their parents to play with me).

After their factory had been operational for a couple of months, they bought houses in Southport and moved the families up from London. Their new homes were just ten miles from Preston and were furnished with the contents of several vans of furnishings from the Mariahilferstrasse apartments. Although emigrants were not permitted to take more than 10 German marks out of the country, there was a loophole that made it possible to prepay a Viennese moving company. They would pack up the apartment contents after the family had left and ship the fully packed moving vans—it was hoped.

The Böhm brothers' efforts were admirable. There they were in a foreign country, having to speak a foreign language, unfamiliar with customs and laws in respect to labour management relations and the weights and management systems, and within months they had established a successful new manufacturing business and a successful life.

With the advent of the battle of Dunkirk in May 1940, the situation turned. As the German army pushed on to occupy Belgium and France, the enemy alien status of all German and Austrian nationals became more restrictive. The Böhm family lost their freedom of movement and could no longer leave the immediate neighbourhood or travel to London without a police permit. Once the Germans reached the English Channel, the families could not even have radios in their homes. Uncle Joele wrote in his memoir:

We went to the Preston Hotel to listen to the news. It was then that we heard the famous Winston Churchill 'Blood, sweat and tears' speech. I will never forget its tremendous impact on the crowded audience in the hotel lobby. It was a gripping manifestation of unshakeable confidence in the man Churchill. I heard voices around me say, 'Now everything will be all right. He's taking care of it'.

During the last week of June their friendly police commissioner warned them on the quiet that all enemy aliens would be interned in a camp on the Isle of Man in the Irish Sea. Joele wrote:

After all we had gone through, the idea of internment was intolerable for us. It meant separation of our families because these camps were separated by sexes ... It also meant the loss of our considerable investment in our factory, which could not continue for a single week without us.

It is so sad to read Joele's accounts; their enormous disappointment and frustration after putting down roots and making such huge commitments to life in England.

Our firm intention had been to stay in England for good. We therefore had not been interested in the American visas, which we had finally received in January 1940 (after nearly two years of waiting) and which we had shoved in a bottom drawer. We now took them out. Just in time, because mine expired on July 10th, Victor's and Richard's [cousin] a month or so later, and we knew the US consulates usually refused the extension of expired immigration visas ...

Once more they packed all their worldly goods and furnishings to ship to America. The factory had to cease operating immediately and the inventory and plant needed to be sold as quickly as possible, which they did with the help of their accountant. Joele and Ali were lucky to obtain tickets on a ship at short notice, just before their US visas expired. He wrote:

I had to leave on the next boat with space still available. Richard and Victor had another month before they could leave.

Joele and Ali took passage aboard a 10,000-ton passenger ship called *Homeric*. They sailed away from Liverpool on the 8th July 1940, just two days prior to their US visas expiring. Joele wrote:

After 10 days of zigzagging [to avoid attacks] through the Atlantic without naval escort and under blackout against the swarming Nazi U-boats, we arrived in New York harbour on July 18.

Victor and Richard arrived in the US a month later, in mid-August 1940, leaving Gertrude and the children behind. Victor's plan was that they should follow him after he had settled in America and prepared for their arrival. Constable Smith continued to care for the family, permitting Gertrude to travel to London to pursue the extension of their visa applications at the American Consulate. This took several frustrating visits during which time she experienced air raids and tedious days sitting in the consulate waiting room without being able to see anybody.

American entry visas were only issued for a very limited time period and it was almost impossible to get one without documentation for an assured passage with a set date of arrival in the US. It was a catch-22 situation because the shipping line was reluctant to issue tickets without a valid entry visa, and even so, they could be rescinded if the vessel was required for war purposes.

The Böhms' accountant helped to a novel route from the UK to the US via South America. These tickets were unlikely to be rescinded due to war-time requirements but there was a complicated conundrum still to solve. For such a journey they needed to locate a neutral American ship with a firm arrival date, and a South American port willing to provide a transit visa for a US-bound ship. At the end of the day, the single means of getting the families out was providing US dollars to support their applications.

Six months after Victor's departure, in February 1941, Gertrude and the children were lucky enough to secure a place on the *Andalucia Star*, a combined passenger and refrigerated cargo ship that sailed between the UK and South America. Britain depended largely on its supply of beef and mutton from Argentina, and the ship transported passengers on its outward-bound journeys to South America.

The journey was challenging. The ship navigated precariously out through Glasgow's estuary surrounded by large numbers of warships, destroyers and battleships. The vessel moved along in torpedo-avoidance mode, zigzagging sometimes sharply every 3 to 15 minutes. Henry wrote:

This constant turbulence, like a sea storm, took some getting used to by holding onto rails, managing food at mealtimes, etc. The ship was equipped with guns of various descriptions. This lasted for the whole 18 days during which the BBC news broadcasts and occasional German propaganda broadcasts were received. At night the ship steamed ahead without navigational or any other lights. All cabin portholes and other openings through which light might escape were, of course, tightly closed and covered at night in order to conform to strictly enforced blackout regulations.

This continued until they arrived in Montevideo where they would change ships to sail to New York. On the way they stopped at the port of Santos on the Brazilian coast where Gertrude and her three children were the only ones of their party allowed to go ashore, probably because they had left Vienna before their newly issued German passports were stamped with the 'J'. The Brazilian and the Argentinian governments were pro-Nazi at that time. They spent the night in São Paulo where they had arranged to visit the family's friends, Tini and Fritz Feldheim, who had secretly smuggled Gertrude and Victor's valuable jewellery out of Vienna during the spring and summer of 1938. They did this for other friends, too, by travelling to Vienna with fake jewellery and leaving with genuine jewellery.

After travelling north for several more days they finally reached New York Harbour where they were reunited with Victor. Life was never the same for the Böhm brothers in America because they did not have available funds for a new entrepreneurial effort, or the conviction that this was the best way to proceed. Joele and his cousin Richard went to work for a large hat manufacturer while Victor found a job as technical head of a small hat facility.

Before leaving Britain for good, Joele and Victor had travelled to London to say goodbye to their mother, Clara. They were so impressed by her indomitable spirit. At 78 years old she had been stripped of her assets and forced to flee from the chaos of Vienna. But throughout this ordeal she had maintained her exacting standards, albeit somewhat downsized. Joele wrote:

[Clara] was simply admirable in the way she took to and adjusted to all the excitement of these days and the drastic changes in her daily life and circumstances. She takes no notice of world events and keeps her head firmly embedded in the sandwiches and cakes she served for tea, and the family do their best to shield her from any problems.

The farewell was not too emotional as Clara and her granddaughter, Clarisse (Leonie's daughter), were awaiting their US visa approvals. They could not have known that Clara's arduous journey out of Vienna had reached its end.

7

THE 'ROMANTIC REPUBLIC' OF FRANCE

There is, however, the story leading up to Clara's escape to England which needs to be told. Back in mid-November 1938, two months after Victor and Joele Böhm had left Vienna, my great-grandmother, along with her widowed daughters, Leonie 56, and Hedl 54, and Leonie's daughter Clarisse, finally received their exit visas, too. Like many German and Austrian Jews, they travelled to Paris, thinking it would be safe from Hitler's forces and an interim measure before they could return home. Also, France, like Belgium, was still taking Jewish refugees. The women took what they considered 'modest' apartments in the Hotel Royal in the hills of Saint-Cloud, about 10 kilometres from the city centre.

Saint-Cloud was one of the wealthiest communes in France, a delightful and historic enclave close to Paris. My aunts' apartment had a small balcony which offered charming views of the Sacré Coeur, Notre Dame, the Dôme des Invalides and the Seine. For a time, it was a kind of romantic existence; they wrote about enjoying delightful picnics with various other fugitive Viennese family members. In fact, Leonie and Hedl fully expected to lead a long, charming and peaceful life there, albeit without the privileges they were used to—it was after all Paris! Meanwhile, their sister, my grandmother Sofie, was the last of the five siblings still trapped in Vienna along with my grandfather, Arthur.

My mother's sister, Pauline, was also in Paris at this time and was keen to see her newly arrived grandmother. When she knocked on the door of the Saint-Cloud apartment, there was so much noise that for a while no one could hear her. On entering, it was to a scene overflowing with people and food, spread across the two rooms. Trays of delectable profiteroles, pain au chocolat, tarte tatin, mille-feuille and macarons from the local patisserie were being served on every available surface, including the beds, while the kettle whistled on the single-burner Primus perched on the bathroom sink.

Clara, with finger-waved hair the colour of silvery ashes, round metal-framed glasses perched on her nose, sat in her armchair in her familiar pose—head tilted, right hand resting across her abdomen supporting her left arm, forefinger resting on her cheek, and gesturing only to make a point in consideration of the discussions and issues of the moment. It was almost like old times as she supervised her reduced dominion of family and assorted Viennese refugees.

But it was not truly like old times. A war was lingering in the wings and there was much anxiety as the family waited for their US visas, an important backstop should things go wrong in Paris. For great-aunt Leonie there was an added worry: her eldest daughter Anne was in dire straits in Czechoslovakia, having contracted tuberculosis before the war. She was being treated in a sanatorium about 60 kilometres north of the family home in Sternberg. But at this time no effective antibiotic treatment was as yet available; the therapy was principally fresh air, nutritious food and exercise. She was not permitted to have close contact with her children because of the risk of infecting them, and sadly, she was not improving.

Grandfather Arthur sent my parents regular reports about her progress. On the 10th October 1938 he wrote that Leonie had received an urgent letter from Bohemia saying that Anne had suffered a setback and she should be prepared for the worst because both of her lungs had become infected:

Hans [Anne's husband] talks a lot about Anne's illness. He gave us a great deal of joy with his visit. He is a good man, and he came to Vienna just to visit us after the recent difficult days [Germany's annexation of Sudetenland, which included Sternberg, occurred on October 1, 1938] and to see if there was anything he could do to be helpful to us. Anne believes she faces bed rest for the next one and a half years. One really hopes to keep her alive and that she can stay with the children. On a political overview Bohemia is now in close association with Germany. There is also a big wave of anti-Semitism.

A month later Grandmother Sofie, who was still living in Vienna, was able to visit Anne and her family, and wrote to my mother:

Early tomorrow I am going to Sternberg and with a heavy heart I am leaving Papa alone for two days. But I regard it as my duty to see Anne once more as the only one left in the whole family [who can do so]. It is possible at this time to travel to Zwittau [3 hours' travel time from Vienna] without any document. There Hans can pick me up in the car. I know that talking to someone in the family will mean a great deal to Anne and I want to see the children once again.

On the 15th April 1939, Sofie wrote that Anne was a bit better and free of fever, but she was wracked with worry regarding what lay ahead. The German army had invaded Czechoslovakia just a month earlier and she was concerned about the future of the factory, and whether the children would be able attend school. Sofie wrote:

Everything there is still in the air. In her condition, leaving the country would be impossible. So, what will they do if they are forced to leave?

There was nothing her mother, my great-aunt Leonie could do to help. She tried desperately to get a flight from Paris to visit Anne in the sanatorium, but it proved to be impossible; she was trapped. Moreover, for the first time my two great-aunts were compelled to earn a living. Both had been wealthy women who had lived in huge homes designed by the best modernist architects. Out of the three sisters, Leonie was the more attractive and spoilt daughter, whereas Hedl, and my grandmother Sofie, were more unprepossessing. In their previous lives, they barely knew stress and had never experienced hunger. Poverty would have been just a word they knew.

To their credit, and to Great-Grandmother Clara's horror, the sisters set about creating a business making chocolates from their home. They even took private chocolate-making lessons from the head chef at Le Cordon Bleu cooking school in Paris. Production went into full swing and pots of boiling chocolate, fancy fillings and packaging boxes consumed the small apartment. Clara objected strongly to the very idea of her daughters having to work for a living, not to mention the constant mess in their apartment. As repugnant as it was to her, this was not a battle she would win since their future was so uncertain.

Soon enough and just before the Nazis invaded France, Clara was whisked away to London thanks to the efforts of Joele and Victor who were now settled in the UK, so the transgression was no longer under her nose. Joele had organised a small flat for Clara with a bedroom and sitting room in Bayswater Road near Hyde Park. An elderly Viennese refugee was engaged to be her housekeeper and companion. From a lifetime spent in a 15-room apartment on the second floor of an exclusive Viennese address, where she conducted seasonal balls and customary Sunday family dinners for 30 or more people, our formidable matriarch was now jammed into a tiny flat.

Those dinners dated back to the time of the Austro-Hungarian Empire and continued throughout the World War I. In later years, my grandmother reminisced about those happy times when the entire extended family would dine and laugh together around the large oak dining table. For such big gatherings every family was required to bring their own servants to ensure that everyone's needs were attended to. After dinner they would play bridge and chess and a boisterous card game called *Schwarze Katze* (Black Cat).

Who knows what happened to that grand table that held the energy of an intimate family life? However, Clara proved to be most adaptable, soon reinstating a semblance of that Viennese life in her reduced space, with refugee friends and acquaintances. Joele wrote: 'Mother was happy and satisfied and had no complaints'.

Like the French leadership at this time, Leonie and Hedl felt a sense of security living behind the Maginot Line. War had not yet been declared, although French visas were limited to just weeks. Their ongoing visas were made possible by Clara's nephew, George Khuner, who was an executive of International Lever Bros.—Unilever—and worked from the Paris office. Corruption was rife within the Third Republic of France during the 1930s and George was an influential businessman. According to Joele:

[George] had the necessary connections and knew where to make supporting 'donations' to obtain French visas almost instantly. Even though they were valid for just 10 days, he was confident they could be extended indefinitely …

French visas would be the least of their worries, however. In the early days of May 1940, an air-raid siren sounded as the occupants of that small Saint-Cloud apartment lay sleeping in their beds. Leonie heard later that morning that Hitler had invaded Holland. During the six weeks from the 10th May, German forces defeated the Allies across France, Belgium, Luxembourg and the Netherlands. At this time, 350,000 Jews were living in France and more than half of those were not citizens. Many of these Jews had emigrated from eastern Europe after the Great War and now thousands more were fleeing Nazi-occupied territories.

The ensuing invasion and occupation saw France divided in two; the German army held the north and a new government under Marshal Philippe Pétain held the south, with its headquarters in the insignificant town of Vichy. For the Jews, it was to become as bad under Pétain as under the Nazis. Jews were dismissed from their jobs and their freedom of movement was restricted. Later, many were arrested and sent to concentration camps.

On Whitsun Monday came the news that all German and Austrian Jews up to the age of 55 in Nazi-occupied France were to be interned in two days' time, which meant Hedl would be taken because she was 54. Then the ruling changed and the age limit was removed. The sisters had to find a way out of Paris, and immediately. By now the air-raid sirens were blaring thick and fast but no one headed to the shelters because the bombs were not yet dropping on Paris.

Meanwhile, my grandparents Sofie and Arthur, having escaped Vienna by the skin of their teeth (in July 1939), were on a convoluted route to Australia. They had sojourned in Italy and were now in Zurich. Letters to my parents told of how sick with worry they were because there had been no word from either Hedl or Leonie for some time. Pauline was also on their missing list and they desperately needed to make contact with her so they could coordinate their travel to Australia. They wrote to my mother on the 19th April 1940 telling her that Pauline's travel visa had come through and that the three of them were due to board a boat out of Europe at the beginning of May. One month later Sofie wrote:

I am still too close to the terrible events in Europe. I am terribly worried about Pauline, Leonie and Hedl ... Pauline has dawdled so long that she couldn't take the April boat anymore. The May ship was postponed from the first to the 15th, and then to the 18th and she has her ticket for then ... Otherwise I don't know what her fate will be and when I will see her again. You can imagine how worried I am and at the same time it is all so unnecessary. Since the middle of March nothing has stopped [Pauline] making the crossing. If she doesn't swim, I suppose I won't hear anything from her for months.

The occupation of France rolled on and the fighting continued, the streets becoming a terrifying cacophony of shooting, bombs and sirens. Belgian refugees began streaming into the country, the train stations were jam-packed, and vehicles choked the roads loaded with every household item, including mattresses, piled on the roofs. Jewish people were forced to wear a yellow star on their clothing.

On the 3rd June, the air-raid siren sent out its dire warning once more while Leonie and Hedl were having breakfast. Hedl rushed to the balcony and watched as the first German bombs hit Paris. The sound was a grumbly thunder. Its clap killed 254 civilians working in and around the Citroën automobile factory and a thousand more were killed and injured across the city. The sisters scrambled into the shelter and considered their escape options.

Days later, they packed a large set of trunks to ship in advance to Bordeaux, avoiding those streets that were humming with the perfectly synced, goose-stepping German troops, and the Champs-Élysées, where a carnival of roaring tank, car and motorcycle and sidecar battalions paraded. The Germans overtook Paris's time and space. Clocks were reset to Berlin time and the Third Reich flag flapped above French government buildings. Street signs on the main boulevards turned to German and hundreds of thousands fled the capital for the relative safety of the countryside.

The following day, Hedl and Leonie visited the American Consulate, hoping there might be some movement on their visas. They were informed that none would be issued till July. The situation felt hopeless. After the war, Leonie wrote an account of those experiences:

In a café we wrote letters to [family in] the USA and London—a kind of final goodbye. Across from us at the Gare St-Lazare, crowds were piling up. Many cafés were surrounded by police in steel helmets searching for spies. We decided to leave Paris the next day, no matter what.

The German High Command appropriated the cream of the city, occupying the best hotels and restaurants, the theatres and brothels. Paris became their pleasure centre. Such was their munificence, each of their loyal soldiers was promised one visit to Paris, and *The German Guide to Paris* was published bi-monthly for those lucky enough to escape the front for a bit. Even Hitler got his day in the city of love; on the 23rd June 1940, the day after France signed an armistice with Germany, he visited all the great Parisian monuments. It was reported to be one of the highlights of his life.

Italy declared war on France and England on the 10th June. The following day Paris woke to a heavy fog. Leonie wrote that the insides of their nostrils were black but there were more pressing concerns than wondering what the source of it might be. Finding a porter to take their luggage to the station was near on impossible because there was indescribable panic with everyone trying to leave town.

Carrying a few small suitcases, they took a streetcar (tram) to Versailles to pick up their cousins with the intention of continuing on to Chantiers railway station nearby. But the cousins were running late and by the time they arrived at the station, the conductors had abandoned their posts. Even single seats on a horse-drawn carriage were at a premium. As Leonie wrote:

So, we started out on foot. Seven people, doomed to failure from the beginning. Every attempt to find a cart or baby carriage for our luggage was futile.

They joined a long stream of refugees at place d'Armes, the square opposite the palace of Versailles. It seemed too risky to take unknown forest trails so they trekked through danger zones including the army barracks, military checkpoints and airports.

The dreary but perilous trudge continued, kilometre after kilometre, their bags feeling increasingly heavy. They managed to buy an old wheelbarrow for 150 francs but the load was too heavy for one person to push. They spent the rest of June journeying through all weathers—drenching rains or scorching heat. Food was often scarce and sleeping happened mostly in stables. Occasionally they were given a bed in houses along the way where a residing soldier was absent for the night.

Eventually, they reached the town of Rambouillet, around 45 kilometres southwest of Paris. When French military guards discovered that these two older women had walked from Paris, they took pity on them and led them to a barn where they could rest a while. Then they drove them to the railway station, which was packed with people. No one even knew whether the trains were running, so people took whatever vehicles they could to get to take them to Chartres, 42 kilometres away.

Leonie, her cousin and her cousin's two children got a lift on a two-wheeled cart where they sat on a pile of manure behind a drunken driver. They soon discovered that the driver had another destination in mind. The last thing they wanted was to be separated from Hedl and the other cousins, so they dismounted and trudged back to Rambouillet station where they were all reunited.

Sombrely, they waited for a train that might never come. Then the whining of propeller engines came into earshot and soldiers shouted, 'Allongez-vous sous les arbres !' *Lie under the trees!* They hit the ground, burying their faces in their rucksacks to protect their eyes as the machine guns rattatatted overhead. After that, they took refuge in the town's school. Leonie wrote:

We were tired and hadn't eaten for a long time. Katrin [their cousin] went into the street and returned triumphantly with two big bottles of hot soup with pieces of pot-au-feu. Bread was not available. We all ate and immediately our spirits rose. We took off our wet clothes, dressed for the night in the few dry things left and lay down on the paper-thin layer of straw. Our classroom started to fill up. Men, women, children and dogs were put in every vacant space on the floor. Of course, there was a lot of noise, snoring and the smell of garlic, but we still had a few hours' sleep.

Finally, and almost unbelievably, a train arrived. They found seats in the corridor of a first-class car. Inside the compartment were four railway employees who had abandoned their jobs. As the women looked on, the men spread greasy wrapping paper across the seats, pulled out their pocket knives, slashed their hard cheese and *saucisson* (cured sausage), lavished their baguettes with butter, and enjoyed their breakfasts, refusing to make room for them until they had finished their meals.

Many hours later they arrived at Chartres, just as the Germans were attacking. Enemy bombs missed both the station and the town. Then it was on to Saumur. They had not eaten for some time, so they took a break and bought food and underwear and sent postcards to the family to let them know they were still alive. They needed new shoes, too, but these items were unavailable. They bought tickets for Bordeaux while the Germans continued to barrage the area with air raids but the shelters were overpacked, so my two aunts took their chances and waited in a field for the train.

There was less than standing room on the next train that they were able to board. Every carriage was overpacked, but they managed to squeeze in. This journey was filled with a myriad of dramas as people fainted from lack of air, or food and water, and air raids forced them to exit and run for cover. The slow train was a smelly caterpillar as the days passed; caught in a futile frame, sometimes going forwards, other times back, as air raids loomed overhead.

Food became scarcer and the dispossessed became more depressed and exhausted. Eventually, most of the passengers got off including our hungry, grubby Hedl and Leonie. On their swollen, sore feet, they and their cousins walked in the burning sun to the next village. When they finally spotted La Roche from half a kilometre away, they were too tired to continue, instead collapsing in the field, dazed from exhaustion. Leonie wrote:

We crawled the uphill way from the station into the village, a trip that later we had to repeat very often. The first large farmhouse was overcrowded with French soldiers. We didn't even try to ask for quarters there. A few houses further on, we saw some women in an open kitchen window. In answer to our question as to whether we could spend the night there, they said no. But after we took a few more steps they called after us that we could sleep in the hayloft of their barn. We were overjoyed and settled down satisfied with the milk and bread, which our new hosts placed on a table in the courtyard for us.

As they ate, they watched their hostess in the doorway of her house, tears welling in her eyes as she said goodbye to her husband, who was off to join the British army. While they felt very sorry for her, they only had energy for eating. Again, they would sleep in a barn and make their beds with a pitchfork. But sleep was interrupted that night when four French soldiers returned to the farm, drunk and scared. Their officers had deserted them so they had become helplessly exposed to German air raids.

The following day Hedl and Leonie were invited to stay on at the farmhouse. At this stage, there was no point in moving on because nowhere was particularly safe. They adapted to the daily routines and Leonie wrote that for a time, they enjoyed a relatively peaceful interlude.

We had fine weather and everything looked friendlier. We became acquainted with the house and the inhabitants. Fernande was looking after the kitchen, Mme Bottreau was running around the house confused using a magnet to collect straight pins that were strewn about her sewing room. The 82-year-old grandmother was sitting in the kitchen staring vacantly. In the house every bed was occupied, the larger ones doubly ... Eventually we were asked to eat in the dining room with the family.

One evening when the four soldiers did not return, Leonie and Hedl were upgraded to their quarters.

It was a large ground-floor room with a brick floor and completely unfurnished. Along the wall was a large pile of straw which had not been changed nor turned since the soldiers had left. Gun shells, which were buried in the straw, were found only weeks later when our room was cleaned. This was now our apartment into which we gratefully moved.

Soon after, the peace was ruptured by an explosion; a nearby bridge had been dynamited. A few days later German troops marched down the road and pilfered food from the abandoned houses. This region was now occupied. Facing the scenes of defeat, Leonie walked 12 kilometres to a village to get some shopping.

Endless rows of German supply vehicles came toward us, everything moving in the direction of the coast. To the right and left of the road lay discarded French gas masks, steel helmets and weapons lay in heaps. One had to be careful not to step on live shells ...

Soldiers regulated traffic in the town. All large buildings were occupied by German staff and marked by the flags with the crooked cross. The artificial rate of exchange was in force, but the merchants didn't yet know what this sell-out really meant ... Tired and depressed, I returned home.

By the end of July, they received a family letter with news that buoyed them. Leonie's son Thomas had made it to England, and their brothers, Victor and Joele, and their families had arrived in New York.

Life continued relatively peacefully in La Roche. No one showed animosity towards them for being foreigners; everyone just got on with their daily work. Then, on the 15th August, an air squadron flew overhead towards the west, heading to the fiercest battle of the war—the Battle of Britain, or Black Thursday. The Luftwaffe launched a series of air raids aimed mostly at Royal Air Force (RAF) bases and the entire RAF was engaged in defending London and Britain's south east. It was a critical battle and marked a turning point in the war. Winston Churchill gravely announced that, 'Never in the field of human conflict was so much owed by so many to so few'. Leonie wrote:

We counted 53 planes … We guessed that this was an attempt at invasion of England. The newspapers kept silent. After a short time, there were large military transports in the opposite direction. 'Ils ont des mauvaises têtes,' [They have bad heads] said the people with great satisfaction. It seemed the invasion had failed.

Who knew how and when this devastating war would end? Leonie and Hedl could not sit by complacently and hope; they needed to find out whether their American visas had been approved. They decided to take a chance and return to German-occupied Paris. There were no restrictions on travel within the occupied zone so the train journey back was relatively simple. They arrived in Paris in the evening. It was a depressing sight; Paris was now a spectre of its former glory. The streets were dark and empty and German soldiers occupied all the fine restaurants.

The trip the following morning to the American Consulate proved fruitless; they were still not giving attention to visas. However, there was a letter waiting for them with devastating news—Leonie's daughter, Anne, had died in the sanatorium on the 28th August 1939. She was just 32.

Hedl cradled her sister in her arms as she wept and wept, guiding her into a tiny café nearby where there were no German soldiers. Seeing their distress, the waiter brought them espressos and shots of Benedictine.

'You must be strong. We cannot give in to this now,' Hedl told her sister.

Days later they were summoned to the prefecture where a policeman advised them to get out of town the best way they could. They returned to La Roche in time for the wine-making and harvest festivities; and by October there was exciting news from the local American Consulate in Bordeaux. Their US visas had been processed. However, it soon became clear that the Germans would not allow them to leave. Then more bad news: a telegram informing them of their mother's death. In early September Clara had been stricken with pneumonia in the midst of the air Blitz on London. She had been well-attended by their doctor from Vienna but became progressively weaker, and died of heart failure on the 19th September 1940 with Leonie's daughter, Clarisse, at her bedside.

8

THE IMMIGRATION MINEFIELD

Keeping ahead of the German army was all very well, but where to go was often a conundrum because immigration laws were another minefield in this escalating war. The story of my aunts can wait for just a few moments because it is worth noting how those parts of the world not plunged into war were responding to refugees. In July 1938, in Evian on Lake Geneva, delegates from 32 countries assembled for a nine-day international conference to deliberate over the refugee problem. Although there was a general expression of sympathy for refugees, most countries, including the United States, Canada and Britain, offered excuses for not granting entry to more people than their quotas dictated. In fact, the US president, Franklin Roosevelt, did not send his secretary of state or any other high-ranking official; he sent a friend of his, businessman Myron Taylor, to represent their mighty country.

Even efforts by some Americans to rescue children failed. The Senate refused to support the Wagner-Rogers bill to admit 20,000 imperilled Jewish refugee children in both 1939 and 1940. Anti-Semitism wasn't just a European phenomenon: racial prejudice, including anti-Semitism, was rife amongst US State Department officials too.

The attitude of Australia's government was no better. Australian Cabinet Minister, Colonel Thomas White, stated that, 'As we have not real racial problems, we are not desirous of importing one by encouraging any schemes of large-scale foreign migration'.

Nonetheless, that year Australia took a thousand more Jewish refugees than they had the previous year, largely as a response to the horrors of *Kristallnacht*. That one night of destruction convinced the Australian government to change its policy and accept 15,000 Jewish refugees over the next three years.

These responses from the major countries turned out to be a juicy feast for the German propaganda arm of the Nazi government that stated grandiosely how astounding it was that foreign countries criticised Germany for their treatment of the Jews, but none of them wanted to open the doors to Jewish refugees when the opportunity was offered.

By the time of Leonie and Hedl's sojourn in France, more than 250,000 Jews had exited Germany and Austria. The US took 155,000, the UK 40,000, 8,000 refugees entered Palestine, 14,000 went to Switzerland, and 15,000 went to France.

Britain's quotas made provision for the entrepreneur. They would accept people who could enhance the nation's industry, which was how Victor and Joele were able to get their British visas. Australia was also not keen to receive the 'detritus' of the European war. It, too, was in the depths of economic depression and government-assisted immigration had just about ceased. Certainly, there were hefty disincentives for non-British migrants. They needed a guarantor and £500 landing money to gain entry.

But at the time of our migration in 1938, there was increased pressure on governments to accept German Jewish refugees. The Australian government reduced the landing fee to £50 for those with guarantors and demanded £200 from those without. My parents and I did not suffer the traumas of many Holocaust survivors. Nevertheless, like all refugees, we were not exactly made to feel welcome and, as a matter of policy, refugee-ism was considered to be a burden.

Another avenue for a European exit, albeit tricky and expensive, was a path through Moscow, then a trip on the Trans-Siberian railway over the Russian-Manchurian border to China.

Interestingly, Shanghai became something of a safe haven for more than 10,000 Jews from 1938 to 1945.

For Hedl and Leonie, the situation worsened as the Germans tightened the noose around the Jews in France by widely distributing anti-Semitic propaganda. Aunt Leonie wrote:

Through posters on the walls in Chinon [a nearby town], the Jews were ordered to the prefecture. The Vice-prefect, who had previously spoken to [their cousin] on several occasions, had simply advised her, 'Filez !' [Scoot!] And on top of it, he had given her the address of an inn at the border, the proprietor of which made it his business to transport people across the border.

They contacted the inn proprietor, Monsieur Meunier. A few days after making contact, he suddenly appeared to inform them that they should travel alone to the border and he would meet them there. He took care of their jewellery and luggage, promising to send it on to them.

On the 25th October, as they waited in a furniture removalists office for several hours, someone mentioned that the Germans searched vehicles. This made Leonie very anxious about the US$ 1,000 in her luggage, so she decided to leave it to be taken care of by Monsieur Meunier. They departed at dawn in the removalist's private car, which towed a van filled with passengers. Late that night they arrived in Evreux, which abutted a huge German border camp.

The following dawn a primitive ferry took them to the other side of the river, then they caught a train bound for a spa near the border.

It was a charming resort with a good hotel which was completely occupied by German troops. At the long lunch table, a well-dressed young man sat opposite us and wanted to talk but we were awaiting Meunier and wanted to remain undisturbed.

Meunier appeared punctually and sat down to eat. He mentioned that very soon a milk wagon would stop here and would take us along. The coachman was told that the two of us were Meunier's aunts … We sat down on the little stools … under the cover of the wagon. In front of us were large cans full of milk, which we would have to deliver on our way.

At a turn of the road, in true terror we saw the partner from our lunch table; beyond any doubt he was from the Gestapo … We made ourselves as small and as invisible as possible under the canvas. In the meantime, Meunier, on his bicycle, had caught up with us and brought with him the Gestapo man who in fact was just a poor devil, who like us, wanted to cross the border but had even less courage to do it than we had.

I can imagine this 'poor devil' would have been terrified of being detected by the German army. As a deserter, he most certainly faced execution by firing squad. Leonie and Hedl arrived at a farmhouse to find, already seated in front of the fireplace, Meunier, his father-in-law and the suspected member of the Gestapo. After some refreshments they were led out to the yard where Monsieur Meunier indicated that beyond a group of faraway fir trees was the free zone. They were to make the journey there alone and he would rendezvous with them.

It wasn't a particularly long walk, just across a couple of fields, but it felt surreal to these two older 'peasant ladies', heads disguised by lacey cream bonnets, meandering with baskets to fill with wildflowers. Wooden stakes decorated with German colours to the right of them indicated the demarcation line. They reached the fir-tree forest and to their great relief, Monsieur Meunier was waiting at the border. He had with him Monsieur Barillet, a man with whom they marched another 8 kilometres to his home in Preuilly-sur-Claise, a village filled with French soldiers. He put them up for a few days, and once more they were in for awkward sleeping arrangements.

The old man started with preparations for the night. With uneasiness, we learned that we had to sleep in the only large room next to the kitchen … He gave us impeccably clean bed linen and left the room so we could get ready for bed.

When we were lying in bed, he entered the room, disrobed as much as he thought necessary, put on a white night cap, lit his pipe and went to [his] bed.

'Bonne nuit, mes dames.'

'Bonne nuit, Monsieur.'

Then came a final meeting with Monsieur Meunier to arrange the last leg of the escape.

At dinner the following took place; the turning over of our jewellery and money and also the settling of our account, namely 10 percent of everything, and everybody was satisfied about it … The next morning, we drove to Chateauroux, and from there we joined the endless train of travellers, of wanderers, but we were no longer the hunted ones.

And so it was that the sisters boarded a ship in Nice and sailed to America. Events change people. Leonie, who was always considered (by my mother, at least) to be a rather selfish woman, had changed considerably after experiencing life's tenuousness and her terrible losses. My mother, with whom she spent her remaining years, said that she had transformed into the kindest, most thoughtful person one could imagine.

9

CAPITALISTS OUT!

Meanwhile, in Sudetenland, Leonie's son-in-law Hans and his three children, Arthur, Heidi and Rudi, were having a less difficult time under the Nazis. Two months after Anne's death, Grandfather Arthur reported:

His [Hans's] mill is running well and his looms have been changed to the new automatic system. His children are healthy and they think lovingly of poor Anne.

Although Anne and Hans's marriage was arranged by the family, it had been a successful union. Anne was born in 1907 with a physical handicap. The left side of her body was not as developed as the right and the left leg was not properly aligned with the right one. When it came time to finding her a husband, they needed to look no further than their own business. Leonie's husband, Arthur, had taken over his family's textile factory, Heeg & Friedmann, which was founded in 1850 in Sternberg, Moravia (now Sternberk, Czech Republic). It bore the 'K.K.' or *Kaiserlich Königlich* designation, the imperial and royal warrant of appointment, which meant they were suppliers to the Austrian Imperial Court.

Heeg was an earlier partner but when in 1870 he was bought out, his name remained so that the company would appear less Jewish. The director of the mill, Hans Klimes, began his career there as a fabric designer but through talent and hard work, he was eventually promoted to manager. After Hans and Anne developed a fondness for each other, their marriage was arranged when Anne turned 19. Thus in 1938, when Jewish businesses were being forcibly seized, Leonie was able to sell the factory to her son-in-law, Hans. He went on to make it highly successful.

Hans was not Jewish, and as this difficult story evolves, it proved to be of some use to their children who were classed as *Mischlings* (a term used by the Nazis to describe people who were half Jewish and half 'Aryan'), once the Germans took Czechoslovakia.

The Nazis allowed Hans to keep his factory running despite the fact that his late wife had been Jewish and his children were *Mischling*, because they needed it to produce fabric for their military efforts. The children could attend school but only until they were 14 years old. In his autobiography, *An Adventurous Pilgrim*, Hans's youngest son, Rudolf (Rudi), recalled his childhood view of the occupation:

The German army marched in, 'Isn't their goosestep grand,' I asked my classmate Fritz …

As an unwilling citizen of the Third Reich, I had to greet my teachers with an outstretched hand salute and say, 'Heil Hitler' … Hitler touched me in a number of personal ways … First and foremost, he condemned me to death, together with all the Jews and half-breeds. I had to study *Mein Kampf*, and memorise and celebrate his birthday. There were occasions I had to sit and listen to his shouting speeches. That was painful because we could not comment or react.

By the age of 14, Heidi was sent to Vienna because she was no longer permitted by the Nazi authorities to attend school in Czechoslovakia. In Vienna she attended boarding school where she was accommodated with some of the children of the Austrian monarchy. However, when they discovered she was half Jewish, she was expelled, which happened in every subsequent school she was sent to. Both she and her brother Arthur spent the rest of the war, from 1941 to 1945, in hiding with Viennese families, while Rudi remained with Hans who was still in Czechoslovakia running his business.

Although the final battle in the terrible war took place in Czechoslovakia and continued even after the official surrender of the German army on the 8th May 1945, a new battle was on its heels. Two days before, on the 6th May, General George Patton led the American Third Army to victory over the western portion of Czechoslovakia, while the Soviets liberated Prague during the Prague Offensive. When the Germans were defeated, the Third Army halted its advance and Czechoslovakia was divided between the Soviets and America till the end of 1945.

Initially, I knew little of the Klimes' family ordeals. My mother had told me that Hans escaped to Canada in December 1948 with his two sons. In 1994 when I visited Toronto, they filled in some information gaps and conveyed the fact that their trials under the Soviets were far worse than their experiences with the Nazis. Once the Soviets took power, the country lurched onto a violent path towards Soviet satellite-hood and life became intolerable. The Russians turned the country upside down as the German army retreated, with Sternberg, where Hans and the children lived, becoming a site of murder, theft, rape and destruction. Rudi wrote:

I had survived Hitler's Holocaust. Could I accustom myself to life under Stalin's Iron Curtain that was fast descending on us? ... I was at a loss as to where to turn. In our family, we did not talk about our fears.

During this time, Hans counselled the children not to go out onto the street because they would be shot by soldiers. Sternberg had become lawless. Nazis fled in cars, trucks, bicycles or on foot as the Russian juggernaut rolled in. Rudi remembers that the local cigarette factory across the street from their home was set upon by civilians. Cigarettes became currency in the collapsed economy. He was just 13 and wanted to join in the fun.

'We do not steal. We do not need their cigarettes,' his father told him.

Those early days were rife with danger. As a businessman, Hans was at considerable risk of being shot or deported to a Siberian gulag—capitalists were considered to be a scourge on society, and Heidi, who was 17 by now, was likely to be raped, or worse. So, the family gathered their bedding, clothes and food and hid in the loft under the factory roof. They stayed there as long as they could while the Russian soldiers puffed out their chests and established their dominance through systematic and indiscriminate, sickening violence and rape.

In terms of daily life, everything stopped: the mail service, electricity, police, buses and trains shut down. The Czech currency was near worthless although diamonds, pearls and gold held their value. Hans had a safe in the factory where he kept money and family valuables, including expensive jewellery, which were gifts from Anne's family. A few days after the Soviet army rolled in, Hans' accountant was held up at gunpoint by an officer and ordered to open it and empty the contents into two flour bags.

A month passed before two armed soldiers burst into their stylish 13-room house on the site of their once lucrative factory and stole all their belongings. They took all the furniture, which included exquisite Biedermeier pieces, and ordered the family to vacate. Hans and the children rolled up their bedding and everything they could carry in their cardboard suitcases and moved to an assigned one-bedroom apartment to co-habitate with bed bugs. The Klimes family became one of the impoverished multitudes in the now Soviet-ruled Eastern Bloc.

Some weeks before their move, Hans was ordered to attend a short interview with the Russian authorities. He was taken to an overcrowded barn filled with local businessmen and the pungent smell of cow dung. From there they were forced on a march to Siberia, a distance of more than 5,000 kilometres. This kind of journey is hard to imagine. Even the soldiers must have been sorely pushed.

After three days, Hans outwitted the guards by feigning a heart attack. He let his body collapse into a ditch, seemingly dead. A soldier kicked him hard but he remained motionless. After everyone had moved on, Hans headed for the woods and made it back home three days later, sick and starved. Soon after, he was arrested again by the KGB, this time on suspicion of collaborating with the Nazis. Although they questioned him under duress for several days, the charges did not stick and amazingly, they set him free.

Life settled into a semblance of normality and for the next two years Hans supported his family by working as a textile teacher in a town some distance from home, while his two boys studied at a textile school. The US relatives had for some years tried to persuade the Klimes family to flee. Finally, after years of enduring communism and having their wealth redistributed to those who had decided that wealth was evil, Hans and his children decided to exit before the Christmas of 1948. They could only leave if they signed papers declaring they relinquished their Czech citizenship and the Sternberg properties. This would mean that they would have no passports and would have to travel with certificates of identity.

Then, just as they were making their final arrangements, Heidi hit them with unwelcome news. She had fallen in love and become pregnant to a Catholic Czech army officer, Mirek Rohel. Hans was absolutely furious. Rudi wrote:

A few weeks before [they were to leave Sternberg], Papa had a little ceremony in front of Mutti's [mother's] portrait and read Heidi out of the family for becoming pregnant out of wedlock. Now she was staying behind to deliver her baby and to get married.

Would we ever see her again? At that time, it seemed as though we were saying goodbye forever.

They left with the grand total of US$16, and without Heidi. They flew to Montreal via Prague and London. In Canada, they were classed as stateless refugees. Within a week of their arrival, Arthur and Rudi found night work in a textile mill and supported the family while they got established. For Hans at the age of 61, the adjustment to a new country and a very different culture and language was not so easy, but after just six months he was able to prove his technical skills in the textile industry. He got a well-paid position as manager in a textile business in Galt, Ontario, where he stayed until his retirement. Hans took a short holiday in 1951 and reunited with Leonie and Sofie in Miami. Sofie wrote to my mother about the reunion:

He spoke much and interestingly about the last time in Sternberg, but he barely spoke about Heidi … He knows exactly that with his salary of $ 5,000 per year, he is greatly underpaid, for he had brought the nylon material to an unheard-of standard. But he put up with it, temporarily, when he had to provide only for himself …

Hans Klimes got his job without knowing a word of English. He described very successfully how one had to get an interpreter in order to negotiate with him. The town of Galt, where he works, is somewhat similar to Sternberg and there he leads a quiet life just as he used to. Therefore, he quite likes it.

As for Heidi, 13 months after Hans and the boys left, she married Mirek. The marriage had to be delayed because the Russian authorities deemed that she was German and as such they would not give her permission to marry a Czech officer. Life was doubly difficult for them because they refused to join the Communist Party, which caused them to be ostracised and isolated from their community. Ultimately, it led to Mirek's expulsion from the army.

My journey to Toronto in 1993 was principally to visit my daughter, Gill, who was studying at Waterloo University. My other mission was to meet the Czech side of the family. I was overjoyed to find that Heidi was waiting for me at Toronto airport. Over the few days we spent with her I learnt that she had eight children and that after she had her seventh child in 1963, she and Mirek decided to plan an escape from Czechoslovakia.

That year, in 1969, they all headed for Vienna on a holiday visa on the pretence of visiting Heidi's family. At that time the authorities would only permit them to leave for a vacation. They filled their cases with clothes, loaded them into the boot of their small Skoda and packed four of their children into the back seat. The three eldest children had to travel alone by train. To avoid raising suspicion, they had to leave everything they owned behind.

After they arrived safely in Vienna they stayed in a tiny apartment while waiting for their Canadian papers to be approved. Then four months later, they received permission to settle in Toronto and the family was finally reunited; and Heidi was reconciled with her father.

10

ALL THAT REMAINS

Returning to Vienna at the end of 1939, very few members of my extended family remained. Still hanging in there at Stubenring 14 was great-aunt Marguerite, the wife of Grandfather Arthur's younger brother, Walter, along with her son, Hans (not to be confused with Anne's husband, Hans).

Some 30 years earlier, the marriage of Marguerite Selinko and Walter Kary had been arranged by their families; the Selinkos and Karys were well acquainted through the trade. Walter and Marguerite developed into a stylish, fashionable and popular couple, throwing regular parties and travelling widely—including to exotic places such as Egypt. They had a hunting lodge in the country, two trendy dachshunds and the latest cars (Marguerite was purported to be one of the first Austrian women in Vienna to drive a car). On the surface they had it all, but one thing was missing: they had been unable to have children. Then in 1927, after 23 years of married life, when Marguerite was 41 years old, she gave birth to a son, Hans. He was the light of their life. Grandmother Sofie never forgot her response: 'Mein Gott, ich habe ein Enkelkind geboren.' (My God, I have given birth to a grandchild.)

Like Arthur, Marguerite and Walter were also dealers in fabric. Their business, Brüder Selinko, was a woollen-cloth wholesaling business that was established in Vienna in 1869. Walter had purchased the business from Marguerite's father, Ignaz Selinko.

Pre-1918, Brüder Selinko was the largest and most profitable textile wholesaler in the Austro-Hungarian Empire. When borders and markets changed dramatically post-World War I after the signing of the Treaty of Versailles, their business needed to adjust significantly in order to survive and they established a new weaving mill in Inzersdorf, 15 kilometres from the centre of Vienna. But now that it was under the directorship of Walter, it often teetered on the brink of bankruptcy. Walter was by all accounts not a good businessman—he would overstretch their capabilities and borrow too much money for expansion.

Then, tragically, Walter was stricken with encephalitis and lapsed into a coma that lasted several weeks. After regaining consciousness, he could neither walk nor talk. Some of his functions returned after rehabilitation and he managed to live another five years. But from the time of his illness, Marguerite and the technical manager ran the business, conservatively and successfully. Walter died in 1935.

By the time of the Anschluss, Marguerite was well adjusted to life as a single mother. When the Nazis arrived, they expelled all the Jewish children from the Catholic School little Hans attended so, undeterred, Marguerite sent him to the Goldschmidt Schule in Berlin, a school that was created for Jewish children who were no longer allowed to enrol in public schools. After two terms he returned and was schooled at home until he finally got a place on a *Kindertransport* (children's transport) in June 1939, for the sake of his safety.

The *Kindertransport* was an organised rescue mission that began nine months prior to the outbreak of World War II whereby Britain agreed to take in around 10,000 refugee children, mostly Jewish, from Germany, Poland, Austria and Czechoslovakia. Once in the UK, the children were fostered and, in many cases, became the only family members to survive. These children were often terribly traumatised by the dislocation from their families and the terror of being taken to an unfamiliar place. And then, of course, at the end of the war came the grief of their losses.

The effect of this could be seen plainly in my family. Some of my other relatives were transported to the UK under this scheme as well. When Arthur's brother, Fritz, was abducted by the Gestapo during Kristallnacht and sent to Dachau concentration camp, his wife sent their only child, 14-year-old Victor, away on the *Kindertransport* while she was trying to get Fritz released. She managed to do so in 1939 and he was able to join his son and wife who were then both in England. They hardly recognised the emaciated man at the dock when they went to pick him up in Dover. Soon after his arrival another blow struck. On the 27th May 1940, Fritz and Victor together with over 10,000 Jews and Nazi sympathisers of German and Austrian origin were declared enemy aliens and sent to the Isle of Man where they were imprisoned until after March 1941.

Victor, however, was lucky as he was taken on by an old electrician as an apprentice and was able to escape the horrors of the camps. Fritz spent his last years in London and died of cancer, a broken and sad man, in 1947.

Also, great-aunt Friedl von Hofmannsthal's two children, Huni and Liselotte, were shipped to England where they lived together under very straitened circumstances and were left pretty much alone to look after themselves while Friedl spent the war years in Hungary.

Friedl told me that when she emigrated to the UK after the war, the children did not come to meet her at the train station. Unsurprisingly, it took them a long time to adjust to having her around. The children would have experienced such complex emotions about their parents after what they had been through, as well as feeling abandoned, afraid, angry and traumatised.

So, amidst the chaos and distress of hundreds of other parents, Marguerite put little Hans on the train from Westbahnhof Station.

Holding back the grief-fuelled tears that threatened to engulf them, the parents waved their children goodbye, not knowing whether they would ever see them again. The hoarse 'her-*chug*, her-*chug*, her-*chug*' of the steam train hurried the children to safety through Cologne to the Netherlands, then up to the Hook of Holland, where they boarded a ship that took them across the North Sea to dock at Harwich in Essex.

Soon after, Marguerite was forced to leave her apartment and go to live with her mother in the Leopoldstadt district, which had become a Jewish ghetto. She got a nursing job at the Rothschild Hospital, every day walking an hour each way to and from work because Jews were not allowed on public transport. During World War I, after Walter went off to fight in Poland, she had trained as a Red Cross nurse, a role she had thoroughly enjoyed.

Letters that Marguerite wrote to various organisations and people who might be able to help her escape were kept by her faithful nanny. Presumably, Marguerite left it too late for them to be sent before she was rounded up along with her mother and sent to Theresienstadt concentration camp in Czechoslovakia—a halfway house for the Nazi killing centres. In addition to the overcrowding, starvation and forced labour (one day Marguerite managed to get an onion, which she gave to her sick and malnourished mother; her mother eventually died in the camp), it allowed inmates to run schools, art and music programs. It even had health facilities.

Theresienstadt was used as a showpiece, or rather for propaganda, to show the Red Cross how well the Nazis treated their inmates. The truth was that if the inmates survived, they would ultimately be taken away to extermination camps.

Marguerite was a nurse in the camp, which saved her life the day her name came up to be sent to an extermination camp. The doctor gave her a shot to render her unconscious for 24 hours and told the German soldiers she was too ill to move. What was even luckier was that the end of the war was near.

On her release in 1945, bloated, feeble and malnourished, Marguerite returned tentatively to Vienna, understandably afraid of what she would find. The city had been bombed 52 times and 87,000 houses had been destroyed. It has been reported that there were more than 3,000 bomb craters throughout the city. Her Stubenring apartment had survived but it was still occupied by an Austrian Nazi family so, despite the overthrow of the German regime, she was unable to return to her home.

Friends in the Leopoldstadt district ghetto, formerly Vienna's Jewish quarter, took Marguerite into their home and cared for her— her physical condition was very poor after enduring years of a diet of bread, potatoes and watery soup. Soon afterwards, she fell and broke her hip but pinning it was out of the question because of her deteriorated physical state. Her life-long legacy was a very bad limp.

When she was well enough, she applied for a visa to visit her son Hans in London. Britain clearly was not keen to entertain any more refugees and her first application was refused on the grounds that she might want to stay in England permanently, which in truth, she did. It seems that one of her relatives worked at the Danish Embassy and he wrote a letter on her behalf on embassy letterhead. This did the trick and she was finally granted a visa.

It was 1947 and a nervous time for both mother and son as they prepared to reunite after so many years. Hans was 11 when he was sent away, now he was 17 and very much an Englishman. Years later when I met him in London in 1982, he told me that he was afraid he might not even recognise his mother when he met her at the boat in Dover. He did, but she was really a stranger to him. What a painful reunion that would have been.

When Hans initially arrived in England on the *Kindertransport*, he boarded briefly with a family in the Gorbals, a poverty-stricken industrial district in Glasgow. Once Britain entered the war he was evacuated and saw the war out with a farming family in Dalbeattie in Scotland, a town renowned for its granite quarries. At the time of Marguerite's arrival, Hans was at university in Leeds where he lived in a boarding house on a refugee scheme. He had grown to love his foster parents so relations with his mother were very strained. As a consequence, she rented a room some 314 kilometres away, with old friends in London. Rationing was still in place, so she paid her way by mending clothes.

Marguerite's attempts to stay in the country came to nought, and she returned to Vienna a year later without Hans. She fought for and managed to have the Nazi family evicted from her Stubenring apartment, where she lived until her death in 1979. An amazing woman, she even managed to restore the business to its former glory. When Hans returned at the age of 24, he took over its management. By then, he had changed his name to John. Grandmother Sofie wrote:

Marguerite was in New York. I saw her for the first time in 18 years and was quite amazed at how unchanged she looked; not even grey hair. However, she does limp badly and walks with a stick, and from behind, she looks fairly crooked. She speaks about Theresienstadt without any bitterness, as if talking about an interesting experience, the memory of which she wouldn't like to be without.

In 1968, my daughter, Diana, and I visited Marguerite at her Stubenring apartment, which was one floor above my parents' apartment. It was the first time I had returned to Vienna since I had left as a four year old. She was the only relative left in Vienna. What a strange feeling it was. I remembered the staircase and the lift; and many memories of my early childhood came flooding back.

The name Kary was still on the door. We rang the bell and were warmly welcomed by our very charming *Tante* (Aunt) Marguerite. She ushered us through the entrance hall to a living room with very high ceilings. It was an overwhelming experience for nine-year-old Diana who whispered to me, 'This apartment is bigger than our whole house'.

Marguerite rang a bell to summon the maid to serve the lavish afternoon tea of coffee and Austrian cakes. Later, we returned to our hotel with a parcel of delicious baked goodies. She arranged to meet us the following day to take Di to a toy shop. True to Kary form, where young children were pampered and spoilt, she instructed her to choose anything she desired in the shop.

11

FOREIGN

In 1939, Australia entered the war, fighting with the Allies in Europe and North Africa. In 1942 they turned their attention to the Pacific War, after the Japanese captured the Singapore Peninsula and bombed Darwin.

In 1940, the Australian government had advised each household to build air-raid shelters. It was unlikely that my father had ever used a shovel before, but he began digging a shelter in earnest, attacking the topsoil in the furthest corner of the garden. For a few weeks we could see the hole getting deeper but then the shovel was left to rust; the heavy clay in the substrate proving too difficult to penetrate. The winter rain set in, turning it into a pool of soft gluggy sludge that was fun for me to play in. I loved sinking into the mud and getting my only pair of shoes clogged with clay. Then came summer and the mosquitoes found the hole to be a congenial place to breed. For several summers it was a memorial to air-raid shelter construction.

Throughout these years, I was blissfully ignorant of the trials of our extended family and the war. As far as I was concerned, our new home was paradise being set in a municipality with lots of green open spaces, so different from today where apartment blocks abound. Our neighbours had a huge property awash with peppermint trees, wattles and pines. Next to them was a small paddock where a horse was kept. For a climber and adventurer, it was a piece of heaven, and in those days you could wander and explore at will. Although our home would have probably been on one of the smallest blocks in the street, it was big enough for our growing family.

My five-year-old world was no longer anchored in Vienna, although I could not yet speak a word of English. My new Australian kindergarten, conducted in a garage, was part of the Margaret Lyttle Memorial School, later known as Preshil. This was, and still is, an independent progressive school in Melbourne based on the philosophies of great educational thinkers such as Rudolf Steiner and Maria Montessori. Initially I was unable to understand what the teacher or the children were saying, nor could I understand why they could not understand me, so I executed actions like biting a playmate to get the toy he was holding.

The weather, the language, the customs, the strange terrain, the diminished financial resources, the newness of faces, all required a huge adjustment. Even though we were so far away from Vienna, we were still tarnished, and even before that fateful declaration of war we became pariahs—enemy aliens on Australian soil, to be eyed with suspicion and fear. People were certainly apprehensive around us foreigners who spoke English with German accents. As such, we were not permitted to own a car, a radio or property, and my parents had to report to the police station every week. But I suppose we were the lucky ones in Victoria because many foreign nationals, including Italians, Germans and Jews, were interned in camps. I enjoyed our weekly walk to the police station, regardless of our new 'untrustworthy' status.

Aunt Liesl and her young son, Alf, would take public transport to visit us from their home in Ivanhoe. Their journey generally drew an audience. People would actually stare at them while they conversed. Alf became so embarrassed that he begged his mother never to speak to him while they were on a bus again.

The White Australia policy set the guidelines for immigration based on pure European ethnicity. However, it seemed that pure also meant speaking perfect English (Australian) and being Christian. Interestingly enough, my parents did not have strong accents because from an early age they had learnt English from their English nannies, and as a consequence, they spoke the language well, with British inflections. Nevertheless, there was enough of the German accent to make them stand out, although physically, neither of them had features that particularly distinguished them from Anglo-Australians. My father was tall, fair-haired and good looking, and my mother was pale-skinned, dark-haired and attractive.

But the fear factor was high in Australia during the war—sometimes people would call the police just because they heard someone speaking German, and Australians were encouraged to be on the alert (shades of John Howard's post-9/11 public exhortation to: 'Be alert, not alarmed'). On one occasion, Aunt Liesl's husband, Erich, was reported to the police as a suspected German spy after he was heard speaking to another refugee, a German Jewish jeweller, in the Ivanhoe shopping centre.

In June 1944, my father made another adjustment to his national status by renouncing his citizenship of Germany and swearing allegiance to His Majesty King George VI, his heirs and successors. Technically he was no longer an enemy alien or reffo, but was he ever that committed to Australia? Not really. In fact, he often talked about his dream of returning to Vienna permanently.

What could any of us do other than keep moving ahead? My father was working in the office of a metal factory and my mother would cook and clean and take care of us kids. For household chores, she never dropped her standards of dress. Her bobbed hair was nicely coiffed and waved, and she wore smart, tight-waisted dresses protected by an apron.

Although she had to do some household chores in Vienna while the maid walked me in the park, routine domesticity was still alien to her. It was interesting to watch my mother clean the house, vacuum-cleaner hose in one hand and book in the other, in a futile attempt to make housework less boring. Unsurprisingly, she struggled to do both—that is, read a story or learn a poem while negotiating tight corners and furniture. The housework took twice as long, of course.

After a day at school I would wonder what project my mother would be engaged in on my return. Handyman jobs were hers because my father had no practical ability or inclination when it came to chores. His refurbishing attempts became family jokes. Mostly his 'fixed things' were thrown into the rubbish bin or required the services of qualified tradesman to mop up. One time when my mother was visiting family in America, my father attempted to cook rice. He accidentally poured the rice down the sink which, of course, caused a blockage. He thought a nutcracker might be a good instrument to undo the drainage pipe. Inevitably, it made a hole in it, which unblocked the sink sure enough, and the sticky rice drained onto the kitchen floor. A plumber was called.

My parents struggled to make ends meet so my mother made our clothes, re-soled our shoes with rubber, and even made things to sell. She attempted to make money by weaving seagrass seats for stools, and then she started making hats. As a younger woman she had tried her hand at millinery in Vienna after finishing school, even though women of her class were not supposed to work. During her late teens she wrote in her diary:

I will never stop looking for a purpose in life and I am convinced that I will never find one, and yet there must be one.

As a young woman, my mother had everything going for her. Because of her physical beauty, she was sought out by Viennese photographers; some would even stop her in the street and ask her to pose for them. She was well-read and intelligent and just like her mother, she had the privilege of a very good education for the time, one that was *de rigueur* in upper middle-class Viennese families. For girls there was an emphasis on German, French and English languages, as well as literature and history. The school day finished at one o'clock, which was when their

English and French governesses took over to make the children conversationally fluent. Then there were piano lessons, regardless of ability or the desire to learn.

Once the school years were over for girls when they were around 16 years of age, private tutors came to the home to continue lessons in piano, German and foreign literature, and the history of art. And art was a lifelong passion for my mother. One of her most bitter disappointments was that her father did not send her to a *Gymnasium*. It was rare for girls to go to university in early 20th-century Vienna, but by the time her younger sister, Pauline, reached school age, she was given every opportunity to pursue ongoing study but was not at all interested.

After graduating from school at age 18, my mother, Hertha, who loved fashion, pursued millinery probably because of the family connection with the Brüder Böhm hat company. This did not satisfy her yearning for purpose or stimulation, in the end. Nor was it a comfortable experience; the class divide became abundantly apparent when the other apprentices questioned her as to why someone of her social standing, who obviously did not need to work, was actually there in the first place. She wrote:

Else [a schoolfriend] is a hopeless optimist and egoist. She is looking for happiness. She doesn't see the ugliness in the world. She doesn't see how many people are jealous. I can't be happy as long as I feel myself envied. I always feel guilty because I am doing well, because I am happier than many, because I have a lot of clothes while others go around in rags.

I always admired my mother for being so compassionate towards the less fortunate. Her healthy social conscience was only able to be fully exercised later in her life because, as a young privileged woman, there were many restrictions on her activities. Nevertheless, she attempted to find a fulfilling enterprise, and for a brief period she opened a hat salon in Vienna, making bespoke hats for ladies. Her sister Pauline wrote in her memoir that it was financially unsuccessful, so she was still reliant on their father's support. Then there was the inevitable marriage, my arrival, a baby who died, and escaping Vienna, so being a career woman was not an option for her. Then, with all the challenges that life in Australia threw up, being a supportive wife and mother was the best she could hope for.

12

THERE'S NO STOPPING A WATERFALL

It was 1939 while the world was in chaos, when I was six and far away in Melbourne, that our little world experienced a joyful invasion with the birth of my brother, Martin. My mother kept her pregnancy from her parents, afraid that her father would tell her that it was the wrong time to have more children, what with all the uncertainties including our financial situation, and the war. She sent her parents a telegram to announce his birth, which understandably, came as a complete surprise, but also delight, somewhat mitigating their deep distress with their worsening situation and the impending European war.

My little brother was very shy with everyone and did not speak until he was three years old, when suddenly he displayed an excellent command of language. From then on, he never stopped talking with his immediate family but was still painfully shy with outsiders. My parents called him *Wasserfall,* which literally means 'waterfall', a term used in Austria to describe people who never stop talking. And he was a handful. He loved to wander. Nothing would keep this angel-faced, blonde, curly-haired escape artist inside the house. From the time he could walk, my mother dressed him every day in a funny little white waistcoat emblazoned with red embroidered letters: *I am Martin Langer. I live at 15 Knutsford St, Balwyn. Please take me home.*

My mother was always out looking for him. The main problem was that he was unable to find his way back home and, of course, he did not yet speak. The vest worked a treat, though—someone usually brought him home.

My mother was also very concerned about Martin's late development, but my father believed there was nothing to worry about and doted on him to the point of spoiling him. He would give my brother everything he desired and refused to discipline him. If my mother tried to institute any behavioural changes, an argument would erupt. If she asked Martin to set the table, my father would do it for him. He never let Martin do any of those jobs that gave him the normal life skills. In due course, even Martin thought it was wrong. He once told me, 'I don't have any respect for Daddy, only for my mother because she worked so hard. My father just spoilt me and gave me everything I wanted.'

Come to think of it, our cousin Alf, Liesl and Erich's son, was also not required to do anything he did not want, so I imagine that this was the example set by my father's mother, Melanie.

Martin and I began our school life at Preshil, but the lack of structured learning did not suit my brother. Early on, his writing was indecipherable: the letters jumped all over the lines and lay upside down, sideways or flat. Eventually, my parents put him into a state primary school where he thrived—learning to read and write, and soon, writing with great skill and eloquence. It was bordering on miraculous given that he was uncommunicative with all but the immediate family.

While it's normal for a child to feel anxiety about being displaced when a sibling arrives on the scene, for me it was doubly difficult because of Martin's parent-consuming challenges. My father and I had always had such a wonderful relationship and he took me with him everywhere. But when Martin came along, he gave him so much more attention and indulged him unashamedly, in a way that he never did with me.

Martin's behaviour was especially embarrassing when my friends came to visit. He would follow us around but avoid eye contact or any form of communication. I tried to be a good sister, even taking him with me sometimes to visit friends, but he would not make it easy for me. On one of these occasions, we went horse riding and although Martin had never ridden before, when we put him on a horse, he just galloped off—I could only imagine what could happen to him and the trouble I would have been in from my parents. There were always problems and I was not very patient, or sympathetic. I often wished that he could make friends of his own.

However, relations did improve between us, probably after the intervention of Aunt Liesl. In 1950, my mother spent 15 weeks visiting her mother in the US leaving Dad, Martin and me at home with a housekeeper. By this time, my brother was 11 years old and I was 17. My father wrote:

Dear Hertha,
Both children are incredibly good, Susi has improved a lot, although only after Liesl talked to her seriously. On the whole, she gets on better with Martin and quarrels are rare. Martin would very much like to give his job up, even though he no longer needs the newsagent's job to deliver the newspapers and is usually home by seven in the morning. However, the expectations of the tips at Christmas time keep him going. It seems to go well with him at school. He did exceedingly well at the last test ... He also admitted he had a friend at school with whom he now plays marbles...
Many kisses,
Your Peter

Perhaps another reason my father was extra indulgent with Martin was because we had lost a child. For a short time in Vienna I had a baby sister called Vera. I was just three years old when she was ravaged by pneumococcal meningitis. In those pre-antibiotic days, meningitis was a death sentence. Vera, whose pet name was Veralein, was born on the 2nd July 1937 and died on the 22nd December that same year. Reading my mother's diary entry describing Vera's final days still tugs at my heart.

Today our little Veralein passed away—at 2.45 in the night ... She was a darling little being. An indescribably happy child, a pleasure for us. Her death has left behind a place that no one else can fill. It had to be like this. I won't ask why. Nobody can ever answer that. I hope and believe the child has everything she desires. Perhaps she is with Muli [Dad's mother who died in 1937]. I should have liked the baby to be like her.

Her health and strength remained strong. But it was a sad and upsetting time during which I was carrying her. I was afraid about her health. She came normally and at the right time into this world. The labour gave me very little pain. She did not weigh much but was well-formed. It was not long till she developed into a wonderfully plump, strong baby. Besides a cold at two months, she never became ill. We were terribly thrilled with every new milestone of her development and every day she became sweeter ...

During the night between 17–18 December she cried a lot. Peter sat beside her for two hours and stroked her. She was so grateful for it. Later I gave her camomile tea and a hot-water bottle on her tummy. She cried quite differently from normal. In the morning I took her temperature; it was 38.6 degrees. I notified Frau Dr Stross who diagnosed a mild attack of flu with a somewhat red throat. She told me that much flu was expected that year, but unfortunately this wasn't the case. The next day, Sunday, she was lively and happy again and in spite of the raised temperature, she spent a good night.

On Sunday morning her temperature was 39.6. Frau Dr Stross was worried and prepared me for the possibility of a lung infection, but felt it might possibly be a bladder infection. At 11am a consultation took place with the paediatrician Professor Knopfelmacher who confirmed her diagnosis. The child was apathetic but still cried terribly each time she was picked up. Temperature around 38.5, urine analysis negative.

During the night between Monday and Tuesday the poor child could no longer sleep, was very restless and groaned every time she took a breath. At 7.30 Dr Stross discovered she had a swollen fontanelle and thought of a brain infection but was still hopeful of only a bladder infection ...

That afternoon the child began to get very restless, thrashed around, groaned and cried terribly. Frau Dr Stross performed a lumbar puncture. The cerebrospinal fluid was cloudy. Tests showed an enormous number of pneumococcus. The case was hopeless for the doctors, but we hoped and decided to send her to hospital [Leopoldstrasse Hospital in Vienna]. There she died. In death she again had her former sweet face, lay still and at peace. She is at peace.

I remember the day of Vera's funeral. The nanny and I were sitting in the nursery looking out the window. She pointed to the night sky and told me that an angel had taken my baby sister to heaven. I got a fleeting glimpse of the angel high in the sky beyond the tree-lined boulevard of the Stubenring and thought to myself: how lucky Vera was to be able to soar so high.

No parent ever gets over that kind of loss. My mother rarely spoke of it, but my father spoke of her often, particularly on the anniversary of her death.

13

THE WILL TO LIVE

Another challenging male came to live with us: my uncle Erich who was married to my father's sister Liesl. Having escaped Vienna, the pair arrived on an auspicious Melbourne day. With a single suitcase between them, they alighted from the ship at Port Melbourne dock on 7th November 1939, Melbourne Cup Day, a month before my brother was born. My father greeted them with, 'It's a holiday today for a horse. It is unbelievable that in Australia they have a holiday for a horse.'

My parents gave them a home for three months while they got their lives sorted. Erich had an annoying compulsion to charge about; he could never keep still. Like a whirlwind he hurried from room to room, kitchen sink to stove, cupboard to table. Although he was very helpful, somehow he was always in the way.

Liesl, whom I adored, was a sweet sensitive person. She and my father were quite different in temperament and physique. Although they were both fair-haired and blue-eyed, the physical similarities ended there. My father was sporty and would climb a mountain at the drop of a crampon. Liesl, a year older, was short and inclined to put on weight. As far as exercise went, she might go for a two-hour afternoon stroll, but only when on holidays.

After the death of their parents, Liesl had lived alone and unmarried in their apartment with just the one servant. When it came to marriage, in terms of Viennese tradition, she was a late bloomer. At the age of 32, there were no suitors in sight and she was on the verge of old maidhood. This worried my father terribly, so he took matters into his own hands and secretly contacted a marriage agency.

As cupid and kismet would have it, she was matched with Erich Müller, a lawyer who had divorced his first wife, an opera singer, and had also recently lost his mother. Liesl and he got on famously, nurturing their friendship as they played piano and violin sonatas together. After their marriage they lived contently at Lobkowitzplatz until they came to Australia. Throughout their long and happy relationship, Erich's mantra was always that his Liesl was like an angel.

Leaving Austria, her home and family was tough for Liesl; she cried every day in that first year. Despite this, and impressively, she just got on with fitting into Melbourne life, even attending the local Presbyterian church where she was taken under the wing of the devout Miss Cowperthwaite, a woman whose devotion was so profound, she even managed to quietly expire in her pew during a church service one Sunday.

When it came to religion, like many educated professional European Jews, the Langer family never practised their faith. When Liesl was a child her governess would sometimes take her to services at St Stephen's Cathedral, so she grew up quite confused about which religion she belonged to, but her regular attendance at the Ivanhoe Presbyterian church services gave her a great sense of belonging to a community. The frequent afternoon tea parties she held for some of the church devotees—confirmed old spinsters with limited views and profoundly boring topics of conversation—were occasions I liked to avoid.

Liesl was able to put her musical skill to good use as she had kindergarten teaching qualifications from Vienna and was renowned for her use of music in the classroom, so it was easy for her to find work in Australia to supplement their income. She adored children and they adored her. As a child I loved her because she spent time playing with me, and as I grew up, she listened to all of my problems—and, likewise, with my children. Her house was always open to family and friends and her regular afternoon teas, with cakes from the nearby Swiss Cake Shop, were always a treat.

Portly, good-humoured Erich Müller loved Australia from the day he arrived. He borrowed £400 from my parents—quite a large sum at the time—and bought a milk bar with adjoining living premises at 125 Upper Heidelberg Road in Ivanhoe. He worked hard, long hours, and ate sweets, cakes, chocolates and coffee with *Schlagobers* (whipped cream) seven days a week. He ate day and night, retiring by 8.30, but still eating until he fell asleep—often with a lolly in his mouth.

What kept his weight in check was a love of sport, particularly tennis, and he rode his bike everywhere before they were able to buy a car. He had also developed a love of horseriding during his time in the horse artillery in World War I. We would often go for rides together in Ivanhoe where there were still lots of unmade roads to ride on.

Erich made us laugh a lot with his mispronunciations and mistranslations from German to English. One great example that we'd quote for years afterwards occurred when Liesl became pregnant and suffered from morning sickness. Someone phoned her and Erich answered, explaining, 'No, sorry, she cannot come to the phone at the moment because she is breaking'. The German word *'brechen'* has two meanings, to vomit or to break.

While they embraced their new life in Melbourne with great enthusiasm, their beloved homeland was descending further into madness. Erich's father and sister were murdered in concentration camps. I can only imagine the guilt and distress that this would have caused. By now, Vienna was blacked out, Austria was no longer an independent country, and its borders were being closed. A few members of my family still remained on Austrian soil to contemplate their fate. One was my great-uncle, lawyer Ludwig Gallia, my father's favourite uncle. Liesl's farewell to Ludwig had been miserable. He made a gut-wrenching plea to her not to abandon him there. But what could they do? Liesl and Erich had their visas and they had to leave immediately. She did her best to reassure him that they would soon be together in Australia, but Ludwig was no longer optimistic about finding his way out.

Conditions worsened as the Nazis introduced new regulations for Jewish lawyers where they were to be known as consultants and permitted to work only in very limited areas of the law. Considerable sums of their income had to be contributed to the support of 'deserving' non-Jewish colleagues. More than likely it went into Nazi coffers. Restrictions progressed to disallowing them to practise at all. In fact, most Jewish professionals including doctors, lawyers and civil servants were sacked from their positions.

Ludwig wrote to Liesl soon after she left Vienna saying that his chances of joining them were diminishing fast because it was becoming increasingly difficult to obtain a permit. He said that he was only reconciled to the sadness of their leaving by the expectation that at least they would find a good home in Australia.

It is amazing how history sometimes unfolds and crawls out of the recesses and crevices of life to form a story. It took years to build a picture of Ludwig from the trickling of family accounts and letters and the discovery of various documents.

Another snippet of his story was revealed in 1952 when I was staying with his sister, great- aunt Friedl in London. I learned that Ludwig, who had never married, had a daughter. He had become romantically involved with Therese Bokesh, a young woman from a family of modest means who lived in a village outside Vienna. The two met and had a love affair while he was in the army and Therese became pregnant. He wanted to marry her, but she refused. Nine months later a daughter, Luise, was born.

The Gallia family made every attempt to hush up the situation but Ludwig would not shirk his duty. He was determined to provide for them in the best way he could. As well as paying all the expenses for the baby he bought Therese a business—a coffee shop in a village close to her home. In addition, he continued to pay her expenses till the time she married another man. Therese and her husband went to live in Mürzzuschlag, a small town about 85 kilometres southwest of Vienna.

Therese's husband wanted to adopt Luise but Ludwig refused to allow it and in 1929 he formally adopted her himself. She became Luise Gallia and was brought to live with him in the Gallia family home so that she could attend a good high school. There is no evidence that she was unhappy about this decision, although it cannot have been easy to be taken from her mother and placed into a new family. From all accounts, the Gallia family was welcoming and accepting. When she completed her schooling, Ludwig persuaded Luise to study accounting and then join the family business. She stuck it out for a while, but hated it, deciding to study pharmacy instead. More detail came to light when my cousin, Tim Bonyhady, received a letter from Luise's grandson, Andrew Jakins, in 2015, who lives in South Africa. He wrote that shortly before Therese died, she told Andrew that Luise, being a country girl, never felt she fitted into the Viennese, or the privileged sophisticated lifestyle, of the Gallia family. Friction developed when Ludwig disapproved of her choice of boyfriends and tried to marry her into a Jewish family.

Between 1934 and 1939, Luise and Ludwig drifted apart. When Hitler annexed Austria, she reverted to her mother's maiden name, Bokesh, which was a good move given that her mother was not Jewish. She moved to Wiesbaden in Germany where she married a man who subsequently died in Russia in 1943. According to great-aunt Friedl, she joined the Nazi party and would have nothing further to do with Ludwig or the family. This broke his heart, of course. Andrew Jakins believed that Ludwig did not mention Luise in any formal documents, in order to keep her Jewish heritage a secret—for her protection.

Luise remarried and had two children, then the family emigrated to South Africa in 1952. However, sometime before she left Vienna, she contacted Ludwig's sister, Friedl von Hofmannsthal, to apologise for her behaviour. There were a number of ways in which poor Luise might have been harshly judged. Well, there was the Nazi thing, but she was also given every opportunity to have the most privileged life with a loving father at a time when being an illegitimate child was not considered to be acceptable.

As the momentum of the Nazi occupation built, Ludwig, who was already a very sensitive man, became increasingly disheartened about his future prospects. He was terrified of being trapped and alone in Vienna's deteriorating conditions, or worse, being sent to a concentration camp. And the prospect of making a new start in Australia at the age of 61 also filled him with trepidation: he would not be able to practise law and he could not imagine what else he could possibly do to make a living. To compound all this, the news of Luise joining the Nazi party proved too much for him to bear; in early March 1939, he joined the ranks of an estimated 1,200 Viennese Jews who took their own lives. He overdosed on barbiturates. Grandfather Arthur wrote:

Vienna, March 4, 1939

Dear Peter,

Alas my news will cause you great sorrow, but you must accept it with courage. Your good Uncle Olu [Ludwig's nickname] could no longer bear this life and is from today no longer. No one noticed anything extraordinary yesterday; he attended ongoing conferences and commissions and, in the evening, went to bed showing no emotion. In the morning he was found still alive in his bed, a doctor and the ambulance were called. He died in the Rothschild Hospital without regaining consciousness ...

Your uncle had not expressed any serious intentions about suicide and no one was prepared for it. However, he took a sufficiently large amount of Veronal, which he had saved up. He did not suffer during the process of dying and we should accept his decision which he made in full consciousness, positively.

It is too terrible what we have to endure; it is almost impossible to start a new profession, a new life, at the age of 61. No one really knows how many people commit suicide, for old people there is hardly a more rational choice. Uncle left a last letter, which I have not seen, and I do not yet know about his funeral.

Dr. Weissman will settle his affairs; he is very attentive to your aunt's [Friedl] needs. Your uncle often spoke of you and Liesl in these past days; he was very attached to you and would very much have liked to live with you both in Melbourne, but he wanted a living profession of his own. He knew there was no possibility, hence his decision. We shall take care of your aunt and try to console her. In his farewell letter he asks for no obituary, no burial: he is to be cremated so that nothing of him should remain …

If you wish to deal with anything judicial yourself, write to Dr. Weissman. However, I will engage him to act on your behalf— send him a Power of Attorney, also one on behalf of Hertha. The matter of the Stubenring house is still unresolved. Aryan lawyers are no longer permitted to act for Jews. Sleeping and dining cars and air travel for Jews is forbidden. No wonder Olu had enough. For doctors it is equally horrible, and what about merchants, industrialists, employers, workers? It gets more cruel day by day.

With regard to my affairs, I have had to give in altogether but I have received only promises for permission to leave …
Papa

Ludwig's last will was written on the 4th March 1939. It seemed he felt so worthless and hopeless that he wanted to be obliterated from history:

I am to be burned. No one is allowed to be present at the resting place or the burial. My ashes are to be taken out of the urn and dug into the ground. No stone or any other memorial is to be erected. No notification of my death must happen.

Somehow life balances out the challenges and in June of 1940, my parents and Liesl and Erich's grief was offset by some wonderful news. Liesl was pregnant. Their son Alfred was born in February 1941. The pregnancy was difficult and Liesl haemorrhaged after giving birth—so much so that a number of blood transfusions were administered, one of which was directly from another person in the room. Alf was a much loved and molly-coddled child. He developed asthma at age three, which sent Liesl into a spin and she fussed over him even more obsessively in order to protect him from every seen and imagined problem. Alf was so indulged that his parents served him breakfast in bed every day until he left the family home to get married.

14

JAIL TIME

Even when things are difficult, it is important to remember to be grateful. Yes, everything is relative. There were money worries and health concerns, but for our small family cohort in Australia there was safety. While my father was unhappily working in a factory, my mother was learning to be a domestic goddess, and Aunt Liesl was 'breching', my grandparents were still trying to get out of Vienna. They had two sticking points: one was settling their estate and accounts with the Nazis, the other was that their youngest son, Andreas, was in Dachau concentration camp and they were not going to leave without him.

Life following the Anschluss was complicated. Initially, the Nazis did not just haul all the Jews off to the camps—they set about dehumanising and humiliating them first. To begin with they plundered their homes and businesses and forced them to do activities such as wash the pavements with toothbrushes and clean up horse manure with their hands. Simultaneously, Jews were stripped of their dignity and their estates.

For the Nazis, there was much wealth to be had. This meant that those who owned property struggled to obtain the Austrian exit visa: no Jew could leave the country without first being relieved of all of their businesses and assets. Businesses were sold for next to nothing to Nazis and their sympathisers who generally ran the assets into the ground because they had no expertise. As for the sale of my grandfather Arthur's considerable enterprise, he wrote:

I suspect that the whole purchase of the business was only a guise to enable her [the woman who 'purchased' his business] to undertake smuggling and other crimes.

Soon after the Nazis rolled into Vienna, Grandfather Arthur, and his sons Otto and Andreas, were arrested and imprisoned in a lockup at the infamous Elisabethpromenade. They were crammed in with so many other Jewish men that they were unable to even sit. The courthouse prison had largely assumed the role of dispatch centre, and Andreas was soon dispatched to Dachau, then Buchenwald. It is unclear why he went to Dachau while the other two were released, but given what I know about his particularly difficult personality, I suspect he probably opened his mouth once too often. The Germans had plans for Arthur and Otto—there was much wealth to be seized.

Many times thereafter, Arthur's doorbell rang during the night and he would be re-arrested. It became a feared ritual. He even kept a satchel with a toothbrush, razor and comb by the door to take for his jail time. However, they sent him home each time, probably partly because of his ill health and age, but mostly because of their plans to appropriate his estate.

In the meantime, Sofie and Arthur did all they could to comply with their new business obligations to the authorities. On the 4th August, Arthur received a letter from the Assets Authority in which they gave him a week to offer his declared foreign assets to the nearest branch of the Reichsbank.

August rolled onto December and in Arthur's correspondence to my parents, he reports frustration that the settlement of his affairs was not moving forward. Then his lawyer became ill with the flu and could not attend to anything. Daily, the situation in Vienna became increasingly threatening. Passports for Jews now had to be marked with a 'J' and all Jews, be they secular or religious, were made to wear a yellow star. Arthur's business was eventually taken over, his assets frozen, and he and Sofie were forced to take other families into their apartment. They could no longer use public transport or even walk in the park. Arthur wrote to my parents:

We are in despair over every incident like this because nothing has been achieved since December 15. Matters about our departure go up and down. I don't want to be too hopeful but neither do I want to run our chances down.

The following February another letter came from the head of the Assets Authority, giving Arthur three days' notice of a meeting, 'in regard to your Assets Declaration with relevant document and identification papers.'

There was no getting around it: to exit Vienna, the toll had to be paid and my grandparents' toll would be a treasure trove.

Some years ago I applied to the Austrian authorities for the 30-page asset document that my grandparents were required to compile. Their assets included residential and commercial real estate, stocks and bonds, bank accounts, jewellery and artworks, complete with valuations. An excerpt from the confiscation order of the State Secret Police (Gestapo) reads:

The Property of Vienna 17, Neuwaldegg 41 [my grandparents' holiday home] was confiscated in favour of the German Reich. In accordance with the announcement of expatriation in the Reichsanzeiger, the department for the confiscation in invalid assets, Finance Office Moabit-West at Berlin NW7 is responsible for the declaration of invalidity.

Dr. Karl Muenzer, Vienna 1, Landstrasse 1, was appointed property administrator.

The State Secret Police [Gestapo] requests that you give no authorisation of sale or offer and place the necessary documents for the registration of the whole property at the disposal of the property administrator.

Sofie Kary registers in her VA (i.e., Vermögensanmeldung—registration of property) under 11 a family home at Vienna 17, Neuwaldeggerstrasse, 41

Arthur Kary registers under 11 a rented property at Vienna 1, Lugeck 4

Otto Kary registers a factory with land at Markt Fischamend—a half share

And the list goes on to strip every asset and Reichsmark from them. A note on the file states:

Ref: Arthur Kary, Vienna 1, Stubenring 14, d.o.b. 2. Dec, 1874
Sofie Kary 6. Dec, 1882
Arthur Kary declared that he was satisfied with the basis for the calculations for the tax on leaving the Reich as RM 1,040,000 and renounced any right of appeal ...

Come the 4th March, Arthur wrote that he had given in to the Nazis' wishes. Files reveal that after calculating his assets, his *Reichsfluchtsteuer* ('Fleeing of the Reich Tax' or 'Reich Emigration Tax') was estimated at a quarter of this sum and he had to pay it by the 15th March 1939. He had the right to object within a month but if he lost, the cost of the appeal would be charged to him. The letter concluded with the following threat:

This step will not however delay the procedure and if the full amount is not paid within the month, charges will be laid, an arrest warrant issued and widely distributed to police, customs and others.

For the next few months there were regular visits from the Nazi officials. Arthur wrote:

They happen so often that it no longer causes us much tension. After they invite me to go there in a friendly way, I had to provide a signature which did not alter my lot but I did receive a few promises. Maybe this time they will be kept!

In the meantime, news from Andreas in the concentration camp had pretty much ceased:

Andreas, the poor thing. We have received no letters and ours don't seem to reach him.

Eventually they received a printed form with Andreas's signature and a health certificate, which allayed their worst fears—at least he was alive. At one point they were informed that he had been moved from Dachau into Buchenwald and, in a letter to my mother, Grandfather Arthur wrote:

Andreas the poor fellow wrote a very short letter from Weimar which states that he is healthy and really nothing else. Further he sent a power of attorney with instructions to try for any foreign entry visa. Since everybody wrote the same letter, one must presume that the inmates hope to be released if these visas can be obtained. For this reason, we immediately obtained a Mexican visa, however I am very sceptical.

Andreas's fiancée, Netty, meanwhile was doing whatever she could to try to secure his release. Like so many others, she queued for hours at Nazi offices, pleaded with the authorities and offered bribes. She even travelled to Berlin to obtain a visa for Italy. But time goose-stepped on and the despair in my grandparents' letters was palpable as progress froze somewhere in the ether. Sofie wrote:

Papa, Netty and I only have one thought, Andreas. We wait and hope every day and there is no space for any other thoughts than Andreas. Only when he is finally here will we set everything in motion again to get him away.

On the 15th April 1939, after a year of negotiations and bribery, Andreas was released; a joyful special edition family letter announcing it. What was most peculiar was that my grandparents initially made it sound as if he had been to a holiday camp.

Yesterday evening an unexpected call came through from Leipzig and we were soon connected to Andreas who joyfully informed us of his impending arrival. Early morning, we were at the railway station to pick him up. We found him in good shape, tanned to dark brown and in the best mood. He said goodbye to his numerous friends, who all seemed to love him dearly, then we brought him home where a bath and a plentiful breakfast followed. He was starving for news and wanted to know everything. He seemed completely healthy and had preserved his good humour throughout his ordeal.

The last days of last week were taken up with Andreas. To go by his face, he absolutely doesn't need to recover. His skin is shiny and taut and he has taken on the appearance of an athlete. We absolutely don't have to worry in that respect. He talks a lot about the past and then the signs of the war psychosis begin ...

Of course, he arrived without any luggage, not even a parcel. You can easily imagine our joy and that of his fiancée ... The formalities [paperwork] in Vienna are almost completed and I am not afraid that the authorities will delay him for very long ... You cannot even think how lucky we are today and what worries have now left us.

When I read this letter, I already had a fair idea about the inhuman horrors perpetrated in Dachau, and concentration camps generally. It seemed incredible that Uncle Andreas, a Jew, got out of there tanned and looking like a Greek god after 14 months, but the reason would later come to light. A week after his release, on the 22nd April, Netty and Andreas were married. It was a modest affair held at a shabby location on the Zirkusgasse, a road in Vienna, conducted by a 20-year-old bureaucrat.

In the following 'Children's Newsletter' from Sofie, dated the 28th April, she tells my parents about the wedding:

We just came back from the local city office that for us is in the Zirkusgasse. Andreas Israel and Netty Sara were married there and required to sign the register that way. [All Jews under Hitler's regime had to take on Israel (males) or Sara (females) as their middle name]. Thereafter they exchanged eight-carat rings. Papa and [his brother] Heinrich were witnesses. I was only a spectator. After 34 minutes everything was properly completed by the 20-year-old bureaucrat. The newlyweds went immediately to a photographer, and then celebrated their marriage with sandwiches and wine at Csesurewsky, a restaurant. The big evening meal consisted of Kupferberg Gold [sparkling white wine] and a chicken soup because one can't get anything else. However, Andreas is at present not at all spoiled and therefore to him all food tastes good.

As they waited for some resolution from the Nazi authorities they tried to live as normally as possible, but clearly there was a new normal. Arthur and Sofie wrote on the 22nd June:

A walk through Vienna gives one a very strange feeling, especially the Wollzeile [a shopping street] is not recognisable. Many shops are completely shut, all remaining Jewish establishments have, with few exceptions altered the company signboards. On our company signboard still remains, 'Kary, Established 1864', but the business cars already have the signage Seiden-Hollenstein, [Hollenstein Silks, Hollenstein being the new owner]. Otherwise I hear nothing about our business. The shops if they are managed by German firms are without exception markedly altered ... In the inner city the majority of closed [Jewish] shops are used to enlarge other shops.

Andreas is absolutely radiant. At meals he eats three normal portions and then finishes off that of his Netty ...

Netty is already running away at 7.30 in the morning. Where, cannot be established, then she returns to make telephone calls, then she disappears again. It's a lot of work to organise leaving the country. In the meantime, Andreas disappears again, also without anyone knowing his intention. Both come back very late ... and one cannot even talk to them. How these two are supposed to come to manage and organise a household is quite a mystery to us. At any rate it is certain that Netty at present has shown no great interest in cooking and housework, but in these times, it is understandable and pardonable. The main thing is to take as many beautiful things as possible with you and soon to land many thousands of kilometres away from Vienna.

Andreas and Netty finally received their exit visas, and on the 8th May 1939, departed for Zurich with jewellery sewn into their clothing. The following month Sofie had a letter from Andreas in Abbazia (then in Italy, but now in western Croatia and called Opatija) telling her that he was diligently learning English. She wrote:

… it would be the first time in his life that he is industriously learning, so I am a bit sceptical but perhaps he realises that it is important to his future prospects.

It was hard for her to believe because Andreas had been expelled from every school throughout his childhood.

Then Arthur's resolution came: his remaining assets were confiscated and later placed into a locked account labelled 'Proceeds from Jew Elimination'. Despite the fact that they had permission to leave, Arthur continued to push back their departure in a pointless bid to retrieve some of his estate. Their older son, Otto, who had already made it to Miami, was getting a very clear picture of events in Europe, and insistently urged them to get out immediately. This seemed to outrage his father who continued to stall, putting their exit visas and lives at risk. Sofie, who always had a tight grip on her home and family, seemed to be unravelling with worry, writing to Pauline:

The last days in Vienna were dreadful for me. I thought I had people following me. I was afraid that for some stupid reason or other our passports could be blocked and I got frightened at every sound and voice.

Finally, Arthur gave in when Sofie threatened to leave without him. He had to accept that the Nazis now possessed the larger part of his fortune, including the Lugeck Building, and that he needed to get on with making their final arrangements to travel to their ultimate destination: Melbourne, Australia. My mother had already helped them decide on a location—the seaside suburb of Brighton, an affluent address that would suit them well. Although she wrote advising Sofie to reduce the amount of furniture they might want to bring, despite that, they required a crate larger than 6 square metres.

On the 15th July, just two hours prior to their departure from Vienna, a plain-clothed official, probably Gestapo, appeared at their door, threatening to confiscate Arthur's travel pass and passport. Sofie was now beside herself. According to Arthur:

I had to go to with [the official] to the Schottenring office and I just managed to reach the train before it left ... It concerned proceedings initiated by a creditor whom of course I had referred to the locked account. Sofie's nerves were not together.

Evidently, the daughter of a creditor whom Arthur had referred to his locked account, wanted him arrested. For some reason, fortune smiled on him this time as the commissioner abruptly turned down the woman's application.

The farewell at the railway station was wrenching, with friends, Arthur's brothers, the housemaids and even our beloved Scottish terrier, Putzi. Not till the train pulled away from the station would they be relieved of bad news. Arthur's brother Heinrich informed them that the container with all their carefully chosen possessions had not received its travel permit. There was nothing they could do but leave him to deal to with it. All Sofie and Arthur could take were their suitcases and 10 marks each. Although they had money from international businesses in foreign accounts, their spending from now on was to be more frugal until they knew what was ahead.

Their first stop was Abbazia, a seaside resort town on the northern Adriatic coast, where they were reunited with Andreas and Netty at the Lakatos Sanatorium, a fashionable health spa. Abbazia had been part of the so-called Austrian Riviera where members of Austro-Hungarian royalty and nobility used to come and luxuriate in the elegant hotels, villas, and sanatoriums. As they waited for further travel authorisations, the Karys spent their time restoring some physical and emotional wellbeing and relishing the simple pleasures of being able to swim in the sea or sit on a park bench, ordinary rights that had been denied to them under the Nazis. Their nerves slowly relaxed and the sound of a doorbell was no longer a cause for alarm.

But the stream of miserable news was relentless. Brother Heinrich wrote constantly from Vienna. He and his wife, Mitzi, had been forced to take in non-paying tenants 'with kitchen and bathroom rights'. He wrote that they were considering leaving their home as any Jews who stayed behind were subject to such treatment. On top of his own challenges, he had to deal with the remainder of Sofie and Arthur's estate. The process of shipping their furniture container to Australia had halted. More likely the Nazis had stolen it. Heinrich was finding it very difficult to cope.

Even more devastating for Arthur was the news that his business, in the hands of the Nazis, had no employees left who were capable of running it. This confirmed his belief that it had become a front for criminal activity. He took some satisfaction when he learned that justice was being meted out to the woman who now owned it. He wrote:

[T]he person who has taken over my business, who had in no way behaved in a decent manner, now has her residence at

Elisabethpromenade [the jail where Arthur had previously been interned] where she belongs for a long time ...

In this way, this stage of our existence, and also the previous lives of our children, are over. Mama and I hope that our children, who are now in the most actively creative period of their lives will soon successfully prosper and thrive. We trust also that they will enjoy thinking back to their Vienna period.

A few weeks later, Heinrich's communication suddenly ended. Arthur was beside himself with worry, and soon after he discovered that Heinrich was interned in Theresienstadt. The next time he heard news of his brother, he learned that he was dead.

15

IN LIMBO

Days and weeks passed in Abbazia while my grandparents enjoyed enchanting concerts under the canopy of the stars. The sanatorium continued to fill with more Jewish Viennese escapees, many of them acquaintances. There was a lot of socialising and gossip, including some outrage at the apparent laxity of the many female fellow refugees. Sofie wrote:

Ladies my age go around here like mad things glaringly bejewelled with red or platinum blond hair, in shorts or just short backless summer clothes in the most glaring colours.

Arthur was still not well. The stress, the stroke, the terrible losses had taken their toll and Sofie had to tell friends that he must not be disturbed. She, herself, was not averse to making up a fourth at bridge.

Travel permits continued to be a source of concern. En route to Australia they planned to visit Clara, Victor and Joele in England, and Otto in the US. Then a telegram arrived from Vienna notifying them that the English visa had to be applied for again in Abbazia because of restrictions that had come into force on 'enemy aliens' after Britain had declared war on Germany and its allies. At this point they wondered whether they should go straight to Australia before it was too late. A visit to a coffee shop in the village to read the latest foreign newspapers provided no comfort. Arthur wrote to my parents:

[P]olitical anxieties are unbelievable puzzles. If one wants to be cautious one would need to seek out a different refuge, but where? Even our future home need not necessarily be safe. For us nothing else remains but to let fate take its course.

My thoughts are much occupied with our coming great journey, the reunion with you being its beautiful destination. We have it so much easier than you who had to travel into the unknown. We shall be sorry to leave in 4-5 days. It is so beautiful here and outwardly peaceful.

As I re-read these letters, I was amazed at their optimism in light of how much they had already lost, and the chaos as the world slipped into war that September. Their next strategy was to try for a permit for the French section of Switzerland:

Andreas has a Swiss resident permit for the time being because a branch of the business was there. In September his quota number for America is due but how is he to get there?

Despite Otto continually urging his parents to settle in America, Sofie and Arthur were still adamant that Australia would be their new home.

I know already that Miami is a paradise. There are however many such paradises in the world and we will stick with Australia in the hope that Australia will be a paradise for us also. First of all, there we have a grandchild and at some point, one has to make a decision.

Another impediment to their plans were the antics of their youngest child, the wilful, self-centred Pauline, who was swanning around Paris. Pauline was expected to migrate to Australia with them, but secretly, she had no intention of ever calling Australia home. To her, Australia was the end of the world. Rather than be upfront with her parents, she simply went off the radar for long periods of time. At the same time, my mother was making great efforts to get her a visa, which was not easy because thousands of people were applying. Pauline's antics were making her very angry.

Pauline was capricious but she displayed extraordinary resilience and gumption during her escapades upon leaving Vienna, which she documented in a memoir for her family.

One month after my parents and I left for Australia, Pauline had been granted her exit visa. Her destination was Paris, where she would stay with close friends. Unchaperoned, and just 22 years old, she departed from Vienna in December 1938, under the billowing clouds of the steam train. Half nervous and half excited about the idea of being independent—she had always been quite rebellious in light of the strict mores for young women—she waved farewell to family and friends and headed into the unknown. Her first stop was Italy. The 10 marks-worth of foreign currency that she was allowed to take was to see her through a boat ride from the Italian border town of Ventimiglia to Menton on the French Riviera, and then a bus ride to Paris. As insurance, she had a return visa, just in case the Italian border was closed. Pauline wrote:

The conductor of the train had been well bribed and promised not to wake me at the border. I was lying down on my bunk, but sleep would not come. What if anything went wrong? The German border guards could send me back to Austria, the Italians may refuse entry ... When the German SS border control entered the compartment, I was fast asleep. They scared me half to death, demanding to see my papers, then leaving without a word.

The train arrived in Ventimiglia in the early morning. Pauline grabbed her belongings and wired home to announce her safe arrival. A short bus ride took her to San Remo where she was to catch a boat to Monaco.

The sleepy harbour of San Remo lay dreaming in the warm winter sun. A few fishing boats lay anchored along the shore, their owners busily mending nets. They were joking and laughing, and always there was one who would break out into song while others joined in with their beautiful Italian voices.

A romantic scene indeed. However, finding a boat to sail the Ligurian coast to Monaco was impossible. Pauline walked to a small landing to find someone who might have information. An old man dozed over a crumpled newspaper in a waterfront shop. He informed her that boats did once ferry people across the bay but that Monaco had closed its borders to the floods of refugees and Mussolini had threatened to jail anyone smuggling people into France. Something was very wrong. Maybe he didn't understand that I had a legitimate Monaco visa.

Pauline returned to the waterfront and offered money to the fishermen to take her across but no one would risk it. They said they would love to help the *signorina* but the fines imposed by the government were huge and they could lose their fishing licence.

The only thing to do was hurry to the consulate of Monaco. She waited in a line that wrapped around the building, soon discovering that thousands of false visas had been issued. The Austrian consul of Monaco had been making a fortune selling them to refugees. Despondent, she wandered through the town.

I watched the crowds. Instead of the usual elegant shoppers, there seemed to be an atmosphere of tension. People in dark travelling clothes stood about in clusters, wildly gesticulating; some were angry, many were crying. Even before I went out to join them, I knew their stories were the same as mine. All of them had been sold the fraudulent Monaco visa.

A frosty evening blanketed Ventimiglia as Pauline continued aimlessly through the empty, ancient cobbled streets, tired, numb and burdened by her predicament and a heavy suitcase. In the main square she sat on a bench and watched as couples, arm in arm, took their evening strolls, until she was overtaken by sleep. At midnight she woke with a start, unnerved by the quietened piazza. She wondered what would become of her. Then she noticed a gambling game across the square.

The owners [of the game] had finished their last round. They had spotted me, I could tell. One or the other kept glancing over to see whether I was still there. Finally, the younger boy walked over.

'La Signora looks so sad,' he said. 'Is there anything I could do to help?' It was the first time since I left home that anyone noticed me, and looking up into his concerned face, I started sobbing; it took a while until I could stop.

These two young men, Serge and Dino, listened to her story and took her to their home, with the promise that they would help her the next day. Pauline tells such a sweet, albeit odd, story of that night.

The small room was bare except for two narrow beds facing each other from the opposite walls, two chairs and a wash basin. They offered me the use of one bed … I fell into a deep sleep. When I woke up it was morning. A bright sunbeam covered my bed. Looking across the room my eyes fell on the two boys sprawled across the narrow bed, their bodies were strapped to each other and the bed post … It had never crossed my mind to mistrust them.

After coffee and a light breakfast of crusty bread and jam, they took her to see their father, a tall, striking man with a mane of white hair and piercing dark eyes. He was holding a meeting in the Hotel Milano. Later she learned that they were goods and people smugglers who hated Mussolini, especially since his recent alliance with Hitler. Pauline was given a room at the hotel.

At breakfast the next morning, my passport was handed around and carefully studied. For a while it was fun to be the centre of attention. Every day I was invited to someone's house to dinner.

There were a lot of conferences with V [the father] in the town park where he and his friends met regularly. My passport went from hand to hand. Everyone was scared—the fascists were tightening security.

Each week began with a feeling of optimism as she waited for a plan to unfold, but nothing ever happened and she was afraid that the smugglers were losing interest in her predicament. Another solution was needed, but she hardly knew anyone. Then she remembered a woman she had met a few days earlier, a friend of Serge and Dino's family. They had got on well, and she had invited Pauline to come for dinner and stay the night whenever she felt inclined. Now seemed to be a good time to see where that might take her.

The woman's villa was near the water's edge, and they spent an enchanting evening dining on the balcony overlooking the Mediterranean. Conversation was casual and pleasant until the woman started discussing politics. She produced a small bust of Mussolini and began cursing the dictator, threatening to smash the figurine. Fearing it might be a trap, Pauline listened without responding on any side of the issues.

As Pauline lay in her bed at the villa that night, a violent storm raged and the waves pounded against the walls of the house, riding the waves of her thoughts which were as tumultuous as the sea. The following morning, she left after a light breakfast. Again, she had nowhere to go. Feeling lost, trapped and afraid, she walked aimlessly for hours in the bitter cold through the tiny, stony streets that seemed to go nowhere. She had an eerie feeling that she was being followed but dismissed the idea—surely it was her confused mind playing tricks. She came across a small library, a warm refuge, she thought. A young man followed her in, brazenly walking straight up to her and introducing himself as Antonio before revealing his credentials—Border Police. Panic laid a path across Pauline's face.

'Don't worry,' he said, 'I have not come to arrest you'.

Antonio declared that he had been keeping a keen eye on her new friends' attempts to get her across the border. He asked her to trust him. From her writing it is impossible to know why she took her next steps. Perhaps she felt so desperate to get out of Ventimiglia that she would take any opportunity, or maybe she was attracted to Antonio. At that point he was not offering an immediate plan of action or even better assurances than the others. Nevertheless, she packed her case and left the hotel without a word to her smuggler friends, who were no doubt left to ponder her fate, and perhaps her ingratitude.

Antonio took her across town to another hotel where she met his friend and collaborator, Enzio. For a few days the three of them lived it up, dining in charming seaside restaurants with evenings spent at the casino. It turned out that Antonio was an officer in the Italian army who had recently fought in the unspeakably cruel and bloody war in Abyssinia.

Finally, a date was set for her escape: New Year's Eve, 1938. She was to walk out of Ventimiglia alongside a male Russian refugee. Their instructions were to walk arm in arm as if they were drunken lovers on their way home from a party. The terrain was rough along the railway track, but it was an ideal route because it was expected that both Italian and French guards on either side of the fence would be drunk from the New Year celebrations. The instructions were: if they are seen, Pauline and her companion should fall into each other's arms and embrace. If a train comes along, they should throw themselves into a ditch.

When the night arrived, they dressed Pauline in a party dress and silk stockings. Of course, she could take no luggage, but Antonio promised to deliver it to her in Paris. The two refugees followed their instructions, and when freight trains rumbled past, they dived into ditches. When they eventually reached a French village, they parted ways. Pauline caught a bus to Nice, then a train

Sue's maternal grandparents and their children. L to R: Arthur Kary, Hertha Kary, Sofie Kary, Pauline Kary, Andreas Kary, Otto Kary, c. 1926.

L to R: Arthur Kary, Netti (Andrea's wife), Putzi the dog, Andreas Kary and Sofie Kary, 1939.

Sue's paternal grandparents, Jakob Langer and his wife Melanie, c. 1903.

Jakob Langer (far left) and Melanie Langer on a beach vacation in Italy with their children Peter (Sue's father) and Liesl (sitting on her mother's lap), and friends, c. 1908.

Andreas Kary, Sue's maternal uncle, c. 1941, USA.

Ludwig Gallia, Sue's father's favourite uncle, c. 1938.

Pauline Kary, Sue's maternal aunt, c. 1962.

Clara Böhm, Sue's great-grandmother,
c. 1930.

Hedl, sitting, and Leonie Böhm, c. 1904.

The Kary family's house on the Ringstrasse, Vienna, 1920's.

The family house in Australia where Sue was brought up, 15 Knutsford Street, Balwyn, photographed 60 years after they sold it in 1954.

Sue's Mother, Hertha Kary (Langer), c. 1950.

Sue's father, Peter Langer, c. 1930.

Sue with her parents and younger brother Martin in Australia, c. 1941.

Sue and her baby sister Vera, 1937.

Martin Langer, Sue's younger brother,
c. 2018.

TRIBUTE TO GALLANT NINE - YEARS - OLD SCHOOLGIRL . . . . .

LITTLE HEROINE, nine-years-old Susi Langer, of Balwyn (above left), who will be awarded the Bronze Medal of the Royal Humane Society on August 30, for saving the life of her small brother, Martin (above right). She is the youngest recipient of this award on record. By running in front of an oncoming tram to push Martin from its track, Susi was hit and received severe concussion and facial injuries. The children were photographed at their Kew schools yesterday.

Press article, newspaper unknown. At 9 years old, Sue (Susi) saved her little brother Martin by pushing him to the side as a tram was about to hit him. Tuesday August 31st, 1943.

Sue, 1954.

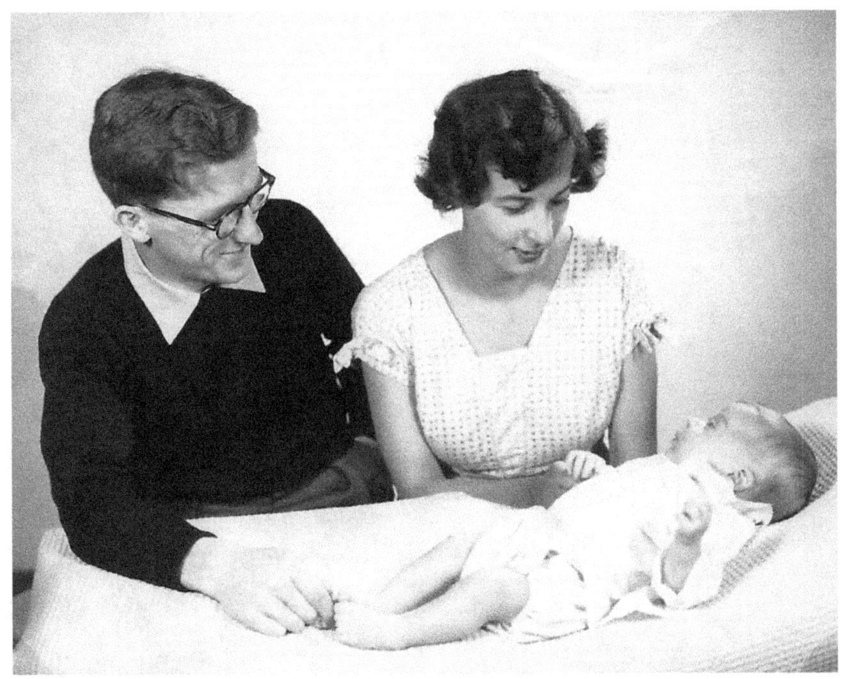

Sue and her husband Laurence Course with their first born Antony (Tony), 1957.

Sue on the day she received an Australian Citizen Award, 1998.

Sue hiking in Tasmania, c. 2002.

Photograph taken from Wynstay Crescent overlooking Darebin Parklands while it was still in private ownership, 1974.

View from Wynstay Crescent 45 years later, 2019.

Sue and Lyn Snowden, friends since their days at Kindergarten at Preshil school, c. 2008.

Parkland founding members Anthea Fleming and Sue, with author Sarah Mirams in 2011. (©Newspix Janine Eastgate)

Sue's family, Christmas. Her favourite aunt, Liesl Muller, sits on the bottom right, 1993.

Sue as a nurse offering support at Caritas Christi Hospice, c. 1997.

Sue with her husband Laurence in Tasmania, 2005.

Phil (Sue's youngest son) and his son Ethan in front of the family Silk trade building in Vienna (now a restaurant), the Lugeck building, 2015.

Adolf Loos (designer), Pair of chairs from the Langer apartment (1903).
National Gallery of Victoria, Melbourne. Purchased, 1994.

Adolf Loos (designer), Desk from the Langer apartment (1903).
National Gallery of Victoria, Melbourne. Purchased, 1994.

Adolf Loos (designer), Sideboard from the Langer apartment (1903).
National Gallery of Victoria, Melbourne. Purchased, 1994.

Adolf Loos (designer), Chair from the Langer apartment (1903).
National Gallery of Victoria, Melbourne. Purchased, 1994.

to Paris and arrived unannounced, in dirty, torn clothes, at her friend's house.

After regaling them with her incredible tale, the room suddenly fell silent. She had arrived without her visa. It was a dire situation for Pauline as well as her friends because they were now harbouring a fugitive—a seriously punishable offence.

The immediate solution was to get her out of Paris forthwith. Her friends found her a job one hour from Paris with a family who was looking for a tutor and governess. This lasted only a week because for some reason the mother took a dislike to her, probably because the husband was being friendly. After this, through overstating her skills, she landed a position as a secretary, at which she failed miserably. Her next job was teaching English conversation to a wealthy businessman who had the connections to get her a French visa.

Throughout all her dramas in Paris, my grandparents, who were at this point just across the Swiss border in Zurich, were sending her countless admonishing and frantic letters. Arthur wrote to my mother:

Apparently, as of today, there is a flight from Genoa to Batavia [Jakarta, Indonesia]. We shall certainly stay in Switzerland as long as possible, definitely not an ideal place either, but at present I don't know of anything better. We are persisting.

By all accounts, Pauline, as the youngest of the four children, had been very spoilt, so unsurprisingly, she was quite immature. As she naively flitted around France enjoying her independence and finding talk of war a crashing bore, she briefly considered marrying one of her French boyfriends so she could stay there permanently. Not wanting to leave without her, her parents missed boat after boat.

By now, Netty and Andreas had arrived in America while Arthur and Sofie were taking full advantage of having the opportunity to partake again in the pleasures of the cinema and theatre in the balmy warmth of September. Time was most definitely running out, however, and their letter of the 16th September from Zurich was despairing:

We are unable to either return to Italy or get to France or England in order to book a ship [to Australia]. We have been declared enemy aliens and our visas and air tickets from Zurich to London and boat ticket to Australia have been cancelled. The refunds were not returned to us, they were sent to Austria where the Nazis will use them.

On the 29th of October, they finally received news that their American visas had arrived in Zurich, including one for Pauline. It took till the end of December to complete the formalities— the paperwork and medical examinations. By New Year's Eve they reached Florence en route to boarding a ship in Genoa, which was due to sail to New York on the 20th of January. Sofie wrote:

We are spending especially lovely days here, Hertha, going to places you will still remember well. We have already been twice to the Uffizi in the Pitti Palace, buried ourselves a whole morning in San Lorenzo, mainly in the manuscript library. I had never been able to enjoy art so quietly. I was always in a hurry to get home and look after the children. So, everything bad has its good side, you only need to know how to find it ...

Write to me soon and in detail. Everything interests me so terribly much, I always live in my thoughts with you. I send you all my best love, Mama.

There was still no sign of Pauline, however, and Arthur was furious.

Because of Pauline, our carefully planned voyage preparations have now fallen into the water. The air ticket from Zurich to London is unusable, the boat ticket likewise. As far as the permit goes, I will inquire at the responsible authority, the English Consul in Geneva. Perhaps an exception can be made for German refugees.

I wondered whether Pauline felt any remorse about her illusive behaviour. She certainly had a lot to answer for at this point. In a world where danger was confronting them at every turn, she had foiled all of her parents' attempts to leave. Arthur wrote another thoroughly miserable letter to his youngest daughter:

I dare not even think that today we should have embarked ...

We delayed our departure for Australia because we wanted to wait for the moment of this anticipated change of opinion in order to travel with you. Only when we saw that you could not make up your mind, and the terrible events which then came, did we have to determine the date of our departure. As you know it was then too late, events overtook us. Our permit ran out, my money was already in Australia. I am suffering a gigantic loss in the exchange rate and the money is frozen.

My mother, too, was furious with her sister's disregard for her family's fate. For most people it was obvious that Europe was about to erupt, but Pauline seemed none to fussed about the gravity of the situation: that the Jews were being hunted and hounded out of every country, that German forces had occupied many European countries, and that she had rendered her own and her parent's resettlement in Australia impossible.

Stateless and homeless, Sofie and Arthur's only hope was to find a way into the US since America had not yet entered the war. They plagued the French consulate for two days to get a transit visa for Marseille, and somehow, they got a ticket for Pauline on the same boat. True to form, Pauline did not respond to their requests to join them and Sofie and Arthur had no choice but to leave without her.

A letter to my mother arrived on the 5th February 1940, from Grandmother Sofie in New York.

Dearest Hertha,

We arrived on the 1st February at 3 o'clock and after a three-hour customs inspection we were able to leave the arrivals station … The sea crossing took place without any mishaps. We had first class accommodation in a big cabin with a bath, and excellent food and service … The weather was very stormy for four days … There were many people from Vienna on this ship; most of them travelled in third class, which was overcrowded with poor conditions. The crossing took nine days. I am glad to be free from the witches' cauldron [referring to Europe], only I wish Pauline was already there too … For the first time in one and three quarter years I can feel truly free and safe.

Pauline did eventually get it together, sailing into New York Harbour on the 18th of May 1940, where she spent time with her brothers before reuniting with her parents in Miami. Sadly, my grandfather's life in Miami was brief. He died one year later, in April 1941. I have no knowledge of the last year of his life or what he died from although I could hazard a guess that the enormous stresses that he had been through had proved too much for his already compromised health. Nothing much was said at the time and all that my mother wrote in her diary was:

On 6 April 1941, my father died. I only found out on 7 May. I won't see him again. May fate be kind enough to let me see my mother again. Sometimes I feel it is unthinkable that we will live through this war. I cannot imagine the end.

As was typical of the women in my family, my grandmother made the best of things. She commissioned her oldest son, Otto, to build her two blocks of apartments at 125 Meridian Avenue, Miami Beach. She lived in one and her sisters Leonie and Hedl lived in the identical block next door until Hedl died of leukemia in 1945. They dined together every night and played Patience in the evenings. Without the privilege of maids, they learnt domestic skills and even made their own clothes.

The apartments, named Earls Court, were a successful enterprise as short-term holiday lets, and they soon became a popular winter holiday retreat for far-flung family members. My grandmother promised to come and spend six months with us in Australia after the war was over and, although there was a lot to do to establish a new life, she kept her word and came in 1946 when I was 12.

16

GUGELHUPF

Being a good *Hausfrau* (housewife) for her *Mann* (husband) required my mother to bake an inordinate quantity of Austrian cakes to satisfy my father's insatiable appetite for these delicacies. In so doing, she had attained a level of domestic industriousness unheard of in our family. From a distance of 16,500 kilometres my grandmother conveyed her concerns about my mother being so consumed by the chores of a maid, writing in March 1939 that she would do all she could to help with household duties when she came to stay.

I am concerned about your tiredness, Hertha darling, and the amount of housework you have to do. Please don't make so many cakes for Peter. I will make a lot of cakes when I arrive in Melbourne to make up for it …

I am quite appalled at all you have to do. Do not take too much on and take someone for two hours to clean. The cooking one can shrink to a minimum and Peter would of course forgo the cakes at present. I would commit myself to making up for it later.

My father's favourite cake was the *Gugelhupf*, a light, yeasted marble cake, that has a long history, and for him I suspect, it was a way to connect to home. This Viennese patisserie staple dates back to late mediaeval Austria where it was decorated with flowers, leaves, candles and seasonal fruits, and served at important community events. History aside, the spongy, chocolatey sweet is scrumptious. Then there was apple strudel, poppyseed cake and Sacher torte. Those sturdy old Austrian cake tins were used every single day. When visitors were expected, my mother hid the cakes to stop them being prematurely devoured.

How things had changed. Just a few years earlier my mother had recorded in her diary that she was less than pleased with her lot, which included her husband, being a mother, and domesticity. This entry was made in Vienna on the 17th March 1936:

I went for a walk with Susi this morning. The child eats very little especially when she is tired. If possible, I don't hit her. When I do it now and again, things only get worse. I prefer to avoid something with quiet and disapproval. In the afternoon I went for a walk with her again. In the evening I was irritated with Peter. We quarrel a lot and I think it is mostly my fault.

I am serious, I think a lot and I am not myself; not pleasant company. I am not satisfied with him because I find he neglects himself spiritually. I suppose I am scarcely the right wife for him. I can't rouse him and can't tear him out of his indolence. We are getting less and less compatible every year, unintentionally. I am choosy and very shy.

Unfortunately, I too have become very indolent and am afraid I will become a good mother with a very narrow outlook … I will try to enlarge our circle a little. Peter doesn't like talking, that is, he doesn't like any social entertainment and yet it brings great stimulation. For Susi's sake I don't want to become a good housewife, which is almost certain judging from a coloured film of my life at the moment. I don't want Peter to become a good provider. I would like him to be ambitious.

In Vienna, my grandmother would not have handled a rolling pin or baked a cake. The role of a traditional Viennese upper middle-class Hausfrau was nothing like that of the average Australian housewife of the time. Being a highly competent Hausfrau meant being the custodian of the keys to her domestic kingdom. Those keys ensured the security of linens, clothes, jewellery and other valuables, as well as the food. *Die Speis* (the pantry) was a cool, dark room adjoining the kitchen and secured by frosted glass doors. No one could enter without Sofie's permission. Grandmother Sofie's keys were secured to a keyring attached to her belt.

Food planning and preparation were important daily tasks because there were a lot of mouths to feed. My mother was one of four children, so the basic menu was for six. Then there were regular visitors and the three live-in servants, as well as the laundry woman and the chauffeur.

The pantry was perfumed with the aroma of spices. Wooden bins were stuffed full of nuts and raisins, ripe cheeses and creamy butter from a local farm, vegetables and fruit from their gardens and large blocks of chocolate, probably for all the Gugelhupfs. My grandmother supervised the daily weighing and regulating of these staples.

Each morning after Grandfather left for his office, the cook was summoned to Grandmother's dressing room to plan the day's menu. They decided what needed to be weighed and what needed to be purchased. Aunt Pauline wrote about the ritual in her memoir.

Frau Marie left with a large black shopping bag and Putzi, the Scottie, on the leash. In summer I often came along on those shopping trips. There was the butcher, Herr Hirsch, whose face and neck were as red as the inside of a rare steak and whose voice resembled that of a bull. He used to scare me until I found out that he could be quite generous with samples of delicious wurst for me and Putzi. His apron was spotted with blood and I would try not to look too closely at the carcasses of slaughtered animals hanging on the wall waiting to be cut up. Mama had a feud with him when the brisket for Papa's boiled beef was not perfect ...

As soon as the cook returned, the weighing ceremony began. Every dekagram and kilo of flour, sugar, coffee or whatever more was needed, had to be weighed. Eggs were counted out, butter was issued, fruit was chosen for stewing. Meantime, the fire was roaring in the huge coal-fed stove that took up the better part of the kitchen. Large earthenware pots were filled with pork and goose fat. Here was feverish activity and only the cook and her helper were permitted in the kitchen.

The entire family would be seated at the dining table at precisely 1.30 p.m. each day for the main meal. Austrian families never waited at the table for the mother to deliver their plate of meat and three veg. It was considered impolite to make decisions for others on the quantity they wished to eat, so serving dishes were placed in the middle of the table and everyone helped themselves. My grandfather insisted on the same meal every other day— beef soup and boiled beef—a monotony to be endured by all except his favourite child, Otto, who was allowed whatever he wanted, which was usually hamburger or schnitzel. I might add that in Austria, boiled beef, known as *Tafelspitz*, was not as bad as it sounds. It is actually a classic Viennese specialty: beef poached in a broth with vegetables and spices and served with sour cream or an apple and horseradish sauce.

Hausfrau was the life-role that any young well-to-do young woman could aspire to. After graduating from school, most young ladies were engaged in a carefully supervised social life until a suitable suitor was found; the hours were whiled away with pursuits such as thinking and talking about attractive admirers, playing bridge, summer vacationing and winter skiing. Servants did all the housework and cared for the family's every need, even the laying out of the clothes one wanted to wear for the next day. If one lost or mislaid an item, one only had to ring the bell—and every room had a bell—and a maid would come running. Aunt Pauline described their servants as little more than slaves who could be treated however the master or mistress desired. My grandfather Arthur certainly did not treat them with respect.

When I visited Tante Marguerite at the Stubenring apartments in 1968, the tenants who had been renting our apartment from the state since 1940, kindly allowed me to look around. Amazingly, those same keys were still hanging above the door. I wondered how they would feel in my hand and whether they still held the energy of my grandmother's tightly run domain. I was so tempted to ask if I could have them.

Now, in a strange land with no extended family support and certainly no maids, what could one do but make the best of it—and make cake. My mother had to cook for us no matter what. Even if she were sick she would drag herself out of bed to prepare our meals. Years later after I had moved into nurses' quarters, my mother travelled to the US to visit relatives for the second time. My father taught himself to cook for Martin and himself—in a manner of speaking. The trouble was he could only manage to cook one thing at a time. This meant he would first cook the potatoes, which the two of them would sit down and consume. Then he would go and cook the greens. Once more they sat down to eat them. Then he would return to the stove to cook the meat.

The Balwyn of 1939 had few conveniences for the busy housewife—no fridges or dishwashers or washing machines, but there were home deliveries. Daily, food was conveyed through suburban streets by horse-drawn carts. The milkman called first in the early hours of the morning before anyone was awake. It was comforting to be woken by the clinking of milk bottles, the clip-clop of the horse moving onwards at the command of the hearty voice of the milkman calling, 'Giddy-up'.

Later in the morning, the baker appeared in his colourful, enclosed cart lined with wooden shelves which were filled with trays of warm bread and rolls. In those days the choice was slim: unsliced white or brown bread, mostly sandwich or Vienna loaves. There was no bread delivery on the weekends or fresh bread in the shops, so on Mondays we had stale white bread in our school lunchboxes.

My parents bought a machine with a handle to slice the bread. Very high tech. Sometimes it cut little fingers and the doctor would be called in to stitch them up. If the baker was in a good mood he would give me a ride to the end of the street. I would wander slowly back home, collecting fallen acorns from the oak trees lining the street and eating any fruit hanging off the trees, whether it was ripe or not, along the dusty unmade path.

More colourful was the Chinese market gardener who passed through at irregular intervals, riding his large black, horse-drawn cart. He was never in a tearing hurry like the baker so customers had time to peruse his colourful array of fruit and vegetables. I watched as he plodded slowly away, vivid red tomatoes dangling like lanterns, sprays of perfumed bay leaves and herbs, and cauliflowers and cabbages bobbing in baskets hanging from the sides. The butcher was more time-efficient, doing deliveries on his motorbike, his sidecar crammed with bundles of orders wrapped in newspaper. And then there was the all-important ice man. He deposited large slabs of ice protected by hessian into the ice chest. The 1940s saw the introduction of refrigerators and the disappearance of the ice man.

Mostly, my mother preferred to do her shopping on her bicycle. The shops were only ten minutes away, and at that time it was easy enough to get around because there were hardly any cars on the road. Even when my parents bought a car after government restrictions for 'aliens' were dropped, she still rode her bike to the shops as did many housewives then.

So my mother did what she could to be a good homemaker and she seemed to adapt pretty well to the new lifestyle, or maybe she just suffered in silence—our lack of money made things very tough. Adapting was far more challenging for my father. It wasn't feasible for him to return to study law in Australia as he had to support the family, nor did he ever really want to be a lawyer. But his salary from the metalware factory brought in only £5 a week, which was near impossible to for us to survive on with £3.10 going on the rent.

17

TIMBER

I sometimes wonder what our lives would have been like if the war had never happened. I would have grown up speaking German, gone to the best schools, married a lawyer or industrialist perhaps. More than likely I would have been a socialite. The war certainly showed us that you cannot take anything for granted.

For me, being expelled from Austria was not such a big wrench because I was so young. Children are adaptable. For my father, having to work in a factory was certainly more than his highly cultured self could bear, but what utterly floors me in hindsight is that he would even have contemplated going into the timber business.

This venture came about at the suggestion of a close friend of his, Stephan Strasser, who had been involved in timber milling in Vienna. Great friends of my grandparents, the Strasser family arrived in Melbourne not long after us in 1939. I remember the day our families were reunited. It took place in a sparsely furnished room somewhere. Lots of coloured balloons were set out for me and their three-year-old daughter Eva to play with. We got on famously, chasing those balloons. No doubt it was a distraction so the parents could discuss topics we should not hear.

For years afterwards our two families were constant companions. One day my father and Stephan announced that they were going to buy a sawmill, specifically the Ajax Timber Mill in Buxton, Victoria. Stephan was to run the mill and my father would be the financier.

Being six years old, the timber mill experience forms a marvellous recollection of my early years in Australia. I recall my father at his desk poring over books on trees and various kinds of wood. Then there were the trips to Buxton, round and round the steep corkscrew drive up the Black Spur, with its immense mountain ash trees that filtered dappled sunlight into the cool, lush undergrowth of ferns; then more curves through the Great Dividing Range. There were hardly any other vehicles on the road apart from an occasional timber truck laden with massive logs. I loved sticking my head out of the car window and inhaling the pristine damp green smells of the Australian bush. For my parents the business venture was not so romantic.

The mill was situated a few kilometres from Buxton along the road to Acheron. Buxton was a tiny town. There were just two buildings—the weatherboard hotel with its flaking green paint and the general store where everything from furniture to food was sold. On one side of the hotel was a verandah leading to the bar where leathered, sunburnt men in their torn, dirty clothes could always be found exchanging news and yarns over a beer. My father often stayed overnight at the hotel but, as he never consumed alcohol, the locals did not welcome him with open arms. Otherwise it was a rural idyll surrounded by paddocks of green vegetables, grazing cows and a tinkling clear stream that flowed swiftly over pebbles and rocks before disappearing into the forest. Being allowed to accompany my father to the mill was such a special treat, an excursion filled with enchantment.

A long rusty iron shelter housed the machinery for cutting the timber which hardly muffled the deafening noise of the fresh logs being fed to the saws, day in day out. Nearby stood the office, a roughly constructed wooden hut, complete with a fireplace and furnished only with a writing desk, a solitary chair and an old creaky bed. A little creek beside the hut provided cool water for the workers, making work in the blistering summer sun more bearable.

I especially loved to watch the draught horses, their coats bathed in sweat as they pulled the freshly cut logs from the pile to within range of the machine's clutches. The timber workers would call, 'Steady, Ned. Woah, Wally'. Their commands rang through the bush. Sometimes, when the horses rested I was allowed to feed them, and as a special treat, I could sit on a horse's back.

When the noise and activity got too much I was free to follow the winding track into the bush. Sometimes I met one of the tractors with a newly felled log dragging behind it. All the lumbermen knew the boss's little daughter in her brown jodhpurs and spotted shirt, the young girl who ambled along the bush tracks or waded in the creek, enjoying the novelty of the world that they took for granted.

When I tired of all my activities I would stop and watch the highly skilled tree-fellers, who, stripped to the waist, were positioned halfway up the tree swinging their axes alternately and rhythmically—whop, whop, whop—until the trunk was almost cut through. Then they executed the final cuts with the saw. The sound of the saw's thrusts, to and fro, in and out, was like the laboured breath of someone dying. Then they would descend and finish the job from the ground. They knew exactly where the tree was going to fall. A thud followed a shout—'Timber!'—and the silent exertion was broken as a tree hit the forest floor. Now it was ready for the draught horses or the tractor to reclaim it and feed it to the mill's maw.

The country workers were uncomplicated, friendly and easy-going. Their solemn belief was that near enough was good enough and they enjoyed nothing better than to boil the billy for a cuppa over a crackling fire. My father told us that they would indulge in this pursuit all day if you let them. When it was time to drive the timber to the city, they always stopped at the Buxton Hotel for a pot of beer, or several. On bad days my father would see the loaded truck still standing outside the pub hours later.

The sawmillers lived onsite in small wooden huts which contained just the bare necessities—no electricity, telephones or even hot water. On the weekends they would return home to their families who lived too far away for a daily commute. It was a pretty spartan life and often their nearest neighbours would be several kilometres away. Each morning their children set out on foot or horseback along the kilometres of dusty unmade road to attend the local school. My father was so different from his employees and I wonder about the kind of relationship he had with them, and what they actually thought of the foreign boss with the strange accent who knew so little about their way of life or the Australian bush. Certainly, my father could not understand their lack of motivation or their unwillingness to work too hard. Still, he really gave the enterprise his full attention, and his best shot.

The venture turned into a misadventure, with my parents losing not only all of their own money but my mother's entire inheritance from her father's estate. My mother could not believe that it was possible to lose money so quickly in what appeared to be an honest and seemingly sound business initiative, but the timber business was tricky. The workers liked their smokos, and the war was raging in Europe so supply shortages were inevitable. When Japan entered the war in December 1941, petrol became scarce. My mother wrote in her diary:

Peter bought a sawmill with Strasser, Strasser as the expert and Peter as the financial backer. Later it came out that one was not an expert and the other didn't have sufficient money.

Peter now began to work this bush while Strasser, who had kept his share in Yelland [another timber mill], withdrew. The partners' co-operation had not been very successful. Both lacked business sense and knowledge …

Peter couldn't pay back the large debts from the results of the bush. He tormented himself and the success was modest. His tractor and his two trucks frequently broke down.

My father sold his share of Ajax Timber Mill to another mill and he was left with a tract of bushland that he attempted to clear and farm. Clearly, he did not have the expertise so he was never going to recover his debts that way.

When I was 12, my mother rented a holiday house somewhere along the Black Spur for our May school holidays. By this time my father had a new and better fitting job as a cellist in the Melbourne Symphony Orchestra. He drove up from Melbourne one day to visit us but in those days there was no such thing as a 24-hour petrol station and it was not unheard of for my father to run out of petrol. He got as far as Healesville before realising he would never make it to the top of the Black Spur. One of his former employees lived in the area and my father knew he kept petrol reserves. The fellow obligingly poured a large can of fluid into the tank. It turned out that he had sold my father water, which rotted his petrol tank. One can only speculate on the former employee's motivation. Maybe he had an old grievance to settle.

Some years later my family drove through Buxton once more. A rusting wire fence enclosed the remains of the sawmill. Under its pitted roof various rusty pieces of machinery lay scattered. The office hut was intact except for broken windows, while nearby lay an old buggy half buried in the soil—a fitting memorial to a failed enterprise.

When it comes to the aftermath of the Ajax Timber Mill, my memory does not serve me well, naturally, because parents generally shield their young ones from the stresses of mistakes and circumstances. Tears were not my family's way. I wonder though what my father thought. Was he devastated? Did he feel like a failure? I felt so sorry for the hopes and plans that ended in woodchips and water in the petrol tank. But my sadness for my saintly mother was greater. She supported him through all the heartache and misfortune and as the years progressed, she had to endure one financial crisis after another.

My father was a complex man. I remember his inconsistent behaviour often creating a feeling of uncertainty and uneasiness in me when I was young. Rules weren't rules with him. When it came to discipline, he was inconsistent. For instance, as a child, if I wanted to play with saucepan lids, he would say no because it was not hygienic; but later that day, he would put them out on the kitchen floor and encourage me to drum on them with wooden spoons.

18

THE CELLO

My Balwyn bedtime memories are of melodious and calming sounds with the music of Beethoven, Strauss, Mozart and one of my father's favourites, the piano part for Schubert's *Trout Quintet* for piano and strings. I was lulled to sleep as my father played the shiny black Bechstein grand piano that made it all the way from Vienna in the huge container with the bidet, rugs, furniture and cello. Perhaps this is why evening is still my favourite time of day.

My father was a wonderful musician. Since childhood he had displayed prodigious talent and perfect pitch. As a child he practised the piano for hours each day, as well as mastering the cello. Music played a central role in the life of the entire family. Melanie, his mother, was also a talented musician who hosted regular soirées with musician friends, and the family regularly attended operas and concerts. Liesl also loved to play, but she was no match for my father's ability. She told me that she lived in the shadow of his brilliance and as a result, became so withdrawn and insecure that she would whisper when guests were around. After she died I helped clear out her home and found her diary where she had written:

Every week in Vienna we had an evening of chamber music in our home. One of these was a Beethoven trio with Peter and two excellent artists. After hearing the music, I went into my room and cried. The violinist, a wonderful young artist, the best in Vienna, saw me crying and came to find out why I was so sad. I said, I only wish I could play too this wonderful music. She went at once to my parents, to ask if she could teach me the violin and she became my violin teacher for many years, and at the same time she became my very best friend. I adored her and I shall never forget my violin, and later viola lessons with her. I was gifted too, but very timid, and I had no confidence that I might even be a good player.

The cello my father owned was quite a piece, having been manufactured by master craftsman Giovanni Grancino. The quality of the instrument was similar to a Stradivarius and no one was allowed to touch it. In 1953 it was valued for insurance at £500.

His opportunity to have a professional career in music arose in 1946 when he was aged 41 and still coming to terms with the timber mill collapse. After a year of unemployment he heard from a musician friend that the Melbourne Symphony Orchestra (MSO)[2] was looking for a cellist. He had already played several concerts with various members of the Victorian Symphony Orchestra (VSO) in the magnificent gothic revival-style Assembly Hall in Collins Street, Melbourne.

Despite the nerves that often hampered his performance, he auditioned and got the position. Considering that the Musicians Union of Australia only allowed 10 percent of the orchestra to be foreign-born, regardless of skill, it was quite an achievement. At the time Bertha Jorgensen had been the orchestra leader since 1923, when she became the first female leader of a professional orchestra in Australia. Bertha's career spanned 50 years which meant she was the longest-serving female orchestra leader internationally.

I asked him once why he had not played professionally in Vienna. He said that the Vienna Philharmonic was of such a high

---

2   In 1934 the MSO was a radio orchestra for the Australian Broadcasting Commission—the government-funded ABC. It was renamed VSO in 1949 and reverted to MSO in 1965.

standard that he never imagined he would get in. Another reason was that they were not so keen on employing Jews.

My father had high hopes that Martin and I would be at least musically gifted, if not of the genius class. He tried to ignore the reality. Martin played violin for a few years and then viola, but bushwalking was more his thing. I did not have such a good ear for music and there are few happy memories regarding my childhood efforts. Although my father was not my official teacher, he saw it as his duty to show me how to practise a piece. He made me dissect the music bar by bar and repeat each bar separately until it was perfect, a practice I found profoundly boring. I can still hear him now storming out of the room shouting, 'She has no idea how to practise! All she does is play things through. She makes the same mistakes time after time!'

Fortunately he was more patient with his private piano and cello pupils; the orchestra salary was meagre so my father needed to teach to supplement his income. One thing I really admired about him was his generosity of spirit. If a student could not afford lessons, he would provide them free of charge. After my parents emigrated to New Zealand, my father formed a chamber music group for younger musicians. He would provide the music, coach them and organise public concerts. The concerts never covered costs and my parents always reached into their own pockets out of the goodness of their hearts.

Music, like my father's big personality, engulfed everyone in our house. My mother assumed the role of making post-performance supper. No matter how exhausted she was, she would be waiting up for my father with freshly baked cake and steaming coffee. On his return from a concert he would amuse us with the events of that evening's performance using his excellent mimicry and wicked sense of humour. This was how we got to know the characteristics of the conductors, soloists and orchestral colleagues.

Otherwise our home became a hub for European refugee musicians and their wives. Wonderful players would delight us each month. My father was the only professional musician so he would lead the ensemble on cello or piano; then there was Bela Fischer, a Hungarian engineer, on first violin, and Austrians Robert Low on second violin and Heini Wight playing viola. Their playing was interspersed with lively discussions about their musical interpretations: the cadenzas, the improvised embellishments, should a note be brittle or staccato, smooth or vibrato or tackled with gusto. The wives relished the music while knitting or sewing.

My mother embroidered a tablecloth on which every musician who came to our house wrote their signatures. It features more than 50 names of people that my father invited back to supper after a performance, and included the regular monthly group of players, MSO orchestra members and visiting orchestral stars such as Hungarian-Australian violinist and conductor Robert Pikler, and Henry Krips, the Austrian-Australian who was principal conductor with the South Australian Symphony Orchestra. Bertha Jorgensen, Alceo Galliera the Italian composer and conductor, and Boris Stupel, the Lithuanian violinist, are among those featured in cotton thread.

It was a wonderfully convivial time although my father often grumbled about Bela Fischer's reluctance to practise his music beforehand. But as his friends were all amateurs no doubt struggling to establish themselves in a new country and probably working long hours at jobs for which they were overqualified, practising would not have been high on their agendas. Nevertheless, it must have been an enormously gratifying way for them all to connect after being exiled from the European cultural life that had been reduced to ashes.

After consuming my mother's sumptuous supper, the musicians drew out their diaries to make a time for their next gathering and my father would hand out a copy of their musical part so they could practise for the next soirée. Initially our family was the only one in the group to have a car so my father transported them to and from their homes in far-flung Melbourne suburbs. Car travel was a novelty, plus it was a time before seatbelts and most cars had bench seats so more people and their instruments could be crammed into a vehicle. I often accompanied my father on these rowdy trips and loved all the attention I got from the adults.

Between the ages of 11 and 18, I had the joy of attending MSO rehearsals and concerts. I got such great insights into the productions. My father and I were a handsome pair as we entered the town hall for a performance, he in his black suit and white bow tie and me in my prettiest frock, often one that Grandmother Sofie had sent. I always polished my one pair of shoes for the occasion— my black lace-up school shoes.

My father's orchestra colleagues nicknamed him, 'the late Mr. Langer', because he was always running late. To make up for lost time he would park his car at the top of Little Collins Street then, with the cello in his firm grip, he would run to the orchestra's home base, the Melbourne Town Hall. Strolling pedestrians scattered on hearing his thudding footsteps accompanied by his, 'shoo, shoo', to alert them that they needed to be out of his way, and fast. It was a highly successful ploy.

Speeding was another way to gain ground. When the police would pull him over, my father would use his title of 'doctor' to his advantage. They assumed he was a medical doctor so they would wave him on without a fine. Austria was very title-conscious. My father had a doctorate in law and so he was still addressed by his European compatriots in Australia as *Herr Doktor*. As a courtesy my mother was addressed as *Frau Doktor*, even though she did not hold a degree. It was the convention in Austria to do so.

Then there were the MSO tours when my father would be on the road for a week at a time. During their downtime the musicians would get up to all kinds of mischief. My father preferred to walk in the countryside rather than being couped up with the drunken mob that his musical colleagues would become; he was not a drinker. We enjoyed his amusing letters about their wild behaviour though.

Oct 22, 1950

Dearest Hertha

The past week went quickly as a result of the tour. It was not as bad as I had thought … We travelled over Bendigo and Kerang to Swan Hill and arrived at 6pm after 10 hours of travelling. During the journey, drink stops were often made and I saw for the first time Tim White in a very animated frame of mind and heard him for the first time talk fluently without any stuttering [Tim White, who had a serious stutter, was first clarinettist in the MSO].

The concert in Swan Hill was very badly attended but the supper which ended it was very pleasant … Next day it was the children's concert at 10am. After lunch we climbed into the bus again to travel another four hours to Mildura 104 miles further. Most of the male players travelled in the other bus and later I was told were drunk in the worst possible way … Of those in my bus, the passengers were only aware of the heavy drinking by the other bus stopping every half hour. At every such stop the drinkers lurched out to satisfy their bodily needs, which they did without any regard for the ladies in the immediate vicinity of the bus.

My father gave up a lot to be a musician; including playing tennis and hockey, to protect his musician hands. In fact, those musician hands also precluded him from chopping the incredibly tough Mallee roots for our two fireplaces when winter loomed. My mother and I did the job instead, our hands not being so precious! The problem in those early days, however, was that we had no idea how to make a fire so it would constantly go out when we left the room for any length of time, leaving us at the mercy of Melbourne's chilly winters. Occasionally we had the assistance of my schoolfriend Barbara Norris who would stay the night and stoke it up magnificently. Thank goodness for schoolfriends.

19

SCHOOL OF HARD KNOCKS

For the most part, any kind of creativity was all but beaten out of children in the traditional state schools of my day. My first few years in Australia were spent at Preshil progressive school. In my later school years there were times when I would appreciate its enlightened approach: children were treated respectfully, and happiness was considered as important as intellect, and boys and girls were encouraged to mingle and learn together. Preshil ran on a shoestring but no child was refused entry if their parents were unable to afford the fees.

Even during World War II we sang songs in different languages, including German. I later heard that German tuition was banned in schools across Australia, in contrast to our school's policies. Parental involvement, including that of refugee parents, was encouraged and they would do artistic activities with us, such as creative movement or play the piano for singing. My mother was enlisted to teach the headmistress, Miss Margaret, the German language. Many years later my mother confided to me that Margaret had no ear for languages.

When I turned nine I pestered my parents to let me follow my best friend Lyn to East Kew Central. So, in 1943 I found myself sitting in the headmaster's office with my mother as he took details for my enrolment into Grade Four. He demanded the following information.

'Father's employment?' A short silence followed.

'He has none,' I said. That caused an eyebrow to raise.

'Well, what did he do before?'

'He was the owner of a timber mill,' said my mother.

'Well, maybe he will do this again,' was the headmaster's brusque reply as he filled in the form.

Even as a nine-year-old I was somewhat affronted by the tone of his questioning. I felt like telling that ignorant man how ridiculous he was being. It had been so hard for my father to come to an alien country where his law degree was not recognised, where he had to work for a pittance in a factory and feed a family of four on that pittance. Instead I pursed my lips and squeezed my hands till they hurt.

East Kew Central was a public school steeped in conservatism and tradition, a place where parental involvement was very much discouraged except for one time when a special dispensation was made because I had won a big award. My parents had the rare honour of being welcomed to the ritual Monday morning assembly held in the open quadrangle. There were no such things as assembly halls in those days so come shine or storm we would be outdoors singing to the king and saluting the flag. That momentous day I was being congratulated for winning the bronze medal from the Royal Humane Society of Australasia for saving my brother's life. I remember the scarcely veiled horror on my parents' faces as they watched us perform the salute-the-flag ceremony, followed by marching around the quadrangle in pairs to the command of, 'Left right, left right, left right'. A reminder that the Hitler Youth was just a whisper away.

That medal I just mentioned was a pretty weird thing to my nine-year-old mind. I really could not see what all the fuss was about. It came about on a warm February day, the 26th to be exact, when I was wounded in action. I had just crossed the tram tracks on my way home from school when I saw my mother and three-year-old brother heading for the shops. I raced over to join them.

'We're going to cross the road in a moment, Martin,' I instructed him as I attempted to take his hand, but for Martin a moment was too long and he dashed off across busy Whitehorse Road and straight in front of an oncoming tram.

The traffic came to a screaming halt and the horrified tram driver worked fast. In a delicate manoeuvre he pulled on the hand-controlled brake, but not too hard because applying too much pressure could lock the wheels and cause the tram to skid. At the same time his foot danced between two pedals: one to sound the warning gong, and the other to apply sand to the rails to create extra friction for the steel wheels.

Clouds of sand dust and the nauseating smell of hot iron permeated the atmosphere as the cast-iron brakes strained, squealed and ground to a halt, but not soon enough. My mother collapsed with fright. Having lost one child, all she could see were her two remaining children about to be killed. When she had the courage to open her eyes, she saw that Martin was unharmed but I was lying unconscious on the road. The only thing I remember is racing after him and pushing him out of the tram's path. The following day was lost.

I was a sorry sight and unconscious as my mother climbed into the ambulance bound for the Alfred Hospital. I had a large gash in my cheek, a cut to my forehead, a nasty wound on the back of my head and severe concussion. Wounds stitched, I regained consciousness 24 hours later in the children's ward, surrounded by rows of metal beds. I had no idea why I was there until my mother arrived and told me what had happened.

Soon enough I was up and about playing with the other children and having a great time. We had the freedom of the ward and all day to play. With scars on my face and a bald patch on the back of my skull, I left the hospital a few days later.

Later that year I received a letter from the Royal Humane Society congratulating me for having saved Martin's life. My mother told me I would get something for my bravery. The only thing I really wanted was a horse. I decided that if they asked me I would tell them that. A week later a profoundly disappointing letter arrived from Government House with no such offer—rather, an invitation to a special investiture on the 30ᵗʰ August 1943 to receive the Bronze Medal of the Royal Humane Society of Australasia. Ponies aside, I had the honour of being the youngest recipient of this award on record.

The Sun, The Herald, The Age and the *Sunday Telegraph* newspapers took photos of me in my new hat secured with a bow under my chin and a jacket that was decorated with the newly awarded medal. Being completely overwhelmed by all this attention, I kept a tight grip on the bouquet of flowers and managed an embarrassed smile. All this fuss because I acted swiftly so that my poor brother would not be killed. Who would not do that, I wondered?

And so they made a fuss of me at the school assembly, but it was soon forgotten. The following week, my teacher Miss White, a plump, stern old spinster with grey hair tortured into a bun, was quick to berate me at the drop of a stitch. (Knitting was actually part of our curriculum.)

'And what is this?' shouted Miss White as she held up my latest knitting effort for the class to see.

I was crestfallen because I had felt pleased with myself for finally mastering the art of plain and purl without dropping stitches. I had even managed to knit the front and shoulder straps of the baby's vest and had started on the back. Sure, the opening for the baby's head was a bit small, but it was the best I could do.

The problem was that my knitting had fallen out of my leather schoolbag into a puddle as I ran to line up for Monday morning's oath of allegiance to King George VI. On the way to class I tried to wash the big, grey splotches out of the white wool as best I could under the bathroom tap, but because it was still on the knitting needles it was ineffectual.

Miss White's voice was a simmering volcano. 'Can you explain what you have done? Never in all my life as a teacher has anyone dared to come to class with such a rag on knitting needles.'

Talk about total humiliation. Miss White picked up her ruler earmarked for the punishment of misbehaving girls like me. 'Come up to the stage, Susi.'

Those six words felt like they were caught in treacle as they boomed through the room. I was given six whacks on the hand. It stung like mad but I didn't cry. The quantity of whacks was dependent on the magnitude of the crime, or the teacher's mood. As for the boys, a rolled-up strap lay in wait next to the ruler. In the clink of a knitting needle the strap could be unfurled and flicked at the offending student.

My knitting was not worth continuing so I was made to stand in the corner near the fire with my back to the class. It was a punishment with a bonus because this was the warm spot. The rest of the large classroom was drafty and freezing cold. Some of the children had to wear gloves in class; many of them had chilblains.

Punishment administered, I was now forgotten and Miss White's suspicious, beady blue eyes darted around the class in search of the next victim. A naughty child was not a difficult find—even talking was a serious offence and deviants needed swift punishment.

Generally I did not do so well at that school. Every month there was a test. The results determined who we sat next to for the next four weeks. My bedraggled knitting had a severe impact on my marks, which were already not great due to my poor writing style and my being behind in arithmetic. I knew for sure that I would be seated next to a boy—the biggest disgrace.

I must admit that even though I was the one who begged to go to East Kew Central, the first year there was a bit of a shock after four years of Preshil's unrestricted freedom. At Preshil every child was considered innately good and never needed to have bad behaviour whacked out of them. Preshil teachers believed that misbehaviour happened because the child was troubled within, and attempts were made to find the cause through patience and kindness. One could talk and wander at will; there were no tests and no compulsion to attend classes.

Those early Preshil years were so important to me. How would life have been without my introduction to the wonders of Rudyard Kipling and the enactment of dramas such as the story of the Pied Piper of Hamelin, or the opportunity to climb trees? Sometimes the teacher would appear, a tiny figure way below calling out to ask if we would like to join in the maths class. I always declined the invitation.

20

FOR BETTER AND WORSE

January was always a bad month for bills and a time when my parents wore long faces. My mother's was the longest because she had to manage the consequences of my father's excessive spending. Once it got the better of her. When I was 12, I found a note my mother left for my father on the dining room table saying that she was leaving him and that he could have the children. I had no idea what was going on. Nevertheless, I thought I would go wherever my mother goes. She stayed and I remember her telling me, 'If I left your father, he would never get over it'.

It is interesting that she continuously suffered from his lack of restraint and yet he was the one who needed to be looked after. This was never more in evidence than when we discovered that he had had a dalliance with a woman in Buxton during his timber mill period.

One morning when I was 14 years old, I got up as usual for school. As I approached the kitchen to make my breakfast of Cornflakes and a glass of milk, I immediately saw that something was not quite right. My parents were quietly upset about something that they obviously didn't want to share with me. My mother was standing by the tea trolley, which had the daily newspaper on it. She flipped it to the back pages, cast her eye over it, and then they said goodbye to me and left the house. Of course I looked in the back pages and found the law court proceeding for that day with the name 'Peter Langer' in it. There were no details, just his name and the name of a woman who was being sued for divorce. The report went something like: Mr ..., 39, has petitioned for divorce from Mrs ..., 30, on the grounds of misconduct with Dr Peter Langer of 15 Knutsford Street, Balwyn.

I stood there unable to fathom the situation but I remember feeling terrible. There was nothing else to do then but ask Aunt Liesl what was going on. For sure, she would know, I thought. Fortunately she had trouble keeping a secret, so she told me that when my father had the timber mill, he had formed a 'relationship' with this woman. Among other things, they had written to each other. In those days when you wanted a divorce you had to have evidence of infidelity. The woman's husband had found the letters. When my father was cited in the divorce proceedings, he confessed to my mother. True to form, she remained the supportive wife and, despite her utter humiliation, she went with him to court.

There had been some issues since the earliest days of their relationship. My mother wrote of them in her diary. Back in October 1932, when my father was considering marrying her, according to Aunt Liesl, he had another girlfriend whom he liked as well. The problem was that he could not decide which one to marry. Liesl said he made the decision by counting the buttons on his pyjamas, like counting the petals on a daisy—he loves me, he loves me not, I'll marry her, I'll marry her not. It was a torturous time for 22-year-old Hertha.

After a long day toing and froing, after a terrible, nerve wracking time for me, after I lost all control of myself the day before, after humiliations and struggles, I wrote him a letter yesterday where I made him the suggestion of finally refraining from the plan of getting married soon. A short time after taking the letter to the post I was told by phone that he had made a positive decision [to marry her] and his letter to my father was already underway.

This news had an unforeseen effect on me. Possibly I had behaved very stupidly. I was mad with joy and there was no other thought in my head. I jumped around, laughed, did some somersaults and behaved like a mad person. The week-long tension disappeared at once.

In the evening when he came, I hadn't regained my senses. Instead of using the situation a little, I showed him in a childish way that I had only waited for his word. To his question of whether I was thinking of taking all the blame for a bad result onto myself, I answered yes. I showed him that his remorse and his fear of losing me had been quite unnecessary.

In far too much of a hurry I suggested going to my father. He was very surprised and embarrassed.

I am marrying for love and in the conviction that it is no sunny clear happiness which is waiting for me. What I have experienced now is only a foretaste.

A few weeks later, on the 8ᵗʰ November, she wrote:

Already engaged for two weeks. I have already almost forgotten what happened before. When I look back, these 10 months seem beautiful to me. I am glad I have experienced them. I have got to know him differently. The many visits, the congratulations, the worries about furnishings and the apartment distract one very much from each other. A little leisure, with each other and also time alone, is necessary. I don't want to forget that I am marrying him because I love him and that I want to be the best for him and help him as far as is in my power. I don't want to be wrapped in the worry of housekeeping and children.

There was certainly an element of self-sacrifice in their relationship. No matter what, my mother made the sacrifice and she had a great capacity to forgive. Otherwise, I know that my father really loved her and relied on her heavily. I remember meeting him in Austria when I was 18, after I had been to stay with Grandmother Sofie in Miami. He had already been away from home for six months, pursuing the cultural and scenic bounty of Europe and taking lessons with cellist, Pablo Casals.

'I miss your mother every step,' he said; and he did write to her daily.

In many ways he was a loving and doting father but he never really grew up to become a responsible adult. His grip on reality was sometimes tenuous which was borne out with extreme clarity when I was first married. My father touched my chin affectionately, looked me in the eye and said, 'If you ever need money, just tell me.'

Where would he have got it from, I wondered?

21

TEENAGE ANGST

For most of my teenage years I managed to block out a lot of my parents' anxieties. I had lots of friends and had become quite self-determined. In my early teens my relationship with my father further deteriorated. We were no longer great mates and, if I am honest, I resented the way he doted on Martin, whereas with me, he was very critical. If I got a B on an assignment, he would say, 'Why didn't you get an A?' My fashion choices were also a source of irritation, although by today's standards, they were quite tame, and he had little patience for my long, and what he considered pointless, teenage phone conversations.

The phone would emit its chirrupy signal and the cry would come: 'Susi, there's a phone call for you'. I would make a hurried exit from my bedroom, sliding along the polished floorboards in the hall to the wooden box where the phone was installed on the wall. Because the phone was in the middle of the house there was absolutely no privacy: the whole family could hear my conversations. My father made a point of rolling his eyes each time he passed me and I could clearly hear his regular complaints to my mother in the kitchen at the end of the passage. Usually it was, 'This is ridiculous! In Austria there is a three-minute limit on conversations.'

As I matured, though, I became more introverted and my self-esteem definitely took a tumble after my third change in high schools. My secondary schooling was always of a good quality, but in those days there were just a few public schools in Melbourne that went to Matriculation level so I had to leave Canterbury Girls' High after the fourth year. My parents wanted me to continue learning piano and persuaded me to go to Fintona Girls' School, where there was a good music program. However, I was not happy there so decided to follow some of my Canterbury Girls High friends to Mac.Robertson Girls' High. It was a lot of travel though—90-minutes each way, each day.

Mac.Rob was, and still is, a government school for more academically gifted young ladies; I found myself studying with some of the most intelligent girls in the state. Although I enjoyed school, in no way did I stand out academically despite my studying nights, weekends and holidays. The more I studied the more stressed I became. But I just could not absorb the material. The final Matriculation exams nearly did me in. Having to sit for them in the vast, intimidating hall of the Royal Exhibition Building on the edge of the city centre, compounded my feelings of inferiority.

At the same time my parents were concerned about me not having a boyfriend and that I had, in fact, become too shy even to talk to boys. In true Viennese style, efforts were made to match me up with the sons of some of their friends, although the idea was not to marry me off at this point as much as to bring me out of myself. The young men were usually considerably older than me and although they tried hard to engage me in conversation, my answers were monosyllabic. It was incredibly awkward.

As teenagers we were still directed not to indulge in sexual activity outside the bounds of marriage. In this way mores had not changed since the 19th century. During my grandmothers' and then my parents' eras, girls were carefully guarded against anything that might compromise their moral wellbeing. The pill was still way ahead in the future and certainly, a sexual relationship before marriage was not considered something nice girls engaged in—you had to stay 'pure' for the future husband. Parents were always worried that their girls would become pregnant. My mother would give me articles to read about not having a sexual relationship without love and the security of marriage.

High schools, too, always fostered the moral high ground; those booming, authoritative pronouncements of my various headmistresses still ring in my ears: 'No girl in school uniform is permitted to talk to a boy unless it is her own brother'.

Boys were forbidden fruit in primary school too—not that we were too keen on most of them. Segregation was practised at any given opportunity. Funnily enough, in the Sunday School at St Barnabas Anglican Church in Balwyn we had the opportunity to mingle with the opposite sex, which is where I met my first boyfriend.

I was 12 and Alan was 14, tall and lean. At Sunday School the saucy rascal passed notes to me: 'Have you got a bike?' or 'What do you like best: chocolate or strawberry ice cream?' Sometimes he was waiting at the tram stop when I returned from school and would often ride his bike past my house around the time I was setting the table for dinner. I would do my chores quickly so that I could be in the front garden in case he came by.

Once he asked me to ride with him to the Ivanhoe pool. Even this prepubescent flirtation was met with concern. My parents were dismayed that I had a boyfriend at such a young age, but it was a very innocent friendship—we didn't ever even hold hands.

I wonder if my great-grandmother Clara Böhm would have objected. Probably, because with the wealth and stature of my extended family came a certain standard of social and familial responsibility, prepubescent or not. In her time and milieu, young women were escorted at all times when leaving the house, be it to go shopping or to and from their piano and foreign language classes. Their reading matter was monitored and they would certainly not know of the sexual and reproductive functioning of a woman or man, let alone be apprised of knowledge of sexual pleasure other than that which would be aroused by a husband.

During the period of my parents' engagement they were not allowed to spend one minute alone. If they went into the garden there had to be someone accompanying them. However, when Pauline reached the same age, much to my mother's resentment, she had much more freedom of movement.

On the other hand, similarly to today, men were not required to be so controlled. Generally, their outbursts of sexual activity, either as bachelors or as transgressors of the marital confines, were greeted with understanding. Long-suffering wives took it through gritted teeth and processed their feelings through controlled emotional outbursts in diary entries.

Viennese girls of my mother's and grandmother's generations were educated in private schools that were akin to finishing schools. But equally important for a woman was a rich and busy social life. When my grandmother, and then my mother, turned 18, social activity was ramped up for the inevitable husband hunt. An important social hub in my family was the Sunday afternoon open house at great-grandmother Clara's home. Clara was an extrovert, a socialite of great charm and wit and, from all accounts, she was once a very beautiful woman with a lively intelligence who loved to entertain. Her home could be likened to a 19th-century Parisian salon and she surrounded herself with people of social importance from many walks of life. (This makes her even more phenomenal in my eyes regarding how well she dealt with her vastly diminished circumstances during the war.) As matriarch, it was Clara's duty to ensure that there would be no humiliating breaches of etiquette.

Her youngest son, my great-uncle Joele Böhm, wrote in his memoir:

While Mother was happy, relaxed and very warm and loving within the family … she kept to a very strict etiquette in every move outside the family, especially in regard to my sisters' every step.

The seasonal balls, a tradition in Vienna for European royalty and aristocracy since 1814, were glittering events engineered to forge the right relationships. My grandmother Sofie and her sisters Hedl and Leonie attended balls given in private homes for 50 to 100 guests during the 'season', as well as select public balls given by charities such as the Red Cross and White Cross. Young ladies, glowing in their beaded and brocaded silks, were chaperoned by their parents who sat patiently at separate tables or in loges until two or three o'clock in the morning, keeping a careful eye on their charges as they waltzed themselves weary. If it was a private event, the hosts did everything in their power to encourage their guests to stay as long as possible. It was deemed a poor party if they did not stay till the wee hours. These activities were a focus until the inevitable betrothal.

Teenage life was certainly different in Australia post-World War II. The excruciating efforts of my parents to extract me from my shell only made things worse, although my shyness evaporated when my friends and I took Christmas holiday jobs at the Heidelberg Military Hospital in Melbourne. I served morning and afternoon teas, then supper to bedridden male patients. They needed someone to talk to and I was there. In those days these war veterans were admitted for long periods, some for years.

One evening a man I had befriended in the Spinal TB unit invited me to accompany him to the cinema that was situated in the grounds of the hospital. He was 32 and I was 18. I thought he was far too old for me but I felt sorry for him because he had been confined to his bed for months.

I cannot remember the film but I vividly remember what happened afterwards. As we were walking back to the wards, he took the opportunity of a screen of bushes to ask me for a kiss. I said okay because I thought I should say yes. He was the first grown-up male I had been out with and the first to kiss me. I was disgusted because I really did not want to do it. He asked if he could take me out again. I replied, 'No, you're too old'. I cringe when I think about the cruelty of that remark. It would have been very hurtful to this poor man who had spent a year on his back. Maybe I had developed a little too much confidence to say something like that.

22

MY OWN ADVENTURE

The same year as that first awkward kiss in 1951, I completed my final year at Mac.Robertson Girls' High School. My hospital holiday jobs had made it fairly clear that nursing would be my preferred career, but I was not quite ready to waltz into a new venture just yet. Because of the stresses of the past school year I needed time off to achieve some clarity. Naturally, Grandmother Sofie knew about my restless state of mind because the regular airmail communications continued to relay the minutiae of our daily lives across the Pacific and Atlantic oceans. She responded with a marvellous plan: that I should come and spend a year with her in Miami.

To pay for my passage to England then America, my mother hocked her last diamond brooch. Family and friends waved goodbye to me at Port Melbourne dock and threw coloured streamers at the ship, the *Largs Bay*, before I sailed away for the year. The *Largs Bay*, launched in 1921, was a passenger and cargo ship which transported refugees across to Australia from Europe during the war. Prior to being scrapped in 1957, it was used as a film set for some of the interior scenes in *A Night to Remember*, the 1958 movie about the Titanic. Thankfully, my voyage in June 1952 did not entail any such drama, although the seasickness was quite debilitating as we passed through the Great Australian Bight.

By the time we left Perth I was able to escape my hot, airless cabin, and the stench created by the unwashed undies of my cabinmate, an elderly English woman who believed it was essential to wear the same red flannel underwear every day to protect her against catching colds. Cabins did not have ensuite showers so you could only wash in large baths of sea water, and there was no airconditioning on the ship so warm nights spent in a deckchair were much more pleasant. I made the best of it all and got to know many of the passengers during the four-week journey. Evenings were a whirl of entertainment and dancing, while days were spent lazing in deckchairs, swimming in the pool and discussing the ports we would visit. I planned every precious minute of my time at these stopovers so that I would see as much as possible in the available few hours.

We stopped briefly in Colombo, Ceylon, as Sri Lanka was then called. It was the most exciting experience for me: magnificently colourful, the colonial buildings, human-drawn rickshaws, roadside dealers and throngs of people on the cobblestone streets.

My confidence burgeoned as I sailed towards England. I even had a little shipboard frisson on the England leg of the journey with a Maltese guy, even though my heart was quite taken with Czechoslovakian lawyer Milan Kantor, the son of close family friends in Melbourne. Strangely enough, when I returned to Australia a year later, my Maltese admirer wrote me a marriage proposal. I wrote back:

No, I'm not ready for marriage. I need to complete my studies.

Undeterred, he came to Australia and took me to a nice hotel for dinner, but I had to tell him that I was not going to marry him. My parents would never have been happy with someone like him as a son-in-law. Not because he wasn't Jewish, but he didn't have a university degree.

Next stop was Malta where my enamoured friend disembarked. From there we sailed on through the turbulent seas of the Bay of Biscay to Southampton where I caught the train to London. It was a grey, rainy day when great-aunt Friedl von Hofmannsthal greeted me at Waterloo Station and, as arranged, she was waving her red scarf so I could identify her. I had not seen her since I was four, but our reunion was very emotional for her. We caught the double-decker bus to her tiny, dingy Carlton Hill apartment, which was so far removed from her previous life, yet she was very proud of it. The living room became my bedroom. The tiny kitchen was actually under the stairwell so that each time I stood up, I would bang my head on the staircase.

Friedl was a sweet woman, but she had always been very much taken with title and position. Both of her husbands had died. Her first husband was the cousin of the famous writer, Hugo von Hofmannsthal. She still set great store by this aristocratic name and kept his aristocratic patent. She liked to bring it out of the cupboard and show it off to all her visitors, including me, at every opportunity. When she spoke of Hugo, she would say in solemn tones, 'I met him the first time at my engagement celebration in Vienna. Then we were always together at Altaussee (the family holiday home).'

Some years later, as she slept in her London flat, a prowler stole the precious seal, the only evidence of her assumed nobility, which she had treasured and kept safe throughout the long war years. Of course, it was never recovered.

After the six-week stay, a Dutch ship delivered me to New York and into the expectant arms of more relatives. As the ship drifted slowly towards New York Harbour, the clamour of the city was a muted drone, overpowered by the sight of the silhouettes of the towering skyscrapers and the breathtaking, 93-metre Liberty goddess. I wondered if she was a symbol for me too? Was this my time of freedom to explore and be my little family's ambassador to re-thread relationships long separated by time and oceans?

At the Port of New York, the welcome was wonderfully warm from an army of relatives; some I had not seen since I was four and others I had never met, such as my cousin Dennis Stone, the son of Aunt Pauline. He was just six years old and he believed that he was on the wharf to meet the queen. He bowed when I was introduced to him and gave me a bouquet of flowers. I emailed Dennis recently and asked what he was thinking when I arrived way back then.

In February 1952, a few months before my cousin Susi was about to arrive from Australia, young Queen Elizabeth of England had her coronation. We had just purchased our first television and there was extensive coverage of the event. In those days there was no instantaneous coverage. Film of the event had to be rushed to the US by slow plane and then broadcast to the nation. As a 6-year-old, I sat for hours in front of that small screen. It seemed that the extensive coverage made this a most important event.

Shortly thereafter Susi arrived by boat from England. I thought that only famous people got to travel on a big boat. She was young like the new Queen and our family was so excited about her arrival. I guess I put it all together and in my young mind I assumed we were at the pier to welcome the queen.

It was always a source of fascination to me that our family could remain so deeply connected across such vast distance and time, but few of our ties weakened. Certainly, with my mother's family, the deep-rooted commitment to family life has been the glue that holds us still, more than 80 years later.

And so began a year of American life, a year when I became once more enmeshed with my relatives who showered me with kindness and attention, determined to make up for those lost decades. Each day there were parties and dinners—I certainly felt like a queen with all the attention I got.

My mother's younger brother, Uncle Andreas—the one who had survived Dachau—took me sightseeing around all New York's points of interest. He was very kind to me, as he was with any visiting family. He liked to drive everyone around but I could tell that beneath the surface his emotional state was turbulent.

The effect of his experiences in the concentration camp cannot be diminished; however, the way he was raised by his parents also contributed to his lack of ability to cope with a family and life in a new country.

Eight years earlier when my grandparents arrived in America, their first port of call was Seven Springs, Pennsylvania, to visit Andreas and Netty in their new home. Andreas had a job at the Seven Springs ski resort as a skiing instructor and they both seemed content with their new life. According to Sofie, Andreas and Netty were 'greatly loved and very spoilt'. Sofie wrote:

He has earned a very nice sum over the winter and is now trying to find a new project. You would laugh if you heard him speak but he makes himself understood quite well.

Andreas was never able to hold a job down for long and he undertook many business ventures that required him to travel to other states in search of opportunities. Then in 1943 he enlisted in the army at New York City as a 10th Calvary Reconnaissance Trooper, and later with the 10th Mountain Division, then the 86th Infantry Regiment in Colorado and Texas, with other expert skiers.

Sofie's ongoing reports said that he was successful and happy, and that Netty was a good housewife. Meanwhile, they had two children, Clifford and Tim. Clifford, the elder child, was intelligent and independent but Timmy was uncontrollable. Sofie wrote to my mother of the horrors the family endured with him.

I must tell you about the Schatzi's [term of endearment, like sweetheart] visit. First came Netty with the two boys on the 23rd December [1957]. She looked terrible, quite worn out, and the boys although big and strong were very pale. I had reserved an apartment for them, and but for the meals, they were always with me. From 10–4p.m. they were at the beach in my cabana until they were sent away because of Timmy's naughtiness.

He thumped the peaceful people in their deckchairs, dispersed sand over them and poured water over them. Daily there were temper tantrums when one did not allow such things. Especially hostile were the other mothers whose children he knocked over and hurt. So, I took them to other public beaches, every second day to another one where one did not yet know Timmy, and so the three weeks passed.

Although she described the children as being sweet 'in their own ways', they were terribly spoilt by their mother. After six days Sofie said that her apartment was unimaginably dirty. The boys had ruined everything they could—they had torn, scratched and drawn on furniture and walls.

Netty sent Sofie a letter in March saying they will have to move out of their house because of Timmy's behaviour. He had made enemies of all her neighbours, and what was most disturbing was that Andreas would encourage Timmy to get up to mischief.

Daily there are complaints and barrages of abuse. She cannot leave him for one moment to play in the garden because he is a danger to other children. He hits and pushes, and even pushes baby prams over.

Some years ago, Clifford wrote and told me how difficult it was growing up with his father:

Despite Mother's best efforts, the atmosphere was entirely unpredictable, typically loud, sometimes aggressive. Mother's requests of him or attempts to engage him in conversation about household matters usually precipitated disaster that affected us all … I resented his behaviour towards us and our mother, and rarely made any effort to draw him out. Besides, conversations with him directed towards anything beyond furniture, chess or car repair, remained beyond the scope.

Andreas and Netty's problems continued into the 1960s. Andreas became almost totally occupied with playing chess and he could not provide money to his wife. Grandmother Sofie had to bail him out of financial trouble constantly and Great-Uncle Joele, who was head of the family, had to disentangle him from a number of failing businesses. There were many secrets and many lies. Netty was in despair and because Tim was such high maintenance, she was unable to work.

Finally in 1961, broke and miserable, Andreas realised that he could not continue in this manner and he agreed to seek psychiatric help. Family members reported that he changed somewhat and became much more open and better tempered. However, my grandmother and Andreas' brother, Otto, still had to subsidise his household.

Andreas's later years were not reported to us after Sofie's death in 1962. Then in 2013 Clifford wrote to tell me that Andreas had died some years earlier and that he had set about investigating his father's life. He discovered that many of the early reports of Andreas's achievements were either untrue or inaccurate.

I contacted the university that houses the records of the 10th Mountain Division that he was a member of. They sent me what records they could access so I now have copies. There were some surprises. He had always told me he had been a sergeant, for example. The records however indicated that he never rose beyond the rank of private. He was never deployed to Europe with the group, as I was told, and I was not aware that his discharge was murky, coming soon after a transfer to a medical group. I suspect that they saw he was not quite right and let him go.

My family shared little with their children, just bits and pieces occasionally. He told me several times [regarding his time in the camps] that he was a milkman and that secured him some leverage or better treatment, and that the showers actually contained water, as opposed to gas. Perhaps he was thus able to consume milk to add to his meagre diet, which kept him looking healthy.

We know that Andreas was deeply affected by his internment in Dachau. However, there is another disturbing component to his story. I knew very little about his past until I found my grandparents' letters and read Aunt Pauline's memoir.

Otto was the first born of my mother's siblings. Andreas was second, then my mother, Hertha, and finally Pauline. Both Andreas and Otto were fine-looking lads but their childhood faces bore expressions of impudence and self-importance and their behaviour was mostly out of control. Pauline recorded in her memoir that Andreas was a handful from the outset and was cruel to his siblings. One time, when the family was riding in a carriage, Andreas was seated over the top of baby Hertha in her crib, from where he kicked and kicked her as she wept. This was not an isolated incident and rather than subject the babies to any more risks from the boys, a nanny was hired to take care of my mother, then Pauline, in isolation, a safe distance away from them.

Pauline remembered a time when, aged 5, she was playing with her Erector set (which was like Meccano). Andreas came and took over the construction. She was fascinated by his dexterity in constructing the carts, tracks and moving parts. Pauline loaded the carts with blocks and one broke. In a fury, Andreas slapped her hard across her face.

As the boys grew, their antics became more abominable and a streaming succession of nannies and tutors were appointed to take care of them. Reports have it that some ended up in a rest home for a period after traumatic encounters with those boys. One nanny was woken from her sleep by the flashing of a light. She jumped up thinking there was a burglar in her room, and was again thrown into total darkness. The poor nanny ran screaming off into the night, never to return. The next day they discovered that eight-year-old Otto had installed an electrical connector under her mattress with a wire leading to a bulb secreted under her bed.

During their teens the boys had terrible fist fights, which generally took place while the parents were out, leaving the servants to watch helplessly as the boys pounded each other— they were afraid to intervene in case they got belted—usually, they would have to race up to my Great-Uncle Walter's apartment because he was the only one who could break them up. Aunt Pauline wrote that as a rule, the following day as her mother reminisced about the previous night's concert or party, a half-smiling reference was made to the unruly behaviour of the night before. Boys will be boys.

Otto was his mother's favourite son and, in her eyes, he could do no wrong; but the fact was the boys were ill-disciplined by both parents. Sofie let them get up to all sorts of dangerous manoeuvres but made sure she was nearby in case they had an accident.

In adolescence the magnitude of their misbehaviour escalated. One time Andreas got hold of a gun and conducted target practice in their bathroom. Then a Rembrandt on the wall of their holiday villa in Neuwaldegg was mysteriously pierced by a bullet. Pauline wrote:

For such exploitations, punishment was severe but as a whole it was considered normal for boys to be wild and troublesome while growing up.

Their reputations became legendary. None of the schools could contain Andreas, so eventually he was suspended from every local school. His father admonished him at the dinner table for poor marks. Eventually they got him enrolled in a school far away across the Danube Canal near a cemetery. Instead of walking to school, enterprising Andreas hitched a ride on a hearse then stole the school's record book. Now there were no more schools left.

I found a letter that my father wrote to my mother in the Vienna days, where he expressed utter frustration over Otto's antics.

I have no idea what he was getting up to but it was obviously pretty annoying:

The visits of especially Otto get on my nerves. I had to threaten him to make him more bearable. I keep seeing that his character is much worse than I ever thought. This I could bear but I will certainly have to undergo a lecture from your parents because I will once and for all have to stop these stupidities especially because of Susi when she gets older.

Otto turned out to be a very good businessman, but he was not the most popular family member. When he made it to America he set about building himself a rosy future and became a highly successful builder. He even worked on several projects with renowned architect Frank Lloyd Wright. Generosity of spirit did not accompany his financial success. There were several incidents during restitution claims where he believed he was due more than the family believed he was entitled to. He lost the respect and trust of his siblings over these kinds of issues.

When it came to the distribution of wartime restitution money, as executor Joele decided to give Andreas's share directly to Netty knowing that Andreas would recklessly spend the money to the detriment of his family. Andreas was furious when he found out. This was an affront to his position as head of his family. From then on, he would have nothing more to do with the extended family.

As for my mother's early life, she had a much more contemplative and serious nature than her siblings and, from all accounts, Hertha's childhood was not so happy. She was largely cared for by the Fräulein, while her younger sister Pauline, being Sofie's favourite, was heartily indulged.

I often considered the complexities of my extended family that year I spent in the US. After a few weeks in New York, I spent the rest of my time in Miami in Grandmother Sofie's unpretentious one-bedroom apartment with its lovely view of the river. It seemed that she was happy enough then without the stress of the daily management of a palatial home and servants. In a letter written to my mother in 1940, she had commented about the container of furniture they had attempted to send during the trials of getting out of Vienna:

I am glad [the furniture] didn't come. What would I do with it all in a one-bedroom apartment?

The Sofie of 1952 was well equipped for the responsibility of caring for her far less troublesome teenage granddaughter. I attended the University of Miami for six months, lazed on the beach and ate lots of wonderful Austrian fare, such as my grandmother's delicious goulash and dumplings. I sneaked a look at a letter Sofie sent to my mother one time. She wrote that although I was not as mature as American teenagers, I knew how to conduct myself with the opposite sex. This was after an incident with a classmate at the university—short, stout Barry. Barry was kind enough to drive me 90 minutes each way to uni. I did not like him all that much but it was convenient to get a lift. After knowing each other for two weeks he proposed to me. He disappeared after I rebuffed him.

She also wrote that I did not dress with any style unless I was going out with a boy. That was my cue to up my game and dress more stylishly.

Otherwise, it was easy living with Sofie, like picking up from where we left off when I was four and living in the apartment next door at Stubenring 14. She was a quiet, introverted woman who liked to spend hours playing the piano and reading rather than socialising. In contrast, her sister Leonie was outgoing, charming and friendly. The three of us enjoyed concerts, plays, films and dinners together. My mother wrote and warned me not to give more attention to Leonie than Sofie or the latter would get jealous. So I trod carefully.

23

THE GREATEST CELLIST
IN THE WORLD

As luck would have it, in 1951 my parents had just about scraped a deposit together to buy the house we had been renting for 12 years in Balwyn. At that time I had committed to doing a teaching course. I decided to give my parents my entire government teaching bursary so they could fulfil their deposit. Unfortunately, in 1953 my father was dismissed from the MSO and they were left wondering how they were going to pay the mortgage.

Serious discrimination afflicted the music industry during this period. Music critic and musicologist Albrecht Dümling paints a picture of how undervalued overseas musicians were in Australia in his 2016 book *The Vanished Musicians*[3]:

Unlike their Australian colleagues, recently naturalised musicians had to pass an audition to join the Musicians' Union. One newspaper report stated that, 'A newcomer can join the union if he happened to be born in Britain, Ireland or Canada, but he can jump in the lake or work in a pickle factory if he happened to be born in Hungary or Austria.'

The Musicians' Union of Australia did not correct its restrictive attitude. In November 1948 it imposed a freeze on admissions for all musicians who had been in the country for less than ten years

---

3   Published by Peter Lang.

... The union also pushed through a rule that no more than 10 percent of the members of any orchestra could be born overseas ...

The policy ... resulted in many dismissals ... After re-auditioning ... he (Peter Langer) was rejected on account of the ruling above. Langer's dismissal meant he had to sell his house. To improve his chances as a cello teacher, he undertook several months of study with Pablo Casals ...

The news reached me in Miami, and even though I felt terrible for my father, I was happy to be residing in less drama-filled waters. Starting a new business venture was out of the question—business clearly was not my father's forte. At one point their financial situation got so bad that my parents sold Watkins toiletries door-to-door. I was never allowed to tell anyone about it because they were so embarrassed and would go to extraordinary lengths not to be discovered by anyone they knew. A family friend lived in one street on their round so my mother would take her out for lunch while my father covered the sales.

In 1953 my father, devising a more creative and, according to his view of the world, sustainable solution to enhance his future earning power, travelled to Europe to study with Pablo Casals, then regarded as the world's greatest cello virtuoso. The idea behind this venture was that learning with the maestro would enhance his prestige and skills, meaning he would be able to attract more students. Did he have money for the trip? No. He sought the sympathy and financial support of his old schoolfriend, Stefan Frohlich, who lived in Vienna. On the 9th January 1953, my father wrote:

Dear Stefan,

I received your letter of Oct. 19 and thank you very much for it. This quick response is due largely to a change in our local life situation and our various future plans, for I have been sacked by the Australian Broadcasting Commission and have lost my position in the orchestra. There is no point going into the reasons for this dismissal as they are unclear to myself and apparently of a personal nature.

In order to strengthen my self-confidence, friends and colleagues assured me at least that factual reasons did not come into it, as my standard is considerably higher than that of the local average players. Whatever, the loss of my activity has very much depressed me as it was a very pleasant and well paid one, giving me a good reputation as a teacher. Now I have to start again to find a new income which is not easy at my time of life. Over the last four years I had given up all associations with business or found any interest in it, basing my existence solely on my work as musician and teacher ...

At first Hertha and I wanted to move to Canada as quickly as possible in order to start again. Our intention caused such a reaction from friends and relatives here in Australia that we decided to wait before leaving. It was generally declared that we should have a very hard beginning there, added to which came the different climate, and that there were no prospects in music there, and that it would take years before we should again achieve a secure home. [In fact, my mother did not want to move to Canada or anywhere else.]

I myself would be glad to turn my back on Australia, the earlier the better ... Canada seems to me the most suitable place for our second emigration. The biggest difficulty lies in the transfer of money. Officially one cannot at the present time, take away more than £800, which would be just enough for our keep in the first six weeks. From the moment of landing, therefore, one must start at a post, not begin to look for one. This might be possible for a factory worker, hardly for such as myself ...

[W]e have very little money; although we are owners of a house, we still owe a lot of its purchase price. Its sale would produce some money but would not solve the problem of where to live or what we should do to earn our living.

Since a few days ago the following plan has emerged. I now play the cello many times better than you were familiar with, and my ability for Australian orchestras is more than sufficient, I have no illusions about my actual level/standard. On the other hand, I am convinced that I can still learn more. I will, therefore, try to contact Pablo Casals and become his student for about nine months. He lives at present in the south of France and works almost exclusively as a teacher. I have already booked my fare to Europe and if I succeed to get together £ 500 to £ 600, I'll be leaving on February 25th. If Casals doesn't accept me, I'll go to Vienna to study. In either case, if I can realise the fare, I shall be staying in Europe till the end of 1953 ...

During my absence Hertha will have to manage on her own, but this should be possible by partly letting our house or by some other means. Right now, the situation looks bleak, naturally, but once we see things developing, one way or another, we shall feel better ...

Right now, we have only a little money in Austria, but some is still to be expected [through war restitution]. May I assume that if necessary, you would put at my disposal in Vienna a few thousand Austrian Schillings, which I could either pay back in Vienna, (perhaps after one year), or in £'s, somewhere ...

It would of course, interest me to hear what you think of all these plans and whether you might make a different suggestion for our future ...

Perhaps you can write soon.

The heartiest greetings to you all from Hertha and myself.

The next question was how to raise the capital to travel and live in Europe for at least nine months. Much to my mother's chagrin, it seemed that the only way was to sell the house and buy a cheaper one. Given that my father was keen to begin this new adventure, and selling the house would take time, he hoped that Stefan would make an immediate offer of money.

8th March 1953

Dear Peter,

As I am in somewhat of a hurry, I'll limit myself to the immediate necessaries. Enclosed is a letter for my man/deputy in Vienna whom I have already informed. I have on purpose not mentioned an amount, but I imagine you will need S4–5,000 [Austrian Schillings] per month for three to four months. That is, between 15,000 to 20,000 over a particular time. According to my information he should be able to supply you with this without major difficulties. Don't worry about the return of this money: you will do it how and when you can, so don't, please, limit yourself unnecessarily …

My father sailed off to Europe leaving my mother to manage the financial mess. Listen to the melancholy of the first movement of Beethoven's String Quartet No. 14—that will express how she felt. She sold our brick house and bought a cheaper, weatherboard one in a cheaper neighbourhood—Surrey Hills. It was not such a nice place, but it had a large living room to accommodate the grand piano, the upright piano, reams of musical scores, a couple of cellos, my brother's violin and viola and the richly woven Arabian rug covering the whole floor. She then took in boarders to help with expenses.

But relinquishing our Balwyn home was very emotional for my mother. On the 29th June 1953, she wrote in her diary:

Tonight is the last night and I am saying goodbye to this house that has known us for 14 years. The house that saw our first years in Australia … It has seen sadness and heard quarrels and many thousands of times have I done all the housework … I will find it hardest to forget the view from the kitchen window, the wide outlook onto the magnificent evening sky, and the sunrise. The street was wide and beautiful and gave me such pride and calmed the spirit. Goodbye dear house, and don't forget us.

My father landed in Marseille then travelled by train to Casals' hometown, Prades, in the French Pyrénées where he had lived since leaving Spain after the outbreak of the Spanish Civil War in 1936. Casals was born in 1876 in the Catalan region and demonstrated prodigious musical talent early: by the age of four he could play flute, piano and violin. He started the cello relatively late—when he was 12—and enjoyed a brilliant career until his death in 1973 at the age of 96. When my father encountered him, he was 76 years old, with a career still in full flight.

Pablo Casals, of course, had no prior knowledge of my father because, for whatever reason, he had not written to the maestro to request that he be taken on as a pupil. Instead, my father simply arrived at the Grand Hotel in Prades and expected to be received.

'Can you please give me the address of Pablo Casals?' he asked the proprietor.

'Do you have a recommendation?'

'No,' my father replied.

'You cannot go to Casals without a recommendation,' said the incredulous proprietor.

I know my father would have regaled him with a long story about how he had travelled all the way from Australia to be taught by the maestro, and taken him through the history of his own musical career until he got a result, which he did: an introduction to Casals' pianist, Eugene Istomin. Istomin, too, was somewhat dubious about my father's chances of getting a meeting. Casals was unwell at the time and rehearsing for an upcoming festival.

On the 28th March, my father wrote:

In any case the Maestro will see me on Monday and then I will know more. I will practise in between. The cello and I are in bad form.

Between practising, he explored the beauty of Prades. His appointment with Casals was constantly postponed due to the maestro's health issues. Regular letters to my mother told of his delightful day-to-day experiences:

The village has about 8,000 inhabitants. The people live exclusively from the fruit and grape harvest and seem not to exert themselves, so general happiness rules … The temperature is warm between 10–4 pm, otherwise really cold … The fruit trees and chestnuts are in bloom and with the background of snow-covered mountains. It is a splendid picture …

Eventually, his lessons began. He wrote:

On Saturday I was finally received by Casals. He was not in good health but particularly nice. He talked perfect English. He immediately declared himself ready to teach me without hearing me play … He gives the impression of an outstanding and gracious person who wants to help where he can …

It [the second lesson] was completely devoted to technical matters … I cannot tell you how happy I am that Casals is answering a lot of my questions which occupy me again and again and that he takes so much trouble with me. He also found the way I use the bow incorrect, but was very happy with the corrections I made which he instigated. I am not supposed to do more than two and a half hours a day, which is exhausting enough. Luckily my fingers are just as agile as 37 years ago when I began to play the cello …

I had my third lesson the day before yesterday. As always, I was in a good mood afterwards. This time especially as Casals was more satisfied. I see enormous improvement in this short time and have more confidence … I am practising 3–4 hours a day. The rest of the time I read a lot, and have finished a novel of Balzac …

Casals is trying to get through the whole area of cello technique. Although he looks old, Casals is 100 percent at his peak mentally, his playing is colossal, his ear unbelievable. The brilliant fluency which he has is astonishing, as is the way his fingers obey the most difficult acrobatics. As a teacher he is very strict …

Otherwise, my life is not very interesting ... I have a lot of correspondence to do and also some copying of fingerings and bowings from Casals's music into my own. I read quite a lot of French books and go for long walks, mostly by myself ... At present we have the cherry season and you can eat big quantities for little money. There are also lovely strawberries, even wild ones in the fields and forests and the apricots are just becoming eatable.

It was an exhilarating time learning from the maestro and being welcomed into Casals' inner sanctum. He was engaged in a social life with a line-up of outstanding musicians who regularly gathered at Casals's house to play and listen to music together. One evening the brilliant American pianist and recording artist William Kapell played the piano. Then Casals played Brahms and Mendelssohn sonatas with Eugene Istomin. My father wrote that at the end of the piece, Casals got so excited with the performances that he smothered the pianists with kisses. Interestingly, two years after Casals' death in 1973, Istomin married his widow, Marta Montañez Martinez. Marta was 25 when she married the 81-year-old Casals.

After his seventh and final lesson, Casals declared that my father had improved greatly and was playing a much purer sound, then he handed him the bill. The total was £98 sterling, a small fortune. He did not have the money so he asked William Kapell to pay the tuition fees for him. Kapell was about to tour Australia for three months and my father told him that my mother would reimburse him when he got to Australia. Then he wrote to ask my mother whether she might have that amount at her disposal by then.

My mother did manage to pay Kapell when he came to Melbourne, probably out of proceeds from the sale of the house. But there was a cruel twist to this story, however. The final leg of Kapell's Australian tour was a recital on the 22nd October 1953 in Geelong, outside Melbourne, where he played Chopin's Piano

Sonata No. 2, otherwise known as the 'Funeral March'. Just days later, he flew back to the United States. Tragically, however, when the plane attempted to land in a San Francisco morning fog, it hit trees and crashed south of the airport, killing everyone on board, including Kapell.

Back in Prades, my father lamented that he was unable to continue the lessons with Casals because he felt there was so much more to learn. But the maestro had no more time due to his own busy performance schedule. Plus my father needed to return home. Soon after though, musicians began arriving in preparation for a music festival in the town, and Rudolf Serkin and Pablo Casals were about to make a recording of all of Beethoven's cello-piano sonatas. How could he miss this incredible opportunity? So he delayed some more and attended every rehearsal, writing to my mother:

There are quite a few musicians here now, one of them the pianist Rudolf Serkin, the brother of Will Serkin of Melbourne. He and Casals are at present recording all the Beethoven cello-piano Sonatas for Columbia and I am listening at every rehearsal. All the rehearsals and the actual recordings are taking place in an old abbey church, parts of which have been built in the 9th century under Charlemagne. This church is about two miles from here, in a lovely valley with high snow-covered mountains in the background. Round the building are meadows with high grass and a multitude of spring flowers as we knew them in Austria.

24

THE SINS OF THE FATHERS

It was with great sadness that I bade farewell to my Viennese-American family in July 1953. The relatives had hoped that I would decide to stay in Miami permanently, but my travels only made me realise how much I loved Melbourne. I sailed off to Europe to meet my father in Austria before returning home. We travelled by bus around the countryside that he loved so dearly. I especially loved the alpine village of Gargellen and its handful of houses serviced by not one, but two churches; the quaint 17th-century baroque Church of St Mary Magdalene and the tiny 19th-century Fidelis Chapel. Innsbruck was equally magnificent with its beefy, white-capped Alps appearing to encroach on the town's ancient buildings and streets. However, most special was the spa village Altaussee, where my family often holidayed before the great escape. Although I had few memories of the place from my childhood, something resonated deep in my heart.

We ascended the nearby Dachstein Mountain because my father always felt compelled to climb to the top of every hill or mountain. We stayed with a woman who let out rooms without bathroom facilities. Every morning she brought up a jug of hot water and a basin for us to wash in. We visited the public bath facilities for a bath. Seemingly, not much had changed since the early 20th century.

In August my father put me on a train to Naples from where I would board a ship to Australia. It was sweet the way he fussed over me at the train station, making sure I had enough food for the trip and telling me not to risk eating Italian food because it was largely unhygienic. He stayed on in Europe and I returned refreshed and ready to settle into nursing training, fully expecting to marry my Prince Charming, Milan Kantor whom I had such fond memories of from our times together. One special night in 1952, before I left for America, he had driven me home from a dinner date. As he walked me to my front door, we could hear my father playing Schumann's Lieder on the piano in preparation for an upcoming concert with Stefan Haag, who was a member of the Vienna Boys' Choir. It was so romantic as we both listened reverently outside the lounge window.

Interestingly, the choir had been stranded in Australia when it was on tour in 1939 and were 'adopted' by Archbishop Daniel Mannix, who employed them as the choir for St Patrick's Catholic Cathedral in Melbourne for the entirety of the war.

Milan was also a good pianist and had dreams of taking it up professionally. Like my father, he had been trained as a lawyer in Europe, although he repeated his qualifications after arriving in Australia. It seemed that my time away had not dampened our feelings for each other. Milan was tall, rakishly good-looking, and had a great sense of humour. When he laughed, his whole face got involved. Although he was more than ten years' my senior, I was besotted with him. My dream was that on my return from America he would see me as an adult, which he did, except it turned out that I was just one among an ever-increasing number of girlfriends. Stories of his exploits with women had become legendary. It broke my heart, but I was not prepared to be one of many. I had to tell Milan that I would not see him anymore, which bruised his ego and made him angry.

Our two families were close friends and I really cherished our relationship. It was terribly awkward though, because every time I saw his mother, she would tell me she wanted me as her daughter-in-law. Then just six years ago, I saw an article in the newspapers about him. One of his children had died. I called to offer my condolences. He told me that he often thought of me and I told him that I had often thought about him too.

My father never wanted me to marry as unsophisticated a creature as an Australian. A year after Milan and I broke up I met a young man freshly arrived from Austria. Alex was the son of Girt Hansa, a Norwegian friend of Aunt Liesl's since long before either of them were married. Girt had stayed in the Langer home while studying music and she and my aunt had become firm friends. Alex was tall and fair-haired with stunning blue eyes. After Liesl and Erich fled to Australia, she and Girt corresponded regularly. Liesl welcomed Alex with motherly gusto.

Our relationship was enjoyable for a time. We both enjoyed orchestral music and had a love of exploring the countryside. However Liesl told me that Erich had made it clear that he wanted nothing to do with Alex.

'His father was a Nazi!' said Erich.

'But he was only a child at the time.'

'Alex was probably in the Hitler Youth movement, too,' he said.

'It's all over now, many years have elapsed. It's ridiculous to treat Alex like this.'

Erich stormed out.

To Erich, Alex was an interloper of the most monstrous kind and he treated him with unbridled hostility. And yes, it was true, Alex's father had embraced Nazism. By the time Hitler had annexed Austria, Girt was married with several children and living in Vienna permanently. After the war she encouraged all her children to emigrate, probably because of her husband's difficulties after his wartime activities.

Alex boarded in the same street as my parents' house. No one was thrilled about our relationship, but for us youngsters the war was well over and we never discussed it. On my weekends free from nursing training we would take the train and go on outings in the country.

A surprising invitation came during my second year of nursing training. My cousins, Gretl and her sister Käthe Gallia, asked me to stay with them in Sydney during my holidays. Having never been to Sydney, I seized the opportunity. Gretl and Käthe were the daughters of Hermine and Moriz Gallia who were major players in the Vienna Secession movement.

The ferry dropped me just under their Mosman apartment and I clambered up steep steps to their building. Their lovely apartment, overlooking Sydney Harbour, contained the dark wooden furniture designed by renowned Viennese architect Josef Hoffmann. The rooms were overpowered by the heavy cabinetry, which was not at all suited to such a small place or the Antipodean light and lifestyle.

I soon discovered that Alex had followed me to Sydney, so for a time we explored the city's iconic attractions together. The Gallia sisters somehow found out about his presence but did not invite him to their home. Soon after, an angry letter arrived from my mother telling me in no uncertain terms that I needed time to myself without him. It was the first time she had ever shown open displeasure. At the time I did not understand what all the fuss was about but in hindsight I realise that my parents were worried that it would develop into a permanent relationship.

Was it the Nazi element or a combination of that and Alex's occupation as a carpenter? I will never know but they need not have worried because I worked out all by myself that he was not the man for me. He was not all that interesting or stimulating so that discord soon developed between us. He got a job at the Mount Buller ski resort and appeared at my door sporadically in the hope that we could resolve the breach, but I had moved on and had no wish to reignite the relationship. By then I was well focused on my nursing routines.

25

AROUND EVERY HOSPITAL CORNER

The remuneration for a trainee nurse was shocking—just £ 8 a month. Out of that, £ 4 each month was taken to repay the bursary we were given to undertake the training. Thankfully, board was free in the nurses' lodgings at Heidelberg Repatriation Hospital, where we were required to live throughout the training. Qualifying for the nursing certificate and graduating to the rank of nursing sister involved a gruelling regimen, and we were required to work five days a week for three years on top of the study.

Nursing at Heidelberg Repatriation Hospital was indeed a well-regimented life—it would be because it was originally run by the army. The hospital had opened in 1941 as the 115th Heidelberg Military Hospital, caring for war veterans and widows. Under the strict control of the home supervisory nurse, everyone was bedded in their own rooms by midnight, and the rooms were tidied with beds made up, with hospital corners, for the morning inspection.

It was Florence Nightingale who, from the mid 1800s, transformed nursing into a profession that was strictly supervised 24/7. She advocated that nurses be punctual, trustworthy, meticulously hygienic and neat, as well as having their sexuality under control at all times. As a result we trainees were well-schooled in etiquette or, as I would put it, subservience. The rules were as follows: always allow a nursing sister to go through a door ahead of you, keep your hands behind your back when questioning or talking to a sister, do what the sister asks without question, only learn a new procedure or go to a lecture if you had completed your work, talking to a doctor was strictly forbidden except to answer a question about a patient, and finally, the doctors' residence was strictly out of bounds. Ignoring the last direction resulted in instant dismissal.

At the Royal Women's Hospital, where I did a three-month placement, chatting with male medical students was considered to be an even worse infraction, except in circumstances where there was a specific question about a patient, and only if the charge nurse was unavailable to answer it. However, the trainee doctors found cunning ways to ask us for dates. One morning a medical student called me over. He was carrying a patient's history. He said, 'Nurse, I can't read this word'. I peered over his shoulder and he was pointing to a scrawled handwritten note:

Could you meet me outside the hospital gate at 8pm this evening?

All I had to do was reply yes or no.

The eight-week preliminary training focused on Anatomy and Physiology and the basics of patient care. One of our first lessons was the practice of bed-making and how to finish sheets and blankets with hospital corners. It took me a while to pass this test because I thought that it was ridiculous to have to concentrate on such a trivial pursuit. As far as I was concerned, if there was a choice between comfort and neatness, the former won.

Neatness would be executed with military precision or the consequences were dire and the Sister-in-Charge had no compunction about reporting minor deviations to the Matron. Being called into matron's office was generally not a picnic. Any infractions would be reflected on your report card which was seen in every ward and department you worked in; for me that included, surgical, TB, chest, psychiatric, gynaecological, paediatric and X-ray. Poor reports would affect your chances of achieving a certificate of qualification.

Major lesson two was how to make a patient comfortable in bed. Our nursing guidelines included how to settle patients for the night by checking that their bottom sheet remained uncrumpled, not only for the sake of comfort but to help prevent bedsores. Unlike today where patients are up and out of bed soon after an operation, patients of that era routinely spent many days, and sometimes weeks, in bed. They were not even allowed to get up and shower or sit in a chair.

The evening ward routine before 'lights out' included the last of the four-hourly back care procedures, which involved washing the patients' back with soap and water before rubbing them with methylated spirits—more bedsore prevention. Hands and faces were washed and tooth bowls placed on the nightstand for false teeth. In those days 80 per cent of patients had false teeth. By the end of our evening round the patients were so tidy in their beds they were like swaddled babies who could not move.

As mealtime approached, we would make sure that each patient was in a comfortable eating position and that their bedside tables were placed appropriately. Food was delivered to the ward in large stainless-steel containers. The senior nurse's role was to dish it out onto the plates because she actually knew how much each patient was capable of eating. The rest of us circulated to help cut up food or feed those who were more incapacitated. Today's nurses have nothing to do with the meals and I have found that it is not unusual for food trays to remain untouched because they are not within a patient's reach.

My toughest placement was at the Royal Women's Hospital, which was at that time situated opposite Melbourne University in Swanston Street, Carlton. I worked in the gynaecological wing, which was an open ward with 20 beds—10 on either side with the nurses' station in the middle. Operations were scheduled one day a week and we had to take the patients to theatre and then return them straight to the wards afterwards because there were no recovery rooms. It was all very challenging, especially when patients had huge operations for conditions such as cancer.

We student nurses had a punishing time there, working long shifts, some that began at 6 a.m. And there was no time allowance for breakfast. Our metal trolleys, laden with kidney dishes, blood pressure cuffs and other instruments of care, clanged day and night with just a couple of hours' break between shifts. Handover to night staff happened at around 8.30 p.m.

Not only were the work conditions poor but the place itself could be quite depressing. For instance, abortions were illegal at that time and unmarried pregnant women had two choices: 'disappear' for a few months to give birth and then have the baby adopted, or have an illegal abortion. These abortionists usually charged exorbitant fees and we heard many stories of infection and resultant permanent physical damage or worse, death. We often encountered young men waiting outside the hospital to ask us nurses if we knew of anywhere their girlfriend could get a termination. I could never help because I had no contact with any such practitioners. Sometimes we would see the devastating results of these backyarders, and some of the gruesome results of self-abortion attempts.

I remember when I was a teenager that people would occasionally come to the door to ask for money to help these women. My mother always gave as much as she could. She described to me how secretive you had to be in such circumstances, and how once it was done, you had to leave the place furtively so that no one detected you. I believe she told me these stories as a salutary lesson. On one such occasion, my mother and I were having a cup of tea and she mentioned again how awful it was to have a backyard abortion.

'Did you have one, Mummy?' I asked.

'No, of course not,' she replied.

For some reason I did not believe her but it was not a comfortable topic, so I left it alone. After my mother died I questioned Aunt Liesl about it. She told me that after my brother was born, my mother became pregnant again, but she already had more than enough of a drain on her emotional resources. The thought of what she had to go through made me even more sympathetic to the plight of women in this circumstance.

For student nurses at the Royal Women's Hospital, the excitement began after work. Whenever possible I would refresh my lipstick, comb my hair, replace my sensible black lace-up leather shoes with high heels and make a beeline for the Melbourne University cafeteria to socialise with schoolfriends who were studying there. That of course was not my only reason for these visits. I hoped to meet a handsome doctor.

My friends were always introducing me to young men, but one fate-filled day I was introduced to a student who was not a doctor— Laurence Course. Laurence was on the short side, but slim and fit. In his tweed jacket, brogues and cap, he looked the proper Englishman, which he was, having only been in Australia for a few years. He intrigued me and sparked my interest as he launched into a discourse about his academic endeavours. A distinguishing feature of Mr Course, even at this first meeting, was his inability to stop talking.

He spouted forth on Rupert Bunny, the subject of his thesis for his Master's, the free lectures he had been asked to give at the National Gallery, and how he dealt with disruptive students at Fitzroy Primary School where he was teaching. I barely got a word in.

It was certainly a strange first encounter. The art world, especially the topic of painting, was of no interest to me. I had never had any aptitude for art—in fact, the paintings I was obliged to do in secondary school were always displayed by the teacher as an example of what not to do. Laurie was interesting and smart but, I thought, he is not really for me. Nevertheless, he continued to pursue me and I guess I was somewhat flattered.

We kept on dating although we had regular disagreements. Our backgrounds were so dissimilar. He was born in London and his family dynamic was very different from mine. Laurie came to Australia in 1949 on a three-year teaching scheme. He completed a year-long teaching course at Geelong Teacher's College, southwest of Melbourne, and was then sent to a single-teacher country school in Nhill, a small town in the Wimmera in western Victoria, halfway between Adelaide and Melbourne. There were many stories to tell about his victories with these children and their sporting prowess under his tutorage. Nhill was sheep-grazing country and he loved to joke that all he ate that year was sheep, lamb or mutton.

I told my mother that I liked Laurie but I did not particularly care if we did not marry. Truthfully, my feelings for him were not that strong. I was not in love with him, nor was he in love with me. Given that neither of us felt deeply or desperately in love, he eventually proclaimed that we were not really suited to one another and suggested I should decide at the next date when we should separate.

The next date came. (We often went for a drive on our dates and I especially enjoyed our jaunts to the country. And sometimes we saw a movie.) On this occasion we were driving around the Botanic Gardens in Birdwood Avenue, South Yarra. When we arrived at the Nurses' Home Laurie asked me if I had considered the separation. Being one not to prolong an outcome, I said, 'Yes, tonight is the end'.

Laurie was stunned, which surprised me, given that it was his suggestion. Was he looking for signs of adoration and devotion, or was he hoping that I would fall into his arms and declare that I could not live without him?

In response, he stuttered, 'What about the book you lent me?'

'Post it or leave it with my aunt,' I responded and, because there was nothing else to say, I got out of the car and left.

Several days later, just as I was getting myself ready for work, the loudspeaker announced a call for me. Somehow, I knew it was Laurie. Should I take the call, I wondered, because there was nothing I wanted to talk to him about. For me the relationship was over—we had both decided.

But curiosity won and sure enough, it was Laurie. He asked if I could meet him to work towards a permanent relationship. It turns out that he was unable to let me go, and to this day I have no idea why I said yes. But there was a connection and there was a lot I liked about him, and I had always wanted to be with someone who was stimulating.

Were there declarations of love? Not that I remember although we probably said it. Till death us do part was not something one thought about too much, the interminable march through life with someone at your side. Being that young, we were not aware that life is a long time. We thought everything would all be all right.

Once the Royal Women's Hospital placement was over, it was time to return to Heidelberg Repatriation Hospital. I was completely 'over' the Women's treatment of us trainees. Matrons were powerful figures in the hospital setting and, thinking back to my behaviour on my last day, I cannot believe my boldness. I told the matron that the trained nurse could jolly-well give the handover that evening because my official time at the hospital finished at 8 p.m. This resulted in them sending a poor report about me to the Repat Hospital, but that did not worry me one bit. Otherwise, nursing was a good profession for me, especially because the diversity of the work made it so interesting and, when I had children, the flexible hours were fantastic.

For the next three months our dating continued and we got on fairly well, although we still argued regularly. His obstinacy should have thrown up warning signs—still, in January 1956, Laurie bought me a little ring and we became engaged. As a formality he asked my father for my hand as my mother and I eavesdropped and giggled behind the closed door. The few months leading up to our September wedding was a happy time—making plans, having a dress made, deciding where to honeymoon. It was also just a few months prior to me finishing my nurse training. And at milestone times such as these, where a nurse was to marry, it was customary to arrange an interview with the matron to seek her sanction. I stood before tall, imposing Matron Hanrahan in the customary manner—hands behind my back.

'Yes, my very best wishes to you, Nurse Langer. I have just been looking up your roster and it seems to me that you haven't done any night duty. From the next roster, you will spend the six weeks before your wedding on night duty,' she told me firmly. There was no point in arguing.

At least in nursing I knew where I stood; rules were rules. Introducing a man like Laurie to the family was more challenging. I wondered if I should warn my parents that he was an unrelenting pontificator, or should I just free flow with this thing? I decided on the latter and allowed them to have their own experience.

My mother was a good listener and was polite in her reception of his long monologues on art—she was an art lover, after all. His cynicism, however, for which he was universally renowned, was not so easy to digest. Nonetheless, she found him to be intelligent and well-read, which were important criteria for a suitable husband. My father, on the other hand, accepted Laurie in a civil, albeit desultory way. They got on reasonably well but kept their distance. From my father's point of view, one thing in Laurie's favour was that he was British which was a step up from being an Australian.

But my father and Laurie were very different. Laurie was never really able to connect with people. He instructed, lectured and spoke his mind, but never his feelings; whereas my father's nature was warm and generous. Looking back, I can see how self-centred Laurie was. I remember one occasion when I was studying hard for my final exams and he called me on the phone. 'I want you to come out with me tonight because I want to discuss something with you.'

I resisted, not wanting to go out at all, but Laurie insisted. He picked me up from my quarters at Heidelberg Repat, and took me to his house in Prahran, which was about 18 kilometres away, to discuss whether he should get life insurance! I was flabbergasted.

But there was no use fighting it. Laurie refused to take no for an answer. Things always had to be his way, otherwise there would be hell to pay, and somehow, I found it impossible to stand my ground in the face of his haranguing.

It was difficult to know whether Laurie was a tad on the autism spectrum or whether his modus operandi was purely due to his life experience. In 1940 he endured the terrifying London Blitz. During those frequent bombings, his parents' house had its roof blown off four times. Many of the houses around them were totally destroyed, many people were rendered homeless and 32,000 died. In 1940, when he was 13, his whole school was evacuated to Redruth, a remote Cornish mining town where he was billeted with two spinsters. They put him to work around their property, including their vegetable garden, to the detriment of his schooling. Later in life, I found research showing that the long-term effects on child evacuees were similar to those experienced by children on the *Kindertransport*, being life-long mental and emotional health issues.

When Laurie was able to return home and to school, he concurrently began training to be a pilot and navigator in the RAF Air Cadet Unit. He then managed to get himself into the glider infantry, an assignment that was none too glamorous but highly prestigious. These gliders were affectionately known as flying coffins. They were constructed with the bare minimum of fittings, which meant there was no insulation from the noise of the towing plane's engines or enemy anti-aircraft fire. Few men were chosen for this incredibly daring job. The glider was attached to a plane and then released to deliver troops or heavy equipment into enemy territory. Air pockets and strong winds created violent turbulence and there was not even a parachute. You had to be physically fit to cope with it and Laurie was a very fit man all his life. On leaving Britain for Australia in 1949, much of London was still in ruins and Laurie felt depressed about the fact that not enough was being done to restore normal life.

Couple all of these experiences with a somewhat dysfunctional family, and you have a formula for a challenging life. But at the time I was not aware of this and floundered in the difficult dynamic that had settled between us.

Laurie did rise in my parents' estimation when some years after we were married, he was appointed to a lectureship at Melbourne University in the Fine Arts Department under Professor Joseph Burke. As previously mentioned, my Viennese antecedents were mostly high achievers, so my parents had high aspirations for their children, either for themselves or through marriage. My father's father, Jakob Langer, became a bank manager while his brother, Leopold became a lawyer and a very affluent one at that judging by the photographs of his house, which was designed by acclaimed Viennese architect Adolf Loos.

Uncle Ludwig Gallia was a lawyer, as was my father, who always came top in the class. It was not usual at that time for women to have degrees, but two of my aunts did. Käthe Gallia had a science degree, and Gertrude Böhm, who was married to Great-Uncle Victor, had a PhD in chemistry. Victor dearly wanted to go to university to study chemistry and engineering, but his father's business partner had died prematurely so his services were urgently required in the Brüder Böhm hat business instead.

I know my parents were disappointed that neither my brother nor I went to university after finishing school, but I was to continue my education throughout my life. Some years after the death of my parents I received a Diploma of Community Health and a Graduate Diploma in Rehabilitation, both of which expanded my credentials and gave me flexible work options while I brought up the children.

So when my new husband got a job in academia, my parents were very impressed, even though I doubt they particularly liked him. Nothing that direct was ever said to me, but I have read the letters now. Grandmother Sofie seemed to know that he was not very handsome, which was a mark against him, and there were a lot of innuendos about him being 'a bit difficult' and not helping me at home.

After I had the first two children, my mother once suggested to Laurie that he could help me a bit more. I really copped it for that. Laurie was outraged and became obsessed, reminding me of it over and over again. 'How dare she say that to me!' he would rage. I had to tell my mother never to say anything like that to him again. There was no point in arguing with Laurie because he vehemently believed in his own opinions and interpretations.

Our January engagement gave us plenty of time to prepare for the wedding, which was to take place on Saturday the 1st September 1956; the day of the football final. We had the choice of a church or registry office, but my preference was for the pomp and ceremony of a church service, not that I was religious. People get married in a church and never enter one again, which was how it was for us. There was no question of us getting married in a synagogue, in fact, the thought would never have entered my head. My parents never installed any Jewishness in my brother or me. My limited knowledge of the Jewish religion came only through reading about it when I grew up, and even today I have no interest in religious or spiritual matters whatsoever, other than in an historical sense.

To please his devout parents, Laurie insisted on us being married in the Church of England. It was a silent tribute that fell on deaf ears because to his great disappointment none of his family members could afford to attend—airfares were exorbitantly expensive in those days. They sent a wedding present though, a silver cutlery set in a beautiful wooden box which became Laurie's pride and joy. He would check after each time it was used to make sure nothing was missing.

As the wedding drew closer there was yet another big family upheaval. My father's scheme to study with Pablo Casals had come to nothing professionally and the financial struggles continued. When he was offered a position in the NZBC (New Zealand Broadcasting Corporation) Symphony Orchestra, it was an opportunity he had to take, so reluctantly my parents uprooted themselves from Melbourne and moved to New Zealand.

The idea of such a move, despite all of my father's previous rumblings about wanting to return to his beloved Vienna or relocate to Canada, was clearly distressing for him and indeed my mother and brother. They wanted me to come, but of course Laurie and I were just starting out together and we had no intention of leaving; I had my nursing job, and Laurie was teaching at Fitzroy Primary School at that stage. My mother was not keen on the idea of leaving me behind, but reconciled herself to the move, saying that my father needed her more than I did, which was quite true.

My father left first for Wellington to secure lodgings. We all farewelled him at the old Spencer Street Railway Station[4] as he boarded the Sydney-bound train to meet the Wellington flight. Once more my mother was left to pack up the house, rent out the family home and make all the other arrangements. Somehow, I managed to distance myself from their concerns for a change and dwell upon my positive plans for the future.

Our wedding and honeymoon were planned to fit in with Laurie's week-long school holiday break. It was a busy time for us because I was completing my nursing training while Laurie worked and studied part-time for the final year of his Bachelor of Arts. The wedding was to be a simple affair as neither of us were in a position to afford anything but the bare minimum. Certainly nothing like my parents' society wedding in 1932, a lavish event where hundreds of guests were entertained in the ballroom of their family home, enjoying food from gold-monogrammed plates. Aunt Liesl offered to host the reception in the small house they had moved to at 76 St Elmo Road, Ivanhoe, which was a great help.

---

4   Now moved to a new location nearby, still in Spencer Street, and renamed the Southern Cross Station. It is the terminus for country and interstate trains but is also a major interchange in the Melbourne Metro railway system.

Probably as a reaction to what I observed growing up in straitened circumstances where my father's profligacy and my mother's thrift and struggle competed for a middle way, I have never believed in buying anything I could not afford. So everything was done on a shoestring; I bought the material for my wedding dress, a pretty cream French brocade patterned with gold coloured thread, and had it made up cheaply by a dressmaker in a simple A-line style with a pretty bow on the 'V' neckline. The veil was borrowed from a friend.

When the wedding day finally arrived, my mother and Lyn Snowden, my matron of honour and my close friend since kindergarten, helped me dress. The photographer came to the house beforehand to capture the pre-wedding highlights and, I must say, I felt happy and in love, optimistic and pretty. As I brought the tulle veil over my face, my mother and I shared an unspoken twinge of sadness that my father and Martin could not be there to see me on this special day. Because my father's orchestra salary was meagre, they could only afford one airfare. Lyn, in her sweet blue nylon dress and pink hat garnished with pink flowers, handed me my bouquet of roses, gave me a kiss, and we all hopped into the car and drove to St James Church in Ivanhoe, where Laurie and his best man, fellow Englishman Jack McCall, were waiting.

The ceremony is no longer clear in my mind—after all, it was 63 years ago—but I well remember the musical program of Bach and Handel that was performed by my father's chamber music quartet and the beautiful voice of my schoolfriend Barbara singing solo. The official photos were taken—I made Laurie stand on a stool because he was a couple of inches shorter than me—then it was off to Bright for our honeymoon. Bright is a pretty little town in northeastern Victoria, situated on the Snowy River and at the base of Mount Buffalo, a mountain my father approved of. The town has always had a 'European' feel and was a popular holiday destination for European migrants in those days and for honeymooning couples.

26

BRIGHT

When Martin and I were children, our parents took us to Bright for a holiday. It became one of my favourite places. As a teenager, I had an experience nearby that bordered on the mystical. My mother had taken Martin and my friend Lyn and me on a holiday to Mount Buffalo. My father was working so he stayed home. We travelled by train to Bright and then took a bus the last lap up the winding road to the Mount Buffalo Chalet. Our family holidays were always walking holidays so the next day, immediately after breakfast, the four of us set off on one of the shorter walks so that we would arrive back in plenty of time for Sunday's midday roast dinner.

The track was not signposted, so when we started back we could not tell if we were retracing our steps. Lunchtime came and went. We were lost. Below us far down in the valley we glimpsed a farmhouse surrounded by acres of green paddocks. It seemed that our best chance was to aim for the house. We followed the path of a nearby water course that made its way down the mountain in a series of cascades.

The afternoon passed all too quickly as we picked our way down the steep descent, scrambling over rocks and holding onto branches so as not to lose our footing. Eventually, as the light began to fade, it became obvious that we would not make it before nightfall. My mother was worried but we three children were having an adventure.

We found a reasonably flat area to sleep for the night and made our beds from bracken. We had no food or drink with us, just two lollies which my mother gave to Lyn and my brother. I have no recollection of being hungry, but I do recall the cold autumn temperatures seeping through my open-weave woollen jumper as we lay close together to keep warm.

At first light we continued our descent, avoiding the steeper sides of the gorge. Later we learnt that there had been a number of accidents on this route. When we finally reached the last hurdle separating us from the farmhouse, the Buckland River, we waded across. Someone on the farm had spotted us several hours before so when four tired, wet, hungry people landed on their doorstep, it was no surprise. They welcomed us warmly, dried our clothes and gave us a delicious hot meal.

The conversation was lively. The owner, Mr Lumsden, had been a journalist in Scotland, but on coming to Australia, he had taken up dairy farming. He drove us back to the bus depot and we returned to the chalet—although we had been absent for more than 24 hours no one had even attempted to look for us. When we returned to Melbourne, my mother sent the Lumsdens a thank-you present, a large history book that we all signed. I often recalled being lost in the bush, but I could not for the life of me remember the exact location of the farm.

Twenty years later, as a married woman with three children in tow and once more on holiday in Bright, I decided to teach the two older kids—Tony, who was 13 and Diana, 11—to ski. Laurie looked after Phil who was nine months old while we headed off in the car to the Mount Buffalo ski slopes. I missed the sign and ended up on the Buckland Valley Road. The bitumen turned into a slippery dirt road. The car skidded and we ended up bogged in the mud against a barbed-wire fence. The farmer, whose name was Rory, was driving a tractor close by. He kindly offered to pull my car out of the mud and suggested we go up to the farmhouse to have a cup of tea with his wife, Gay, while we waited. I mentioned to Gay that I had been lost around these parts long ago. Her eyes opened wider.

'My husband has often talked about that,' she said.

Rory was one of the Lumsden sons who had been there when we emerged from the bush 20 years earlier. The history book that my mother sent was on their bookshelf. From then on, we became good friends: our regular holidays in Bright included a visit to their farm and they also visited us in Melbourne.

It was unsurprising that I loved Bright so much. Apart from the magnificence of the surroundings, my connection to nature was ingrained during my earliest days in Vienna. I know this because my parents would often crank up the old movie projector, oil it in 12 different holes, then connect the reels. A flick of the toggle switch opened a portal into the vanished world of that city and the places of our childhood. My brother and I always enjoyed those virtual trips back in time when we and learnt about the mountains and the Viennese street names. I especially loved seeing our holiday houses—the footage generated such feelings of pleasure, and at a very deep level.

Springtime in pre-1938 in Vienna traditionally heralded the move for our family to the country house for the whole summer. Arranging the sojourn required great efforts. It was not simply a matter of packing a suitcase with swimming costumes, cotton shirts and summer dirndls; the family took all their household goods including linen, tablecloths and even cushions. Mostly, we travelled by train to the summer retreat, and Great-Aunt Friedl would brazenly display her cushions to anyone anywhere because they were embroidered with her deceased husband's prestigious name, 'von Hofmannsthal', and the family's seal of nobility.

My family was certainly spoilt for choice when it came to country holiday destinations, but every year we holidayed at Neuwaldegg, a beautiful town in the Vienna Woods where my grandparents, Sofie and Arthur, owned a substantial two-storey villa with a music room, maids' and visitors' quarters, and a cottage on the grounds where the permanent caretakers lived. It was a glorious time there, swimming in the nearby public pools, picking berries in the surrounding hills and touring through the forests and fields on bicycles. Villa Kary was only half an hour drive from Vienna by car so Arthur and my father could still come after work.

Other times we rented a villa in the spa town of Altaussee, nestled on the shores of Lake Altaussee, literally at the end of the road, and the favoured destination for the Langer family. Beyond it is a walking trail up the Loser Mountain. Beneath the Loser Plateau is a complex of salt mines that weave throughout the region. These became Aladdin's caves for thousands of valuable artworks and artefacts stolen from Jewish people by the Nazis. My great-uncle and aunt Moriz and Hermine Gallia, the grandparents of my cousins Käthe and Gretl Gallia, owned a stunning three-storey, 14-room villa in the town, purchased in 1909, but we never stayed there. Their place was subsequently taken by the Nazis and sold.

Finally, my great-grandparents, Clara and Heinrich Böhm also had a palatial holiday villa in Baden, a spa town just 26 kilometres from Vienna. This was Great-Grandmother Clara's preferred summer retreat and the rest of the family were expected to spend time there too. People came from all over Europe to partake in Baden's sulphuric healing waters. But Clara and Heinrich's villa was on a quiet, grand boulevard, Marchetstrasse 50, away from the bustling town centre. It sat at the end of a long driveway, surrounded by majestic trees and protected by grand wrought-iron gates. The house was eventually trashed by the Russians who took their horses and various farm animals inside. Later it was demolished and now a very stark apartment building stands in its place.

On their return from these delightful three-month retreats, a reception line of servants would be waiting for my family at Stubenring 14 and they would curtsy, kiss the hands of my grandparents, and provide refreshments. The spring of 1938 was the first time in 20 years that we did not pack up and move to one of those destinations.

When Aunt Pauline visited the Neuwaldegg villa before she escaped to France, it had already been requisitioned by the German army and stripped of everything: the rugs, dishes, furniture, piano, and even the inbuilt mahogany dining-room fittings. She wrote:

Horses and soldiers' boots had obliterated the lawns and flowers, and the trees had been cut into firewood. I left without looking back. This was no time for nostalgia.

My special memories were of us sitting in the living room in 1940s Melbourne, often joined by Aunt Liesl and Uncle Erich, where we would watch the Viennese family movies. There would be lively discussion, laughter and lots of 'remember whens', all tinged with nostalgia and sadness about happy times before the escape.

Years later, in 1970, Pauline again returned to the property. The small village street still nestled sweet cottages in its yards, but their old home was a crumbling Cinderella castle, overgrown with wild thorns and vines.

I climbed over the rubble to the entrance and peered into the interior of the house through broken windows whose frames were torn out ... the empty rooms looked deserted, unrecognisable.

As progress would have it, the following day the bulldozers came and now an apartment block has formed a new history.

Married life in 1950s postwar Australia was modest; we had no such luxury holiday homes to visit but our honeymoon in Bright was sweet, and there was plenty of snow on Mount Buffalo. We rented skis and found a gentle slope for Laurie's first skiing attempt. He bet me that I would fall over more than him and he was right. It seemed to be a good start to married life.

27

A PLACE TO CALL HOME

Returning from my honeymoon, Matron Hanrahan was determined that I should experience the full gamut of nursing life before I qualified as a sister. Getting married was often frowned upon by the senior, usually confirmed 'old-maid' nurses in those days. So whatever her motivation, Matron rostered me onto a return to six weeks of night duty until I retired my mauve uniform and white cap and donned the white uniform and torturously stiff white veil of the newly qualified Sister Course.

I was delighted to be finished with my training but now the time I had previously devoted to studying was replaced by the frustrating job of veil care. The laundering and heavy starching of the veil was a painstaking procedure as well as somewhat challenging space-wise when Laurie and I began married life in two rooms we rented from a spinster, in a lovely old Federation-style home in Hawdon Street, Heidelberg. Our living area was her drawing room, elegantly furnished with a beautiful piano, which I played often. There had been some wealth in the past as evidenced by the faded grandeur and the now-defunct switchboards in every room to call the servants. The landlady's father had been a member of parliament, but the money lingered no longer.

When my parents' house in Surrey Hills became vacant, we rented it from them, but only briefly as it turned out. They wanted to buy a house in New Zealand and could not afford to own two places, so Laurie and I organised some renovations to spruce it up for the sale. Unfortunately it was sold for the same price they had bought it for. Sometimes, it seemed that nothing went right for my parents. However, they had settled well in New Zealand and were extremely happy there. The Wellington community was small and friendly and as a couple, they made many friends.

In 1958 we managed to buy our own house at 24 Waverley Avenue in Ivanhoe. The advertisement in *The Age* newspaper read something like, 'South-facing, solid clinker-brick house, three bedrooms and verandah, £4000'.

The purchase took Laurie way out of his comfort zone and for a while his face was set with worry. It was the first time he had ever been in debt. As with many from that era, he did not believe in buying anything unless you had the cash up front. Now he had two mortgages—one from the bank and one from Melbourne Grammar where he was teaching. I had done as much as possible to achieve this commitment and it was the one time I was not prepared to give in to Laurie's wishes. Having a secure home was very important to me. Again, this was definitely a consequence of my years of childhood insecurities around money and having a roof over our heads.

The house was not my ideal but it was a bargain price for a solid brick house and in a marvellous position, close to shops and parklands. On seeing it for the first time, I said to Laurie, 'It's too dark'. Laurie response was, 'We don't have to stay here forever'. Only the laundry was north-facing and flooded with sunlight, otherwise it was gloomy—Australians still seem to struggle with designing for the climate—and 55 years later I was still there.

We took possession with just a few belongings—a bed, a chair, a pot, a pan, a few plates and some cutlery—and we took in boarders to help with the mortgage. My dear Grandmother Sofie sent us a cheque to help us buy furniture, so I bought new bedroom and kitchen settings then hit the opportunity shops. If we had been married in Vienna and the Nazi invasion had never happened, our housing scenario would have been very different indeed! Pre-war, newlyweds in my family had a whole different start in life.

Take my father's parents. In 1902 Melanie Gallia, aged 20, married Jakob Langer, who was aged 36. Melanie was an excellent marriage candidate because she was an exceptionally accomplished musician, spoke six languages, and was the daughter of successful businessman, Wilhelm Gallia. Her intended was born in Prerau, Moravia, now Prerov in the Czech Republic. He studied law and eventually became the director of Allgemeine Verkehrsbank, one of Vienna's major banks, located opposite the Opera House on the Ringstrasse. Aside from being a love match, it was also a suitable match.

The newly married couple moved into the apartment that occupied the entire top floor of Lobkowitzplatz 1 in a building designed by renowned architect Otto Wagner in 1884 and located about 150 metres from the rear of the famous Vienna Opera House. It was fashionable to begin married life among new décor and furnishings. The leading bourgeois families generally commissioned the most famous Viennese architects such as Adolf Loos or Josef Hoffmann, both of whom my family favoured with their patronage. Choosing the right architect was a matter of prestige as well as style. Although they were diametrically opposed in their approach to architecture and lifestyle, both Loos and Hoffmann designed furniture specifically tailored to each residence and its occupants. In fact, Josef Hoffmann designed everything for the Gallias, from the chairs to the slippers his patrons wore.

Prior to his marriage, Jakob Langer had already established a relationship with Adolf Loos. In 1901, he and his brother Leopold operated a chain of currency exchanges in Vienna. They both commissioned Loos to design the rooms in their individual apartments and although each was very similar in style, Leopold's apartment became the showpiece in several books on Loos interiors.

Aunt Liesl always spoke of the home she and my father grew up in with enormous fondness—the grand rooms, the marble staircase and panoramic views of the Vienna Woods, a place so special that Adolf Loos would use it as a showpiece for prospective clients.

When Melanie died, Aunt Liesl inherited all her parents' furniture. She shipped it to Australia with all her other belongings in 1939, installing these sophisticated Viennese furnishings, designed for colossal spaces, into their average, brick suburban dwelling with two small bedrooms attached to the rear of their milk bar. One of the pieces was a built-in 2-metre-high mahogany wall panelling structure consisting of a room divider, long case clock and sideboard. All the elements were sculpted with a grid design, and was a magnificent example of modernist design and craftsmanship. When it arrived at Erich and Liesl's house they needed to remove some of the wall panelling to make it fit into their small kitchen-dining area. They engaged a handyman who redeployed that mahogany panelling as ill-fitting door fronts for storage cupboards. The leftovers were stored in a bungalow behind the house. (It gets worse, but do not fear, there is a happy ending.)

The Loos desk resided in Erich's study where he used it as a bench to create his homemade chocolates. He would heat huge blocks of raw chocolate on the stove, then take the pot of melted chocolate and place it on a pile of newspapers on top of the desk to make his delicious peppermint cremes and ginger truffles. Would Adolf Loos be turning in his modernist grave? I think so. Eventually their son Alf rescued it and used it in his law offices for 25 years. The huge sideboard was used to house their silverware and everyday crockery and cutlery. As for the grandfather clock, it was a poor timekeeper and spent much of its time at the Ivanhoe clock repairers.

One of my dear friends is Terence Lane, an art historian, writer, and former Senior Curator of Australian Art at the National Gallery of Victoria (NGV). He lived about 200 metres from my house in Ivanhoe. Laurie and Terence knew each other well from when Laurie was teaching in the Department of Fine Arts at Melbourne University. In 1989 Terence learned of my family's furniture collection and visited Liesl's home several times to view the pieces. He was very excited to come upon such a rare find in a Melbourne suburban home and requested that she lend her furniture to the NGV for a two-week exhibition of Austrian art and design. Liesl could not understand why anyone would want to take her furniture and put it in a museum. Never for a moment did she suspect that incredible value would be placed upon these modernist masterpieces, which were her 'everyday' furniture. My cousin, Alf, wrote:

My mother rang me very excited and in a panic. She was 85 and living alone. She said she couldn't possibly lend the furniture because she used it every day. Of course, I was intrigued as to why Mr Lane wanted our old furniture at the gallery. I rang and had a very pleasant discussion and after a while I began to get the idea that this furniture might be of some value.

Terence painstakingly figured out how to put the mahogany squares back together again and had them restored to their rightful place between the buffet and the grandfather clock.

Just like Hoffmann, Loos's popularity had waxed and waned during the 20th century, but gradually during the 1970s and 80s, Loos furniture and buildings became more and more popular, as architects and designers throughout the world recognised the importance of Austrian architects.

Then, out of the blue at Christmas time in 1990, we received a letter from Liesl's best friend in Vienna who told us that the Loos furniture was now unbelievably popular and had fetched fantastic prices at a recent auction.

When my mother went into a nursing home in 1993 ... my wife Alva and I placed it in our Caloundra home in Queensland. I soon realised that the heat and humidity of the sub-tropics was no place for 90-year-old Austrian furniture. I called Terence and asked him if the NGV was still interested in it. He replied immediately, 'I'll send up a furniture truck'.

Alva and I were going on a five-week trip to Europe. I asked Terence to arrange an appointment for us in Vienna with an expert on Secession design. We saw Paul Asenbaum who was considered the world's leading Secession expert … He surprised us by saying that we possessed the largest private collection of Loos furniture in the world, as far as he was aware.

During the war and with Nazi looting, many Loos-designed apartments were destroyed and later, often subdivided, with the furniture being destroyed or dispersed across the world. It turned out that the desk that Erich made chocolate on was very valuable indeed.

I was fortunate to inherit the room divider from Aunt Liesl after she died in 2000, plus an Egyptian stool, sometimes known as a Thebes Stool, which is a famous design based on an ancient Egyptian stool from the 18th dynasty, circa 1400–1350 BCE. Another piece that I really loved came from the bedroom of my paternal grandparents, Melanie and Jakob Langer. It is a three-hinged mirror constructed from maple which, although functional and unadorned, is so refined that it allows the beauty of the maple to create the narrative. It told me a story of my grandparents.

Terence Lane did an amazing job of restoring the complicated room divider, but when it came to deciding how to display the furniture, there were no indications as to how the furniture should be arranged because no photos of the interior of Melanie and Jakob's home existed. So, in September 1994, he suggested that Laurie and I travel to Vienna to do some research. In particular, he wanted us to visit the Lobkowitzplatz apartment to get an idea of its layout so that we could visualise where the furniture had been situated.

We discovered that their apartment had been subdivided into smaller apartments, so we went to the Viennese authorities to try to locate the original plans, but they were unavailable for public viewing. The only solution was to rely on photographs of Jakob's brother's apartment, which was very similar and featured in many books.

We also managed to meet the authority on Adolf Loos, Dr Burkhardt Rukschcio. He was astonished to learn that this furniture was still in existence and very excited when we showed him all the photos of the Langer collection. Conversely, when I scanned the index of his book, as well as other books featuring Adolf Loos, I was struck by all the names from my parents' families. Leonie and her husband Arthur's home was featured, plus many other Böhm relatives whose apartments and furniture had been designed by Loos. I can only wonder where all this furniture ended up. Little did Great-Grandfather Jakob know that this furniture would journey across the world and become part of a revered collection in a major Australian gallery.

For me, it was hard to let go of the beloved pieces, these connections to a past life. In the end I comfortably relinquished the room divider by making the donation on behalf of my grandchildren, and my daughter donated the Egyptian stool. Alf also donated some of his collection and sold other parts of it to the NGV where it is now housed: and some pieces are on permanent display.

In 2003 when the NGV was re-opened after extensive renovations, the director of the Louvre was flown out to launch the gallery, and we were all delighted to read in *The Age* newspaper that he had singled out particular praise for the Loos furniture, stating that the Viennese arts collection was world-class. Cousin Alf wrote:

After the official opening in 2011 by the Premier of Victoria, Ted Baillieu, we viewed the Vienna Art and Design Exhibition. It featured 360 exhibits including eight Klimt paintings and a 38-metre Beethoven frieze by Klimt, which required the walls of the NGV to have extra buttressing. Almost all the exhibits had been flown in from Austria, except of course for the Hoffmann and Loos exhibits. There we saw with great pride our old but beautifully restored sideboard. Incredibly, panels of mahogany retrieved from Dad's garage had been skilfully used, to once again join up the old grandfather clock to the sideboard, just as it had been in 1903 in Vienna in the Langer's apartment.

Seeing the NGV exhibition for the first time was eerie, almost like returning to Aunt Liesl's house where I had been a regular visitor for more than 60 years. Her dining room, where so many afternoon teas were enjoyed, was on a platform next to that famous buffet made from rich mahogany. Its three in-built elongated brass candle holders were so beautifully polished, as were the keys that were still intact in its doors. Liesl would polish this piece regularly, keeping it in the condition befitting from whence it came even though that world had been destroyed. It looks rather bare now, though, without the silver dishes and the fruit bowl and the various ceramics icing the mahogany cake.

The great-grandfather clock and the room divider were on display for the world to appreciate as was the Egyptian chair from where my kids had enjoyed the novelty of watching TV at Erich and Liesl's house, many years before we had a television set. The Chippendale chair was Uncle Erich's dining chair and nobody else dared sit on it. These objects were used and loved and furnished happy family times from well beyond my early childhood, in a family place, in a happy Viennese apartment—fragments of the fabric of a disappeared life.

Approximately 880 kilometres northeast of Melbourne is Sydney, where Käthe Gallia, and her sister Gretl and Gretl's daughter Anne resettled after escaping Vienna in 1939, while their brother Ernie and his wife Mizzi went to Melbourne. Ernie and Mizzi didn't ever receive their shipped container which held a third of their family furniture as well as other riches, including a Klimt landscape. However Käthe and Gretl's shipment brought a spectacular collection of furniture, art and *objets d'art*, including a Klimt work of great import and value.

Just to make the connections clear, the parents of my father's mother, Melanie, were Wilhelm and Eugenia Gallia. Wilhelm's two brothers were Adolf and Moriz. By today's standards Moriz and Hermine's story is a bit peculiar but not so for the period. In 1893 Hermine Hamburger, whose father was a wealthy industrialist from Freudenthal, a small town in Silesia (now Bruntal in the Czech Republic), married her uncle—that is, her mother's brother kind of uncle. Gretl's grandson, Tim Bonyhady, wrote in *Good Living Street*: 'She was the eldest child and oldest daughter of his [Moriz] oldest sister, Josefine. He was 12 years Hermine's senior, a conventional age difference for men and women of their class'.

Interfamily marriage was common in well-to-do classes for the purpose of consolidating wealth. Moriz was a government adviser, more specifically *Regierungsrat*, or Imperial Councillor, as well as Commercial Director of the Austrian Glowing Gas Light Company. He worked for wealthy Austrian chemist, inventor and businessman Baron Auer von Welsbach, who made his fortune bringing gaslight to streets and houses, first in Budapest, then Vienna and 40 other cities around the world, including London, Paris, New York and Sydney.

Moriz was richly rewarded for the immense profits he secured for the company and was soon able to build a beautiful five-storey apartment block in the prestigious Viennese street called Wohllebengasse. Directly translated, Wohllebengasse means 'Good Living Street'. Aside from their wealth, it seemed that Hermine and Moriz's union was highly successful and mostly they shared a happy life together. They became leading patrons of the arts, specifically of the Vienna Secession movement of which Gustav Klimt was a founder. This was such an exciting era: the beginning of modernism and the development of modern architecture, art and design. So the Gallias mixed in circles that included some of the greatest composers, writers and painters of the day. Their friends included artists Gustav Klimt, Carl Moll, Ferdinand Andri and Egon Schiele.

In 1903 Moriz commissioned Gustav Klimt to paint a life-size portrait of Hermine. This painting became one of Klimt's most famous. The simple title was *Portrait of a Lady* because it was a common practice of Secession artists not to name their subject. Now it is simply known as *Portrait of Hermine Gallia*. The portrait was first exhibited at a private showing for Secession members and collectors in the Secession Building on the 14th November 1903. Viewing the portrait for the first time was a grand moment for Hermine. It was a modernist symbol of status and wealth.

She was captured in a dress of diaphanous flounces and ruffles that Klimt actually designed. By today's standards the dress is not way out, but then it was a radical departure from the dirndl, or the stiff, controlled full-length dresses with high-necked bodices or shirts that gave women a slimmer, lengthened look. The other unusual aspect was the style of the painting. Klimt usually depicted women as heroic, mythical and sensual goddesses. At some point these goddesses became indistinguishable from their exotic backgrounds, whereas Hermine's setting was more conventional, with a carpeted floor. Most of Klimt's subjects invite the viewer in with their carnal gaze, but Hermine's sensuality is more subtly depicted. Her expression is bordering on melancholy and her head tilts slightly away from the viewer as if she's not wholly comfortable in the world, which perhaps reflects more of Klimt's own state of being than Hermine's.

Although the artist had achieved fame and respect, he scandalised the traditional art movement and the government which considered many of his works to be pornographic. At the same time, he was favoured by Viennese high-society women and it is reported that he usually had sex with his subjects and subsequently fathered 14 'illegitimate' children. What a charmer he must have been in his ill-fitting, full-length blue linen painting smock. Even so, there is no evidence that Hermine was captured by his magnetic sexual irresistibility.

Hermine's portrait made it out of Vienna in 1939 and into Käthe and Gretl's small harbourside Cremorne unit. There the massive 170.5 by 96.5 cm painting, worth an absolute fortune, hung in the living room overlooking Sydney Harbour for 30 years along with an impressive array of paintings by other great artists such as Ferdinand Andri, and a rare print of a portrait of Gustav Mahler signed by both the artist, Emil Orlik, and Mahler. Alongside this was an enormous collection of Hoffmann-designed silverware, enamels and glass *objets d'art*, all jammed into cupboards in the little flat where it once graced a home of palatial scale.

In 1970 Gretl and Käthe, both in their 70s and contemplating their final years, decided to downsize. So in 1972 they sold the portrait through Christie's auction house and two years later it was re-sold to the National Gallery in London for what was then a record price of £20,000. More recently, in 2001, it was re-valued at $11 million. Ironically, during this period, Käthe offered it to the Art Gallery of New South Wales as a gift. The portrait was rejected as a work that was of no value for an Australian audience. One imagines that the museum director would have regretted that decision forever.

Hoffmann's popularity had waxed and waned over the years so when it came to divesting themselves of their 80-year-old collection of Hoffmann furniture, it was not so easy. Again, they offered it to the Art Gallery of New South Wales, but there was no interest. They tried European galleries and none of them wanted it either. Next stop was a leading auction house in Sydney. The appraiser said to Gretl, 'Lady, it will cost a lot to cart this away to the tip'.

In 1980 when Terence Lane heard that the Gallia furniture was available he immediately negotiated to acquire it for the NGV for $25,000. There is a certain irony here because these two architects, Loos and Hoffmann, who conflicted philosophically in regard to the expression of a home and its decor, ended up occupying the same exhibition space on the other side of the world. They had always been vocal in their criticisms of each other over the use of ornamentation, Loos regularly criticising Hoffmann's work as unnecessarily ornate and materialistic.

Both these collections have been hailed as the largest and best collections of Hoffmann and Loos apartment furniture and furnishings outside Vienna. One reason for this is that each derives from a single commission, whereas in most cases, individual pieces come from a variety of sources. Additionally, they are valuable as superb examples of each architect's design philosophy.

The influence of Adolf Loos lives on in me: the guiding principle my parents instilled was that furniture should be simple and plain in design. They considered the ornate antique furniture so sought after in the Australia of my youth was ugly, an attitude that mirrored Loos's beliefs. When my friends raved about antique furniture, I kept very quiet. In my 1950s Melbourne world, wrought-iron, vinyl and Laminex became fashionable. Carved wooden furniture had given way to streamlined, fully upholstered suites, which I liked, and that nice comfy recliner for the tired hubby.

28

A 1950s WIFE

But let me return to newly married life in Australia in the 1950s and beyond. An article I read in a 1950s *Reader's Digest* issue gave very helpful advice on the subject of keeping husbands happy and the appropriate preparations for their daily return from work. It stated that one should look smart, brush one's hair, remove the apron and pop on a nice dress. The welcome at the front door should be cheerful, and one certainly should not grumble about the day. Yes, the good wife's mission in life was to keep hubby happy—the right aperitif in one hand and slippers in the other.

The women of my youth were pictured in magazines and advertisements in their pretty floral frocks with pinched, neat waistlines and full-circle flared skirts, tastefully garnished by colour-matched aprons and complemented by stylish stiletto pumps. As these women extracted the roast dinner from the upright General Electric cooker, they appeared to be reaching the pinnacle of a blissful experience—no need to ring a bell for the servants like my Viennese family did because they were having a whale of a time, effortlessly with all those labour-saving devices.

Conversely, husbands were never obliged to assist with the housework, and so it was in my married life. The only regular housework Laurie felt compelled to do was lawn mowing, which was done according to his discretion and inclination; the height of the grass was immaterial. At first we had a hand mower but Laurie soon came home with a new toy: an expensive motor mower that we could not afford, especially because I was saving hard for a house deposit. The only way I could justify his annoying investment was to start a mowing business on a Saturday morning, on top of all my other commitments. That proved disastrous because the newfangled mowers were notoriously unreliable. Once it coughed, spluttered and stopped, I could never restart it. I never managed to finish a lawn and I certainly could not take money for a job half done.

Laurie's Saturday morning was spent doing *The Age* newspaper's cryptic crossword; he was unavailable to assist with anything until that was complete. His duties also entailed occasionally fixing items around the house, which suited him because he was good with his hands and with woodwork. He built himself a nice shed—a must for every Australian male at that time when virtually all families lived in a house with a backyard—and then a carport. He would first draw up meticulous plans, then set out his high-quality tools in the order he would require them. This accorded with the way he was brought up; his mother, Alice Course, educated all her children to be neat and tidy. I liked this trait. If he took a spade out into the garden it was always placed back on its hook. But heaven help anyone who put anything back on the wrong hook. My father was like that with books. He was always petrified that someone would remove one and not put it back in its correct place.

From the start of our marriage I worked harder than Laurie. When we lived in Surrey Hills, I would ride my bike five days a week to and from Box Hill Hospital, about 4 kilometres away. The cooking and housework amplified when I took boarders into our two spare bedrooms. Then on Friday evenings, while Laurie taught an extra art class at Melbourne Grammar School, I cleaned the house and washed our clothes. Yes, as I write this, I realise how similar this was to my mother's behaviour in her marriage. After all, the care of the home and children was a woman's responsibility. To be fair, this was and still is for many families the way domestic work has been distributed over human history. And at that time, although women were starting to have their own careers, men were tardy in taking up a share of the housework or care of the children. Even now, parents are still in negotiations on these matters!

Four months after I began working at Box Hill Hospital, I became pregnant with my first child, Tony. Matron called me into her office 16 weeks later. I entered gingerly, wondering what I had done wrong. 'Your pregnancy is becoming noticeable and it will be embarrassing for the patients. You'll have to leave,' she said.

This was not good news because it set back my plans to raise a house deposit as quickly as possible. Also, I loved working and was never good at being idle, although four children later I would yearn for some idleness.

Like all of his generation, Laurie was not a revolutionary 1950s father who liked to share the load, and nothing changed with the arrival of children. He would sleep through the night when the children experienced the inevitable disturbances—a cough, a sore throat, a bad dream, a feed. There was certainly no chance that I would get to sleep in after a difficult night. As tired as I might be, Laurie was to be as protected from intrusions, otherwise he would be very grumpy. His typical parting comment after I had endured such a night was, 'Well, never mind—you'll be able to relax all day'. Then he would pick up his polished leather briefcase, put on his hat, and disappear out the front door.

The entire morning routine from the early morning cup of tea to his departure was sacred and had to be observed without interruption, otherwise his whole day would be ruined. I would stumble wearily out of bed, leaving Laurie to doze while I made his tea. Tea preparation was an art that took a lot of instruction, and the uninitiated, that is me, being a foreigner after all, could never aspire to anything more than competence in the practice of this fine British tradition. I had to warm the teapot with boiling water, empty the water then add tea leaves, pour more boiling water into the pot and allow it to steep for precisely five minutes before pouring. Not exactly Einstein's theory but just as vital to my husband's and therefore my wellbeing.

With tea served in bed at seven o'clock along with the morning newspaper, the bedroom door was to be kept firmly shut to prevent the children intruding, and 15 minutes later I would bring his second cup. Then he began his exercises at 7.45 a.m. sharp. Once he was standing on his head, it was time to serve breakfast.

His breakfast was always leisurely, taken with a side of grumbles, often about the state of the breakfast table, which was usually strewn with crusts from toast and the children's cornflakes. Then Gill (aged two) and Phil (aged four), would find the perfect ingredients for an experiment. A cup of coffee on the table was a prime medium to discover how much sugar would fit into the cup. The sticky overflow would trickle onto the freshly polished floor, which in turn was trampled across the house.

'Can't you control these two?' he would say.

The actual breakfast was also a cause for complaint.

'What! Not *eggs* for breakfast, again? I'll look like one before you've finished with me.'

For me it was utter chaos. I would do my best to keep things peaceful and resolve the squabbles as Laurie continued his path through the morning paper and then the crossword. Then it was a rush to jam clothes, towels and sheets into the washing machine before he got into the shower because he was bound to deplete the day's hot water as his mind meandered through the wonders of art, or he pondered over a lecture. Between 9 and 9.30, depending on how the crossword had gone, he got dressed.

The two older children, Diana and Tony, headed off to school before Laurie finished breakfast. Once Laurie left, I continued the unrelenting household chores with the two youngest children constantly underfoot and no mode of transport—only my husband was allowed to use the car, where it stayed idle all day in the university car park.

The afternoon push seemed to come so quickly—make dinner, feed and water the tired children, and prepare the evening meal.

If only I could have turned myself into six pieces—one devoted to each member of the family and a little left over for myself!

In the midst of it all my husband would arrive home complaining of unproductive meetings that dragged on so long that he only managed to have three-quarters of an hour for lunch; even morning coffee was interrupted by a phone call. He would retire wearily into the lounge, shut the door, pour himself a scotch, light up a cigarette and put his feet up. A call for dinner was often unwelcome.

'What? Dinner already? Can't I have a few minutes to enjoy my drink?'

For someone with my independence of spirit and the enjoyment of a career, staying home as a housewife and mother was a challenge, especially with a husband who did not seem to be fulfilled at work or satisfied with his life with me.

I recall when the children were young and he was the art master at Melbourne Grammar School, he struck up a firm friendship with John Brack, who was teaching there three days a week. Brack needed to supplement his income because he couldn't yet rely on the money from his paintings to support his wife and four children. Each Saturday Laurie would go to John's house, where they would spend the afternoon through to the early evening talking, drinking beer and discussing the art world and their place in it. Prior to John achieving his status as a celebrated and iconic Australian artist, he wanted very much to be painting full-time. Laurie, too, believed he had not yet fulfilled his potential in art academia. Years later, he would half joke about being the one Melbourne University staff member who only had a bachelor's degree—in later years most of the people employed there had master's degrees or PhDs.

Spending Saturdays at John's house was never up for negotiation. Sometimes it would be to photograph his paintings if John had an exhibition coming up: Laurie was a talented photographer. If I wanted us to do something as a family, or if I had to work on the weekends, he would tell me to find someone to look after the kids. Occasionally the whole family was invited to the Bracks' and I enjoyed Helen Brack's company. Sometimes we all took a scenic drive up to Upwey in the Dandenong Ranges to visit artist Freddy Williams and his wife Lyn, and she would cook us a meal.

While my husband was in some ways difficult, there was something to be said for the predictability of his rigidity and the stability I felt with him which I never felt with my father. Although he could be annoying, at least you knew where you stood. He managed the finances well and other than the initial house mortgages, we were never in debt. If he had to, he could cook basic food and fix most breakages.

Prior to the children coming along, we were reasonably happy and loving, although our differences were such that arguments were quite common. When the children arrived I think he felt somewhat supplanted, no longer the centre of my world, and our different cultural backgrounds, especially on parenting, created more tensions. He was fond of the children, indeed he loved them, but I guess like his family of origin he was not demonstrative, and he was as firm with them as he was with me. Holiday time, though, was his time to shine as a great father.

Every Christmas and Easter holiday season we all went camping. Camping life began early in our marriage. My very first experience was in Metung, where we parked beside the lake. We had no equipment—it was just the wilderness and us, with the lake for swimming and bathing and our small Austin with layback seats for sleeping. We cooked on a portable gas camping stove and used an old greengrocers' wooden box as a table. Although it was beautiful, the complete absence of creature comforts was not my idea of a holiday. As far as I was concerned, I never wanted to go camping again. On the drive home I got terribly carsick, discovering a few days later that I was pregnant with my first child.

When our first two children, Tony and Diana, were five and three, Laurie bought camping gear: a car-top tent where he and

I could sleep on a rack above the car and the children could sleep inside. Putting the tent up and taking it down was hard work so we would find a place to stay for the whole time and walk everywhere to see the surrounding sights—something we all loved to do and a wonderful early education in trekking through bushland and mountains which has stayed with our children. As the family expanded, Laurie invested in a big tent with a kitchen annex, as well as tables and chairs and inflatable mattresses; it was much more luxurious.

Embracing the outdoor life of walking, fishing, swimming and exploring different parts of Victoria was thrilling and it was wonderful to see Laurie so relaxed on these holidays. He participated fully and came up with great activities to create memorable family holidays. Away from the stresses and demands of daily life, he would become a different person and a very attentive father. My youngest son Phil wrote:

Dad took me camping and we walked together at Wilson's Promontory, often when he was so tired that he could barely stand up. He worked hard and had a good set of values. He had trouble dealing with a world that had done so many bad things. He'd seen things that he repressed and never talked about. As a kid he pulled lawnmowers apart with me and we played cricket. He taught me about woodwork and fixing things. Dad took a great interest in my passion for electronics. He was very supportive when I was at university and generally when things in my life were tough. All of those things influenced me greatly.

Laurie's parents idolised him, which probably had a lot to do with him needing to have the world revolve around him, and wasn't that different from the men in my own family of origin. I understood Laurie much better after living with his family in their two-up, two-down, semi-detached London home for ten long months in 1968.

Decades later, when Laurie retired, I thought it was time for change. I saw no reason why I should continue to do everything around the house and work four days a week. I knew he was quite capable of doing some housework—in fact, when circumstances forced him to iron his shirts, he did it immaculately and he could cook too so he would never go hungry. After all, he had been a bachelor for six years before I married him and had done all his own housework.

So I stated emphatically that I would no longer cook his breakfast or iron his shirts. He was furious and there was an uproar. For weeks he banged around in the kitchen each morning at breakfast time. If I was still home, I just went out into the furthest reaches of the garden till he had settled down. After three months he began to love cooking his own breakfast and experimenting with different egg dishes. He did this slowly and meticulously and sometimes, if we were going out, I would offer to cook breakfast for the two of us. 'I like cooking my own breakfast,' he said, as if he had always done so.

As for ironing his shirts, he never did do any and so he wore them unironed except for very special occasions when I felt too embarrassed to let him go out looking bedraggled.

It made me sorry I had not stood my ground years before.

29

FINAL DESCENT

My father's intellectual success in his studies in Vienna provided no defence against the vagaries of daily life, or his own quirks. A sense of helplessness surrounded him in some situations where a bit of commonsense was all that was required. In a way we could not blame him for his idiosyncrasies because he was a prodigious talent. He began music lessons at three and by the age of 18 he played the Mozart Piano Concerto in D Minor in the Vienna Konzerthaus (Concert Hall). He was a creative, so he moved differently in the world, or certainly in that part of the world.

Although part of his soul resided in the European Alps and Carpathians, he embraced the treasure and beauty of the Tararua Ranges on the North Island of New Zealand. Our family could not help but be compelled by his passion for mountaineering and adventure, and embrace hiking and climbing. Martin, especially, had the rambling bug and it was an activity he enjoyed doing with our father. However, once he was well into his 50s, our father's legs were not so strong anymore and when sorely pushed, they tended to cramp. Having been active all his life, he refused to let the pain and frustration get the better of him, or imagine that he might not have the capabilities of his younger self.

The Tararua Ranges form an 80-kilometre ridge running parallel with the east coast of the island near Wellington. The weather is frequently harsh, and the native bush terrain rugged.

Their panoramic beauty drew the attention of many artists during the Victorian period. The resultant paintings were largely romanticised because no one was game to get too close.

In later years safe paths were forged for intrepid hikers to explore with these relatively recently formed mountains. One pleasant Sunday afternoon, on the 13th September 1964, my parents, Martin, and a friend of my mother's drove to a location near the foot of Mt Kapakapanui. The car was parked next to a paddock close to the Ngatiawa River. They set off carrying backpacks filled with sandwiches and tea, to enjoy the mottled sunlight through the dense forest as they climbed and clambered around giant red beeches, gnarled silver beeches garlanded with moss and feathery snow tussocks at the peaks. Native bellbirds and parakeets hailed the incoming mist till the mountains were reduced to a mere smudge across the sky.

The hike to the peak of the mountain they were climbing should only have taken three to four hours. Martin later wrote an account of the event:

The weather was overcast and quite reasonable for an afternoon's walk. We crossed the Ngatiawa River and headed up the mountain. It was about an hour after that that Mum and her friend became weary and decided to turn around and go back to the car. Me and Dad decided to continue on an unofficial path up the ridge. The weather was starting to close in but I thought we would be protected in the bush.

About one and a half hours later, Dad suggested turning back. I said we could try to reach the summit and Dad agreed. The mist was thickening and when we finally emerged from the bush near the summit, neither of us knew where we were because the mist was so thick. Visibility was just a few metres and it was getting dark and beginning to rain.

We decided to look around for a sheltered spot for the night and kept reasonably warm by huddling together. During the night

I saw lights down in the valley but they were coming from the east, which is the direction of the interior of the range. I was probably suffering from hallucinations.

The next morning in pouring rain, we tried to make our way down the mountain, walking in a stream which soon turned into a waterfall. We climbed down it but came across a few more waterfalls, which we had to negotiate. After about three hours we arrived in a narrow valley where we followed a fast-flowing swollen river, which was probably the Ngatiawa. A bit further on we had to cross that river to continue. Shortly after, Dad's legs were cramping and he felt too exhausted to continue. I left him our pack, although there was little in it of much use, and carried on, hoping to get out that day.

I followed the river for a while before climbing another mountain. I was looking around and not getting far and it was getting dark. I found a fallen log and tried to sleep under it. Early next morning I climbed up to the ridge, thinking the way was up and over. I thought I was walking in the right direction and to my great relief there were views of fields and meadows looking westward towards Waikanae.

I continued down, very soon bumping into people from the search and rescue group who had been out looking for us for some time ...

News of the missing member of the NZBC Symphony Orchestra was all over the media. Terrible storms swept the ranges as more than 50 men searched the southern Tararuas. Martin was found by a flooded creek, freezing cold with waterlogged skin, and covered in cuts and bruises. The rescuers gave him a hot drink and some food before returning him to rescue base headquarters at 8.15 a.m. By nightfall he was reunited with my mother then taken for observation to Wellington Hospital. He was in pretty good shape, but my mother was sick with worry as there was still no sign of my father. Martin wrote:

The total timespan of this ordeal was two nights and a day. There was a stage when I felt I would not come out alive and that experience was terrifying.

After two days my father's body was found lodged in a gorge downstream, trapped by a log in the swollen rapids about a mile from where Martin was found the previous morning. This area was usually avoided by hikers because the stream crossing had numerous deep pools and narrow gorges. It took rescuers two and a half hours to extricate him. I still have the newspaper photos showing the appalling conditions as the rescuers brought the body of my 59-year-old father out on a stretcher.

While all this was taking place, I was completely unaware until a friend read about it in the newspaper. The report said my father was lost. I immediately picked up the phone to call my mother just as she rang me to break the terrible news.

'I'm coming over straight away, Mum.'

I could not fathom that it could be true, and rushed straight to the airport without delay. On arrival I found my mother to be much more in control. 'Why didn't you bring Diana? It would have helped,' she said. Diana was five at the time and my mother felt she would have been a great comfort.

I went alone into the morgue to view my father's body from behind the glass screen. This was not like a viewing in a funeral home; his body was still very much river swept and saturated, even though I had arrived around eight hours after he had been found.

Being a nurse, you get conditioned to dealing with death. You learn to stand back and not get too involved. But this time I felt as if I were in a vacuum. It was hard to breath but still I never cried, and never saw my mother cry. It was something we just never did as a family.

The chapel was filled with friends and orchestra colleagues. Four musicians gave a chamber music performance. That was the hardest part for me to take emotionally. Later, my mother said she believed it was better for my father not to grow old—old age was a concept he could not cope with. I wrote to Laurie while I was in New Zealand:

He always wanted to keep up with Martin in spite of being so much older. If Martin wouldn't go walking with him, he went alone. He had a very good sense of direction but no knowledge of bushcraft. Often, he suffered with terrible cramps in the legs so that he could hardly walk. Mummy believes it would have happened at some point anyway.

My mother was extraordinary throughout the whole ordeal. In another letter to Laurie, I wrote:

Not once did she give way under the strain. She talked to the visitors, listened to their stories, made cups of coffee and thought only of them. Now two hours after the funeral she has driven off to see an old friend who was very upset at the funeral.

The Wellington press also paid him a fitting tribute.

A memorial concert to Dr. Peter Langer by the NZBC Symphony Orchestra (leader Vincent Aspey) conducted by Juan Matteucci at the Town Hall Concert Chamber last night.

The NZBC Symphony Orchestra's tribute to Dr. Peter Langer, who died recently while on a tramping expedition, was a concert which would have given much pleasure to their former colleague. The warmth of the tribute was felt, not only in the playing, but from the audience, which almost filled the Concert Chamber.

Dr. Langer was a member of the orchestra cello section and he played the piano too, in the concerts given by the Chamber Players of Wellington, for whose foundation and programmes he was the moving spirit. His musical influence, however, went beyond his executive skill and musicianship.

It was his love of music, which transcended enthusiasm and became an absorption in everything musical with which he was concerned, that infected those with whom he worked, and won him many friends.

It was the same approach by last night's players that gave considerable enjoyment. The orchestra was reduced to chamber music size to fit both the music and the Concert Chamber platform space, but by switching players in the three works almost every member of the orchestra was able to pay his personal tribute. In fact, those who were not required on the platform participated with assistance in front house chores.

The strings have never sounded better than they did in the luxurious sounds of Respighi's suite of 'Ancient Airs and Dances'. The Haydn symphony was a gem, with Juan Matteucci bringing from the music both its elegance and its lively wit. And if the Bartok lacked a little of its primitive vigour, there was compensation in the vivid clarity of detail.

Proceeds of the concert are to be donated to the Chamber Players of Wellington and the Stepping Stones Society with which Peter Langer was closely connected.

The day after the funeral, we went to his music studio in the city centre to collect his belongings. There stood his cello that no family member would ever dare touch. As I placed it in its black case and carried it outside, I finally understood that it would be forever silent. My father was gone. Music was never the same for me again.

After the funeral, a friend of my mother's expressed concern about how she might manage financially without Peter. This amused her. 'Why should I worry? I've had 30 years' training in financial insecurity.'

My mother wrote to Liesl that she was tormented not to have been with him at the end when he was so isolated, and then she just got on with life. Her remaining years were spent doing all the things she believed she could not do while he was around. Before my father died, she joined an organisation called Stepping Stones, which helped people with mental illness re-adjust and rehabilitate after being discharged from psychiatric hospitals. After his death she took ex-patients into her own home to help them achieve the confidence to live in the world after years spent in institutions. She also became a part-time, then full-time secretary for the organisation. This was fulfilling and comforting work for her.

Prior to my father's death, my mother had worked as a secretary, in addition to any other job she could get to generate an income, not having any formal qualifications from which to build a career. Afterwards, however, she fulfilled her lifelong dream and went to university, completing a diploma in social science with distinctions. She approached her life with a new-found air of self-confidence. She told me that she had never felt freer, even though she missed him terribly. When people asked her if she would ever consider remarrying, she would reply, 'It takes a lifetime to get used to one man; I don't have time to get used to another one'.

30

DOLLIS HILL

In 1968, four years after my father's death. I packed 14 cases and two trunks with clothes, books, toys, linen, table and cookware—everything we might need to set up a temporary home in London. Laurie had a sabbatical and was back on the trail of his hero, artist Rupert Bunny. This was also to be the first time he would see his family since leaving Britain, 19 years earlier.

It was expensive to fly in those days, and we had two children at this stage, so Laurie flew to London ahead of us. Tony, who was nine, and Di, seven, and I sailed for four weeks on the *Achille Lauro*, the ship that transported many thousands of British and European migrants to Australia at the time. On arrival, Laurie met us at Southampton docks on a freezing gloomy, grey day. The weather further coloured my sense of foreboding about what we were getting into here. Then Laurie said, 'I don't remember my parents' house being so small. The four of us couldn't possibly stay there.' By now I was in a state of panic. Surely, we had shipped our household goods in order to set up house independently?

The train took us to London, and we took a taxi to Dollis Hill in northwest London where Laurie was born. The luggage followed in a van. Their street was lined with identical two-storey Edwardian, semi-detached houses; one of them was the house he grew up in, where his parents, Leslie and Alice, and his older sister, Rita, still lived.

When the taxi stopped, an Edwardian door opened and his family appeared. Right from the start the reception was restrained, if not strained. It seemed to me to be as chilly as the February weather. Although they had written to Laurie saying they were looking forward to seeing us, it was not their way to show much emotion or affection. They certainly made no fuss of the children, and served them cups of tea, as if they were adults. It was very peculiar to me.

The atmosphere in the house was so austere that it dampened the children's natural exuberance, so much so that for two days they talked only in whispers in the corner of the room. As far as I was concerned we should lose no time in looking for a place to rent. But each foray into London's rentals left us demoralised as the prices were well beyond our means.

Unbeknown to me, Laurie's parents had expected us to stay with them from the beginning. For Laurie it was not a difficult decision and he adapted remarkably well to all the extra attention he was getting—golden son returns, sort of thing. So, the trunks and cases that we had painstakingly packed were wedged into his father's studio/garage. As for the rest of us, we were squeezed into the already burgeoning house. Laurie and I slept in a three-quarter bed in the tiny spare bedroom where there was scarcely room to stand, while Di slept in the grandparents' room and Tony slept downstairs in the dining room.

Living with the family was, to say the least, difficult to negotiate. My mother-in-law, Alice, was a kindly soul with a great sense of humour and I liked her a lot, but when it came to the household, she managed it with absolute authority and some eccentricity. She believed in good organisation, tidiness and saving anything that might come in handy, including newspaper, especially if one ran out of toilet paper. Newspapers were cut up and a hole was poked through the bundle. Then they were secured with string. In a small house with limited cupboard space everything had its place. But finding that place was quite a challenge as they could be quite unexpected, to say the least. Once I lifted the piano lid only to find the keys stacked with books. What a sacrilege this would have been in my parents' house. On another occasion, before guests were expected for a Christmas celebration, I was about to dump a load of washing in the machine only to find it being used as a repository for several loaves of bread.

A short dumpy old lady who trimmed her own hair as best she could, thrifty Alice, who was a good stick, was always on the lookout for practical, cost-saving solutions to domestic problems as she shuffled around the house on arthritic feet. Her husband was ten years' her junior and worshipped her and her lively intelligence. I realised years later that much of her behaviour came from the extreme rationing of everything during the war years in Britain and for four years afterwards—nine years in total—as well their living through the horrors of the Blitz. These experiences would certainly have created permanent lifestyle patterns and attitudes.

As far as Laurie's older sister Rita goes, we kept out of each other's way as much as we could. She was a thin, hyperactive spinster in her 40s who was not all that nice to me. I had the feeling she thought I might not be good enough for her brother. Who knows? Laurie was very close to her—she could have been jealous of another woman in his life and his being married with a family.

Rita would begin each day filled with energy and the excitement of another day's work at the post office, but before she headed off she would dust and clean the house, racing up and down the stairs like lightning; now with a broom, now with a duster. Her shrill, harsh voice would be well exercised when she discovered that Tony had hidden her cleaning implements, just for a bit of sport.

The Course family got on very well, which was a good thing, but I was certainly not accepted into it. They would all go off and visit relatives without me, and on one occasion, they left me in the car while they went into someone's home for afternoon tea. It was a very unpleasant experience, but I didn't say anything to them— not even to my husband in private. I think I was just trying to survive this very difficult situation and could not face getting into an argument with him over this, although I was hurt and angry.

Laurie was clearly the centre of their world and the children and I were way out on the periphery. Each day when he returned from a day's research work at the university, his mother, father and Rita sat him in a comfy armchair, brought him his slippers and a cup of tea and arranged themselves around him to be enraptured by his endless stories. He revelled in this attention and there was certainly no incentive for him to find us our own place. This was going to be a long year.

Life went on in an endless, less than exciting stream of habitual domestic activity. We ate most meals in the tiny, congested kitchen-cum-laundry, usually with racks of wet clothes dangling from the ceiling above our heads, while the coke heater nearby steamed away. It was like a sweatbox.

My father-in-law, Leslie, had a rather sweet ritual that he undertook each morning: carrying a tray of breakfast up to his wife. It crossed my mind that it would be nice if Laurie did that for me once in a while. Then, in the 'privacy' of their bedroom over the breakfast tray, he would begin his tirade of criticisms of me in his booming voice. He was somewhat deaf so I'm not sure he was aware of how loudly he spoke. Each morning new criticisms were vented, leaving little doubt about his feelings or opinions, about the way I brought up my children. I learnt to turn the radio up loudly to block the broadcast of my latest misdemeanours.

Distinguished-looking, perpetually cookie-cutter British, tweed-wearing, Leslie Course was outwardly well-mannered; and on this level we managed a fragile relationship. The thing I could never understand was how he could not fall in love with his grandchildren. The day after we arrived in London, he took us on a tour of the main attractions and then set up a badminton net for the children. That was the beginning and end of his interest. He worked from morning till night in his cold studio, only emerging for lunch and at the end of the day for dinner. He was quite a renowned sculptor who had created film sets in the 1930s, and his commissions continued into old age. Initially I expected that he would show the children the work he was doing and talk to them about sculpture, but that never happened. Not once. In fact, he took any opportunity to be dismissive and grumpy towards them; but mostly, he ignored them. One day I tackled him over it. 'Do you treat your other granddaughter, Jane, like this?'

'Yes, I do. Just the same,' he said.

'It's time the grandfather thought about what he is doing,' I replied angrily, before storming out.

My parents-in-law's values and relationships with children were diametrically opposite to those of my extended family, whose devotion was unconditional—with a tendency to spoil them. Alice and Leslie, on the other hand, just expected their grandchildren to fit into the adult home environment without any special attention.

There was also a certain inevitability to their disapproval of me—they had actively done their best to prevent any of their three children from marrying and leaving the nest, and had a well-oiled approach to any prospects. They were rude and inhospitable to any potential partner their children misguidedly brought into the house. This would be followed up after the interlopers had left, with the parents making pejorative remarks about their physical appearance or mannerisms. No one was ever good enough. This system worked pretty well until the youngest daughter, Enid—Alice's favourite—and Laurie found ways to leave their protective sphere. Rita was the only one of the three not to make it out.

Soon after we were married, Laurie told me that if we had met in London we would never have married. I thought that an odd thing to say to a new wife. But I finally understood it while living with his family. And it certainly explained why they didn't travel out to Australia for the wedding.

Another less than endearing aspect of life with them was the regular time devoted to discussing how the Jews had taken over their suburb. Did they know I was Jewish, and that my family had escaped from Nazi Europe? Probably, but that would not have mattered.

Sundays were my favourite days in the Course household. Alice and Leslie drove to church in the morning and on their return embarked on their preparations for Sunday dinner, always a delicious meal with roast beef, Yorkshire pudding and vegetables, finished off with a 'pudding' of apple pie and creamy custard. The table was set with the best crockery and cutlery and no one sat down until everything was perfect.

In the kitchen Leslie carved the meat with a sense of style and ritual. I loved watching him sharpen the knife and then carve the thinnest of slices, which he arranged artistically on the meat dish. It was a practice that Laurie, too, carried on throughout his life.

After saying grace, at around 4 p.m., we all tucked in. Laurie's parents had their Sunday rest, then supper followed, after which we all played board games with the children. But the rest of the week was a drudge, and the weather really got me down. The children would go off to school and for a time I nursed at Hampstead General Hospital, doing an afternoon shift twice a week. This meant that I left the children in the care of the grandparents for the after-school shift which was not entirely satisfactory—once, Tony ran away and poor, tiny, arthritic Grandma, who could barely walk, had to run after him.

Then, the respite came. We bought a campervan and escaped to the continent for the summer holidays, despite Laurie's parents being scathing about us taking this trip because they thought we had not seen much of England. The plan was to start in France and then visit Venice and Vienna. However, Laurie loved France so much that we spent almost the whole six weeks there. I was horribly disappointed not to be able to go to Vienna, so decided I would go later in the year, which is what I did.

After ten months, Laurie had arranged to fly to America to visit museums and galleries for the remaining two months of his sabbatical and, disturbingly, he wanted to leave us with his family. I was definitely not prepared to accede to that so, using my own money, I booked flights and, with the children, headed for New York soon after Laurie's departure. Once more we were royally welcomed by my many relatives and, in stark contrast to the previous ten months, the children were overwhelmed with affection.

We returned from America on a ship that docked in Auckland so that we could visit my mother. This would be the last time I would see her in what seemed like good health. Some months later, she had a bowel operation during which the surgeon discovered cancer. The prognosis was poor. Her estimated survival time was just six months. I made her promise at that point that when things started getting to be unmanageable, she would come and live with me.

31

SICK AND TIRED

On our return to Melbourne, Professor Burke, the head of Melbourne University's Art Department, offered Laurie another six months' leave to write his book on Rupert Bunny, but Laurie refused to take it. I could not understand why, but it soon became apparent. Each weekend he would disappear into the study saying he had work to do. However, whenever I went in to see him, he would be doing the crossword.

'I'm having a break,' was his response to my questioning.

Some months later, I was reading the newspaper and saw that art historian and curator, David Thomas, had written a book on the same artist, Bunny. I showed Laurie the article.

'Look at this article! I thought you were writing the book.'

'Yes, David was very grateful to me for all the information I gave him.'

I was so cross because he had told me nothing about this and there had been so many weekends when he said he was working when it was actually all over. It was a tragedy for him that I think he never recovered from—he probably sold himself out to David Thomas because he was just completely overwhelmed at the enormity of turning all the years of research and data into a coherent narrative.

Many years later, after Laurie died, I found a box full of his research on Robert Bunny. One of his friends in the art world went through it to see if there was anything of value. Most of the information Laurie had spent years accumulating was available on the internet by that stage so it had become redundant. It was so sad. Laurie was intelligent and at his peak he worked hard and became highly respected as an expert in art literature and appreciation, but something stopped him—maybe lack of intellectual confidence, maybe the lack of a mentor—prevented him going that extra mile to fulfil his potential.

In 1969 I fell pregnant again with my third child, Phil. That was also the year that my mother's condition deteriorated. She was such a strong-willed woman, so after the diagnosis, she set about living her life to the fullest, despite the pain. She embraced the advice of a doctor in Auckland who recommended a vegetarian, mostly raw and dairy-free diet as a means of curing the illness, or at least prolonging her life; and it did, for 18 months. People tried to comfort me with stories about how cancer sufferers had defied the prognosis to live on for many years. Although their intentions were well-meaning, I resented their efforts to give me false hope. I was absolutely devastated.

As her condition deteriorated, my mother encouraged my brother Martin, who was then 28, to travel to America to be with the family. My father's death had affected him deeply, especially as it would have left him with so many conflicting emotions. My mother wanted to spare him the upset of watching her decline. The time had come to relinquish her commitments to both her son and her work. She told me, 'I just want to be able to concentrate on myself and not have to appear out of pain when I'm not'.

Although Martin had never met any of the extended family, they received him as warmly as they had me. My mother wrote to Joele:

The warmth of his reception by young and old was so surprising to him that it took him a while to believe it. He had to sort out all the relationships of the large family, which was not easy.

Not having a green card, however, meant it was impossible for him to stay there very long so he flew to London to visit Great-

Aunt Friedl. While there, he met Elizabeth, the woman he would marry. He stayed on there, got a job in telecommunications and they settled into a nice life where, in due course, they had two children and still live today. Sadly, my mother did not live to see the son in whom she had put so much love and effort, produce his own happy family.

In September 1969, after my mother had had some chemotherapy, I flew to New Zealand to bring her back to live in Melbourne. I was shocked to see how thin and frail she had become. Although she was still well-groomed, she had stopped colouring her hair, her face looking as grey as her hair now was, and she needed a stick to help her walk. Always the optimist, she felt so joyful about the prospect of seeing her third grandchild into the world, particularly as she had not been able to attend the birth of my first two.

'You must let me help with the new baby or I'll feel useless,' she said.

Shortly before Christmas, the doctors determined that the cancer had metastasised to her bones and that they needed to pin her now-brittle hip, which was in danger of fracturing.

As sick as she was, she still expected to lead a useful active life. However, her final weeks were spent in the Austin Hospital. The specialist, believing she might live another few years because she had already outlived her prognosis by a year, suggested she have the operation to fix her affected hip bones. She didn't recover from the operation, but such was her spirit that two days before she died she discussed the unsuitability of the furniture in the apartment she was renting near my house. 'I must change it when I leave hospital,' she said. It was difficult to share her optimism. At 30 kilograms, she was just a skeleton, skin yellowed with jaundice.

As if things weren't bad enough, her hospital ward was badly managed with psychiatric and cancer patients being located in one room. I considered complaining, but I knew the staff would take it out on my mother by giving her even less attention and making her feel like a nuisance. On one occasion when my mother was in considerable pain, I asked the nurse to give her more medication. I was brusquely told that she had already received her allocated dose of analgesic and was not due again for two hours. One of the younger nurses disclosed the amount of morphine she was receiving which was just a fraction of what I had been giving her at home. My request to see the doctor that evening was refused because visiting hours were over.

'Then I will stay here all night until I have spoken to a doctor,' I retorted.

The staff looked at me in my very pregnant state and decided that to comply would be the best option. Years later, I worked in palliative care at Caritas Christi Hospice in Kew, which seemed a way to somehow compensate for the poor treatment my mother received: patients' relatives often said we were like angels.

A day that I shall never forget is the 12th February 1970. I was feeding two-week-old Phil, and Laurie was in the shed doing some woodwork when I received a phone call from a nurse at the hospital.

'Mrs Course, your mother died,' she said.

'When?'

'During the night, around 3 a.m. Do you want to come in and see the body?'

'No.'

'Well you need to come in and pick up her belongings, anyway.'

I continued feeding the baby. I must have been calm because Phil suckled away happily and then went straight off to sleep. I then prepared myself to deal with the business at hand. What I felt at that moment was anger that the hospital had left it till the morning to notify me, thereby depriving me of the opportunity to be with my mother at the end. There was no point asking them why they hadn't called me in, nor was there any point in me going to see her so many hours later when the nurses had laid her out. During my ten years of nursing at Caritas Christi Hospice, I laid out many bodies. It was such an undignified process, especially leaving the jaw tied up with a bandage to stop the mouth from gaping. I knew the procedure well and how one spent time making the body look presentable, but the person never looked the same. It was better to remember my mother as she was.

My mother survived my father by five years, and by some strange coincidence she was the same age as him when he died, just 59. Reading her early diary entries, it saddens me to think that this poised, courageous, complex, hardworking and selfless woman was never really happy, even as a youngster. On the 26th July 1936, my 26-year-old mother wrote:

To give into one's body, not force it, keeps one young. To give into one's spirit in its tiredness makes one old. It is difficult to get over the tiredness of the spirit. I have become worn out. I have the judgement and the knowledge to see that. I can't read light things, they bore me. But more difficult reading tires me. That must pass. I must not get old, comfortable and small.

With Peter I must fight so that he doesn't get like that. I was looking for someone who would help me to combat the inertia in myself. I haven't found that in Peter. So, I fight for two people. Should man's life be like that of animals? Man's freedom and possibilities are too big for that. We may not rest, there is so much for us to achieve. There are the worries of every day and the little irritations, which take up so much room in me. It must be possible that these worries stay buried and that I can overcome them. It is necessary for me to bring up my child. I want to make a fine strong person out of her. May god help me do so.

That strength was well instilled in me and for that I am grateful, but when she died it wavered. My mother had never discussed her death so there were no funeral plans. Aunt Liesl arranged for the funeral director to come to our house, but I felt numb and ill-equipped to deal with the whole business.

The funeral was small. Martin was in England, so it was just the immediate family and a dear friend of my parents, Dr Fritz Loewe, a famous meteorologist, explorer and glaciologist, who gave a splendid eulogy. Fritz was an extraordinary man. He left Germany after the rise of Nazism and established the Department of Meteorology at Melbourne University. I watched as his tall form hobbled up to the podium. His gait was awkward after losing several toes to frostbite on a research expedition to Greenland in the early 1930s. This never stopped him walking to Melbourne University in Parkville every day from his house in Belmore Rd, Balwyn (16 km each way). Even after he retired in 1960, he continued to work on scientific papers. That daily trek to and from the university continued until he dropped dead on his way home, four years after my mother died. I attended his funeral at the Melbourne Synagogue. That was my first Jewish funeral.

The drive to farewell my mother at the crematorium was a torment, such was my grief. After that I rewrote my will with instructions that I was not to have a funeral and that my body should be given to Melbourne University for research. I have since revised this because I realise that funerals give the family the opportunity to mourn, say goodbye, and express their love for the departed. A fitting tribute appeared in the Wellington *Evening Post* on the 18th February 1970:

Mrs Hertha Langer died in hospital in Melbourne recently. The wife of Dr. Peter Langer, she is survived by her daughter, Susi (Mrs. L.J. Course of Melbourne), and her son Martin, at present in London.

A woman of many interests in the arts, painting, music and the theatre, she dedicated herself for the last 10 years to Stepping Stones Inc. and the assistance and rehabilitation of the mentally handicapped.

She worked unceasingly as a committee member, as president and for the last four years as permanent secretary to the society.

For seven days a week she was available to those who needed her, and the villas of Porirua Hospital and the many welfare organisations of the district will feel her loss.

From her illness in 1968, her main efforts were to see that Stepping Stones Inc. should be established with an efficient controlling body which could continue the work she knew was so necessary.

32

THE DAREBIN PARKLANDS LEGACY

After becoming refugees and resettling in alien countries across the world, my family adapted to a new life without great wealth and privilege. Everyone just got on with it. As for me, I wanted to forge a new family history in Australia, and leave a legacy befitting this land that had always been good to me.

Our family home from 1958, at Waverley Avenue, was a short walk from the Darebin[5] Creek which runs through 33 hectares of land. It forms a boundary dividing the Alphington and Ivanhoe sides and is a major tributary of the Yarra River on which the city of Melbourne was founded. Now if you walk through the grassy woodlands, the indigenous flora, the place where 100 species of birds call home, and echidnas and lizards roam, it's easy to imagine that the Darebin Parklands always looked like this. The truth is that it was very different when we moved into our home.

On our side, the Ivanhoe side, was what was then known as Rockbeare Park, comprising 2.8 hectares of land. I often took my children to play there when they were small. It was an adventure land of frogs and birds, and rocks and great trees to climb; a place where we fossicked and caught tadpoles. We loved it despite the fact that it was very much neglected. The park had been bought by the City of Banyule in 1929 and McCloskey's Riding School had agistment rights, which saved the council having to mow it.

---

5   It is thought 'Darebin' is derived from an Aboriginal word meaning swallow-like bird.

The other side of the river, the Alphington side, was an industrially zoned, privately owned sector of 29 hectares; a mixture of quagmire, dump and industrial wasteland and remnant vegetation. I well remember the early days when the bluestone quarry was still active. They would dynamite that bluestone out of the earth and the impact made our windows shake. Then the rocks were loaded onto carts pulled by draught horses, for road and building construction. Quarry businesses were all but over by the 1960s due to an economic depression and building industry downturns, leaving many, just like this one, to become rubbish tips.

My friends and I often discussed the idea of restoring and extending the park. Then in 1973 something happened that propelled us into action. I was walking on the Ivanhoe side of the creek with my friend, Anthea Fleming—an environmentalist and ornithologist—when we discovered that bulldozers, sent by the Melbourne and Metropolitan Board of Works, were in the process of removing every remnant of vegetation from the creek bank in order to remove impediments to the water flow. We had also been notified that Heidelberg Council was going to fill in the wetlands. We decided that we had to act quickly on both fronts to prevent this disaster, so I raced over to the council chambers to try and stop the bulldozers.

Just to compound matters, we discovered that the government intended to build a freeway through there. The whole situation was untenable to us because it was such an important and potentially beautiful site with a spectacular environmental and geological history filled with places of fascination. Ancient nooks and crannies created by volcanic lava flows date back 860,000 years, when basalt outcrops collided with large bodies of water and cooled rapidly. Within 100 metres of the basalt there is a distinct geological change: 860,000-year-old rock abuts 460-million-year-old rock, giving the landscape two different ecologies. So the varieties of vegetation, spiders, insects and birds are different across the divide, all within a 10-minute walk.

In more recent history, for at least 60,000 years before British colonisation, this area would have been a rich source of food and tools for the Wurundjeri people. The Yarra River and Darebin Creek would never have run dry, even in summer, so fish, plants and animals would have provided a constant and diverse diet, and the rocks and timbers in the area were sufficient for all tools and building requirements.

During the 1800s and throughout the gold rush, the whole Darebin area was taken over for vineyards, vegetable crops and orchards, with Darebin Creek being used to irrigate the crops. Thomas Hutchins Bear purchased 14 hectares of land abutting the creek and, using the nearby bluestone, built a grand house, which is still a family home. Their land was on the Ivanhoe side, and they established vineyards and orchards, although nothing remains of their orchard today.

John Sharpe Adams owned 24 hectares, which was the entire Alphington side of the Darebin Parklands. His family initially established orchards and a dairy farm before discovering that they were sitting on rich deposits of bluestone and basalt. They then established a quarry, which must have been a lucrative enterprise considering the enormous demand of the building boom that the gold rush had created. Some of their mulberry and olive trees remain in the park to this day, more than 150 years later.

As we fossicked and played on the land, it was exciting to stumble upon traces of early settlers: a now-derelict ford and weir from 1845, an original wagon track, and plantings that had survived since the early settlers farmed there. Even a few of the old red gums were still growing along some parts of the creek where once they dominated. It was worth making a huge fuss about this place, and if such a project were to be undertaken today, archaeologists would no doubt be engaged to catalogue the artefacts from European settlement to ancient Aboriginal occupation. At the time, however, we Australians did not consider archaeology as being applicable to such a young/old environment. How things have changed, thankfully.

Nature and history ground me and draw me into their stories. I was compelled to start an action group to restore this precious land for my children and my country. Aided by many other locals, we formed a committee. Laurie, too, believed strongly in the cause and we ran a campaign together. His skills were different from mine; he knew how to talk to politicians and how to use the media.

As it turned out, the bulldozers were there without council permission, so they were immediately halted—what a relief. I organised a growing band of volunteers, augmented by Ivanhoe Grammar boys, to perform the gruelling physical labour in the Rockbeare Park area. We dealt with many species of weeds including blackberries, boneseed, cape broom, box thorn and at least 20 others. Each weekend we would attack small areas at a time, weeding, digging and trimming; burning the refuse in bonfires afterwards. Then there was the tree planting; some trees were donated by the council and some we grew from seeds.

Laurie organised his university colleagues, including Carrick Chambers, who was professor of botany, Jeremy Pike, the head of the Landscape Architecture Department, and the Professor of Forestry whose name escapes me, to visit the proposed area of parklands. Often they would come for lunch at our place with their wives and throw around their restoration ideas before inspecting the land.

On top of that, I doorknocked the suburbs around to create local awareness of the cause, and lobbied politicians. It was an extraordinary experience as I engaged with so many people from all levels of government, many of whom turned out to be wonderfully sympathetic. The months of lobbying turned to years. One time I went to Canberra to find out why our first submission had been unsuccessful. Subsequently, the next one was successful and they kindly provided funding for two parcels of land in Alphington. But we wanted all the land, so we invited the Premier of Victoria,

Sir Rupert Hamer, to visit the park. On a very hot January day in 1977, a bunch of volunteers set up family picnics in different areas so he would think the park was well used. (At that time few people knew about it so hardly anyone used it!) We gave Rupert afternoon tea under a canopy of trees near the creek. He thoroughly enjoyed the mulberry ice cream I had made for the occasion, using the berries picked from the 150-year-old mulberry trees in the park.

A week later he wrote and thanked me, and asked for the ice cream recipe because he, too, had a mulberry tree in his garden. In addition, he made an offer to Northcote Council that they match the state dollar-for-dollar to buy the remaining land. It was an exciting time, albeit an incredibly demanding one. A man ahead of his times in many ways, Rupert Hamer became our patron.

Once the Alphington side was purchased, we waded across the creek to work there. Our resourceful treasurer, engineer Sidney Clifton, spent months designing an arched concrete bridge. It was built entirely by volunteers under Sidney's supervision and Banyule Council provided the funding for the materials. It was opened with great ceremony by two state ministers, with refreshments by a bonfire, one cold winter's day in 1979. It was so unique and attracted a lot of attention. *The Age* wrote an article about it called, 'The Homemade Bridge'. It remains the only bridge in the park and now has a heritage listing.

Darebin Park became an all-consuming passion for me for 37 years; we became pioneers in land reclamation in the urban environment. To see the fruits of our labours today is absolutely heart-warming. Although I became known as 'mother of the park', in reality there were so many people involved in creating it. The Darebin Parklands' Association and some individual volunteers, including me, received numerous awards for the incredible feat we had achieved—a volunteer group of local residents without any formal authority secured 33 hectare of land at a time when developers were getting permission to build over every spare hectares available, especially so close to the city, and we took it from wasteland to parkland. Peter Wiltshire, Ecologist and Chief Ranger, said, 'Sue founded Darebin Park with Anthea Fleming, but if Sue hadn't been whipping the pony it wouldn't have happened. It was her perseverance that got this done.'

Although I am unable to do too much these days, I still attend the association meetings, and it provides me with so much satisfaction to see that the park is much used and loved by local communities and beyond.

We documented the story through photographs, minutes, letters and other meticulously kept records. They now form part of the National Library of Victoria's collection to ensure the project will never be forgotten. Many of the photos were taken by Laurie; he played a big part in documenting the changes to the land. Some of his photos were used for funding submissions to the federal government and some featured in an exhibition in the Architecture Department at Melbourne University. He certainly played a vital part in the reclamation, but as far as our lives together were concerned, things never got easier. As he got older, he became more consumed with the bitterness of his unfulfilled professional life and became increasingly difficult to live with.

I planned to find a way to leave him once the children left home, but then I realised that if I did he would make it his business to make my life difficult. I had watched my friends end up with very little money after divorcing their husbands, so when there were just the two of us left at home, I decided to make the best of what I had. After 39 years of marriage I moved into the extension at the back of the house, a self-contained area with a kitchen, bathroom and living room. We still did a lot of activities together—attending meetings, visiting our children, travelling overseas—and whenever I was home we would eat evening meals together, but much of the time I was busy and away from the house a lot.

I still worked four days a week, met my girlfriends for dinners or shows, and played an active role on several committees and community organisations. During this period, I helped establish the Banksia Palliative Care Service and volunteered at the Migrant Women's Learning Centre at Collingwood TAFE[6]. After my retirement, I became a zoo guide and information officer for Melbourne Tourism. Then there was the Banyule Heritage Advisory Committee where I organised open days, as well as my continuing committee work on the Darebin Parklands' Association. I had a lot of energy in those days. Not so much now.

---

6   A college of Technical and Further Education.

33

MOVING ON

Laurie smoked for more than 50 years and refused to quit, even after the science definitively pointed to its causal link to cancer and other life-threatening illnesses. However, in his stubborn way, he always maintained that there was no proper evidence linking smoking to cancer. In 2006 Laurie and I went to see the doctor because he was experiencing difficulty swallowing. Soon after, he was diagnosed with inoperable cancer of the oesophagus. The doctor was upfront about it being terminal. Laurie was 78 years old. Within a year he transformed from a relatively fit man to being elderly and frail. Chemotherapy was recommended to hold it at bay for a time but that stopped working after several months and the cancer travelled to bone and beyond.

There was no way Laurie was going to give in: he never talked about dying and he remained amazingly stoic till the end, continuing his daily visit to Ivanhoe shopping centre for a coffee and chat with one of the shopkeepers. When he was no longer able to walk unaided, he used a walking frame.

As his 80th birthday approached, he had already well and truly outlived his life expectancy of around a year. The whole family decided to go to Stradbroke Island for the birthday celebration. The day before we were due to get on the plane, his condition deteriorated and he was hospitalised: we did not expect him to return home. True to form, though, my stubborn, opinionated husband left the hospital, with the doctor warning him that he might die on the plane because of the state of his lungs.

'If the English were like you and never took chances, we would never have won the war,' was Laurie's retort.

It was a difficult trip for him, but he suffered his pain without complaint as he spent precious time with our children and enjoyed his time on the beach watching the distant whales spouting and gambolling.

As his condition deteriorated and he became bedridden, the Banksia Palliative Care Association visited daily to manage the morphine. Soon he went into a coma and with Phil and Di by his side, he drew his final breath. According to his wishes, we scattered his ashes in Darebin Parklands.

Over the years that I cared for him, the experience of his forthcoming demise did not change him in any way or bring us closer together. I just watched out for him as best I could and got used to the idea of leading a life alone. Throughout this ordeal, I contemplated my own mortality and discovered that I was not afraid of dying, but rather living too long.

Ten years later, at the age of 85, I went to Spain for a holiday with my son Phil, his wife Annella and their two little boys, Ethan and Bryce. Packing was a challenge, with all the body-sustaining equipment I had to take. There were hearing aids with plenty of spare batteries, the dental requirements, walking props including sticks and frames—the list goes on. Fortunately Phil could hire disability scooters wherever we went.

This new chapter of my life—where my hands are becoming deformed, my fingers weak, my knees and feet having their own troubles, and my world becoming more isolated because of my failing hearing (which must sorely try people's patience)— seemed to be somehow familiar. It felt as if I had heard it all before. Then I re-read Grandmother Sofie's final letters and noticed the familial pattern, the similar hurdles, the connections that have helped form this life of mine, with all its challenges and delights. Here is what Grandmother Sofie wrote to us on the 6th August 1961:

Thank you for the arthritis recipe, I will try it, at least for my knee. The hands appear to be something completely different but what it is will probably only be found out in New York. Here [Miami] the doctors are all stupid and very uninterested unless it concerns an operation. In any case my fingers are quite useless and it is impossible to play the piano. How did the dress for Diana turn out? Now I can't sew one stitch, as I can't hold a needle. If a button comes off it is a catastrophe and I try and sew it on with my left hand …

Then there are things like doing up brassieres, cleaning teeth and putting on a brooch, doing one's hair, cleaning or closing a clasp. All this, one has to learn anew and one takes twice as long to get dressed. In one day, I get so little done that I am always behind. So now you can imagine my present life. I will either get better or I will get used to it. I apologise that I wrote so much about myself. But I am so full of these changes in my life and must first of all get used to them because I can no longer play the piano. I miss it terribly.

The next letter, came six weeks later:

We two old bags [the other 'bag' being her sister, Leonie] are going to see a specialist in New York … Leonie is suffering with neuritis which is giving her a lot of pain. My fingers are perhaps a little better, as I do everything that is prescribed for me … As well I have a stomach upset and a torn muscle in my back which upsets me. I'm often in a bad mood and unhappy to do anything.

The final year of Sofie's life was racked with pain and frustration. The greatest shock came a month later on the 16th of September 1962, when my mother's sister, Pauline, wrote that Sofie had lung cancer. Pauline made the unilateral decision that this news would be kept from her mother so that she would never give up. Even Great-Aunt Leonie, who was Sofie's carer, was not to know the truth. When my mother flew across to see her, she had to invent a story that she was en route to a holiday in Austria. The charade upset her terribly because she was unable to share the process of dying.

All these actions are taken out of love. People agree and disagree; that's life. Someone disregarded Uncle Ludwig Gallia's last wish—that he be placed in an unmarked grave—instead burying him in the family plot. The headstone at the Vienna Central Cemetery (*Zentralfriedhof*) had his name on it. First came Melanie and Jakob Langer followed by my sister Vera Langer, then Ludwig Gallia and, lastly, my father, Peter Langer, after my mother transported his ashes across in 1965. Years later I visited the gravesite. All that remained was the burial plot—the headstone had fallen over and the groundskeeper had removed it.

After my father's death, my brother placed a memorial plaque on a rock in the Tararua Ranges which Laurie and I visited in 2003. Martin guided us through the wilderness, unsure that we would even find the spot because so many years had passed. After a long hike and four river crossings, where we locked arms so as not to be pulled over by the current, we came face to face with the plaque. It read: And a light shineth in the darkness. Peter Langer 1905–1964.

History moves on, ashes to ashes.

As a nurse in aged care facilities, I had fed, washed and cared for many elderly people who were powerless and had little quality of life left. I watched as Aunt Liesl slowly descended into dementia. When I was in my 30s, the thought of old age petrified me, so I decided that it would be a good idea for me to die at around the age of 60. To a 30-year-old, 60 seemed old. When that time came, in 1993, I made no mention of my 60th birthday to anyone, hoping no one would notice. I was in Connecticut, visiting my once flighty Aunt Pauline, who was dying a slow, uncomfortable death. That was when she gave me a copy of her memoir, which provided great insight into her life and the historical period from her birth to her early 20s when she escaped Vienna. What a beautiful legacy it was.

I am grateful that I lasted through my 60s because I did a lot of satisfying things during the following decades. I could watch with pride as my four kids made a success of their adult lives, and I have been able to enjoy my grandchildren growing up. Then I was free to travel, sometimes with Laurie, sometimes alone, and often with my daughter, Gill, to far-flung places such as South America, Turkey, Israel and the Solomon Islands.

Well into my 70s and still in good health, I listened as friends tallied their barrages of medical tests. I did not believe in spending time at the doctor looking for every life-threatening disease just to keep me alive a bit longer.

The novelist Rosamunde Pilcher[7] said that, 'You don't stop doing things because you get old; you get old because you stop doing things'. This certainly resonates with me. Those years beyond 60, beyond 70, and now beyond 80, gave me the opportunity to return to the dark recesses in the cupboards of my life and reconstruct my family's history.

History re-forms us and moulds us. From the purity of the birth state we become the daughter, the wife, the mother, the widowed old lady. My home at Waverly Avenue was sold in 2013. It was the right thing to do although it was an awful wrench to move out of the community I loved so much. I was 79 and still in good health. Having worked in aged care had taught me that preparations for old age needed to be made early, so I booked us into a good retirement village 14 years earlier.

After the sale, the house seemed sad and abandoned, so I would find an excuse to return to it every single day until the new owners took possession. The journey from my new digs filled me with pleasurable anticipation. I would reach Heidelberg Road in Alphington, once an unmade road, now a busy street, then proceed

---

7   A prolific and highly successful British author, some of whose books were adapted to television. Born 1922, died Feb. 2019.

over the Darebin Creek Bridge, up the hill and over the railway bridge. I would go till I saw the bold green church spire, not quite of the magnitude of St Stephen's Cathedral in Vienna, but sufficiently imposing. In no time I was back in Waverley Avenue with the Darebin Parklands stretched before me.

Laurie's home-built workshop had seen the last of his obsessive neatness and, strangely, the emptiness seemed to suit the house. Perhaps it was sighing with relief after bulging and stretching to accommodate four children and us. It had teemed with life till it was worn almost to the frame—wallpaper tatty and woodwork on door frames and skirting boards chipped and battered by young children and, in another era, Laurie's walking frame. For a while I was sad, feeling as if I had abandoned my yard, my trees, my house—but really, it was not the place so much as the life and the living of it.

Would I have done anything differently if I had my time over? Would I have not married Laurie, or returned to live in Vienna? The answer is no. There are always things one could do differently, but I am happy with how I have managed my life.

Now, to my current home, another historic monument: Rushall Park Retirement Village in North Fitzroy, Melbourne, established in 1869; a village of delightful old stone cottages. I live in a modern construction on the property but history resides in layers in this place. A painting hangs above my dining table—a watercolour painted in 1910 by Rudolf Schmidt. It depicts a scene outside the apartment block at Stubenring 14. This picture keeps me connected to the home my grandmother lived in where she brought up my mother, and where I spent my first four years of life. I get lost in the ancient scene, people strolling, women in long skirts and dresses impossibly shaped by hoops, bustles and corsets into the acceptable hourglass silhouette. A horse and cart have ceased trundling along the side street, and a red tram has ended its history outside our home on the famous Viennese Ringstrasse where Sigmund Freud among others, strolled daily. It is a lost life, an epoch that has been painted over with a single, dark brushstroke.